Introduction to Process Economics

Introduction to Process Economics

F. A. Holland

F. A. Watson

J. K. Wilkinson

University of Salford and
Partners in Salchem Associates,
Consulting Chemical Engineers

JOHN WILEY & SONS

London · New York · Sydney · Toronto

Library of Congress Cataloging in Publication Data:

Holland, F. A.
Introduction to process economics.

Bibliography: p.
1. Profit—Accounting. 2. Cost accounting. 3. Decision-making.
I. Watson, Frank Alfred, joint author. II. Wilkinson, John Keith, joint author. III. Title.

HG5681.P8H64 338.5′1 73–14380
ISBN 0 471 40619 8 Cloth bound
ISBN 0 471 40613 9 Paper bound

Printed in Great Britain by William Clowes & Sons Limited, London, Colchester and Beccles

Preface

This book is suitable both for bachelor degree courses and as introductory material for scientists and engineers in industry. The increasing competitiveness of modern industry makes it desirable to devote considerable thought and effort to reducing costs. In order to do this, technologists in industry should be fully aware of the relationship between technical and economic factors and, in particular, of those factors which have the largest effect on profitability.

In the past, scientists and engineers have tended to concentrate their efforts on the technical side of industry and to leave the financial side to other specialists. Even design engineers involved in making estimates of the capital and operating costs of process plants have frequently left the overall profitability assessment and investment decision making to others. This approach is no longer advisable for a company or for an individual desiring to be successful in modern industry.

The emphasis in this book is placed on overall profitability estimations rather than on costing techniques. Part 1 deals with the basic mechanics of profitability estimating and Part 2 shows how this basic information is used to assist the decision maker. The importance of the time value of money is stressed and the main emphasis is placed on those methods of estimating profitability which are based on the time value of money. The most common are the net present value (NPV) and the discounted cash flow rate of return (DCFRR). These methods consider net annual cash flows A_{CF} rather than net annual profits A_{NP}. This has the advantage of avoiding having to consider depreciation as an operating cost since these methods implicitly make provision for the return of the original capital outlay. Furthermore, it is net annual cash flow rather than the balance sheet profit which gives a company command over its resources.

The material in Part 1 can be taught in a course of forty class contact hours. It is suggested that a further twenty class contact hours are needed for Part 2. Homework problems are provided for each chapter. The authors are grateful to their own students whose constructive comments have resulted in the modification and development of a number of these problems. The material in this book can be taught in the second, third or fourth year of an engineering degree course.

A significant proportion of the material in this book is based on information that the authors published previously in *Chemical Engineering*. The authors are grateful to the editor of that magazine for permission to make use of this previously published material.

A great debt of gratitude is owed to Miss Barbara Buckley who has typed and retyped the manuscript several times.

F. A. HOLLAND
F. A. WATSON
J. K. WILKINSON

Contents

Nomenclature

a, b, c, d	general coefficients in polynomial and other equations
A	annual cost or annual payment, \$/year
A_{A}	annual tax allowance exclusive of depreciation, \$/year
A_{BD}	balance sheet annual depreciation charge, \$/year
A_{CF}	net annual cash flow, \$/year
A_{CI}	annual cash income, \$/year
A_{D}	annual depreciation charge, \$/year
A_{DCF}	net annual discounted cash flow, \$/year
A_{DIV}	annual amount paid as dividends to stockholders, \$/year
A_{DME}	annual direct manufacturing expense, \$/year
A_{FE}	annual fixed expense, \$/year
A_{FGE}	annual fixed general expense, \$/year
A_{FME}	annual fixed manufacturing expense excluding depreciation, \$/year
A_{GE}	annual general expense, \$/year
A_{GP}	gross annual profit, \$/year
A_{IME}	annual indirect manufacturing expense, \$/year
A_{IT}	annual amount of tax, \$/year
A_{ME}	annual manufacturing expense, \$/year
A_{NCI}	net annual cash income, \$/year
A_{NNP}	net annual profit after tax, \$/year
A_{NP}	net annual profit, \$/year
A_{P}	annual processing cost, \$/year
A_{S}	revenue from annual sales, \$/year
A_{TC}	total annual capital expenditure, \$/year
A_{TE}	total annual expense, \$/year
A_{TFE}	total annual fixed expense, \$/year
A_{TVE}	total annual variable expense, \$/year
A_{U}	annual utilities cost, \$/year
A_{VE}	annual variable expense, \$/year
A_{VGE}	annual variable general expense, \$/year
A_{VME}	annual variable manufacturing expense, \$/year
B	constant in Equation (6.5-1), dimensionless
(BEP)	breakeven period, years
c	general function of several variables
c_{L}	hourly wage rate, \$/hour

c_{ME}	cost of manufacture per unit of production, \$/unit
c_{RM}	cost of raw materials per unit of production, \$/unit
c_S	sales price per unit of production, \$/unit
$\bar{c}_S$	mean sales price per unit of production, \$/unit
c_S^*	optimum sales price per unit of production, \$/unit
c_{TVE}	total variable cost per unit of production, \$/unit
c_{VGE}	variable general expense per unit of production, \$/unit
c_{VME}	variable manufacturing expense per unit of production, \$/unit
C	cost, \$
C_B	amount of loans and bond capital invested in company, \$
C_{EQ}	cost of a major item of process equipment, \$
C_{FC}	fixed capital cost, \$
$\bar{C}_{FC}$	mean fixed capital cost, \$
C_K	capitalized cost of plant or equipment, \$
C_L	cost of land and other non-depreciable costs, \$
C_O	amount of ownership capital invested in company, \$
C_{TC}	total capital cost, \$
C_{WC}	working capital cost, \$
(CR)	capital ratio defined by Equation (5.2-1), years
(CRR)	capital return ratio, dimensionless
(CSR)	contribution sales price ratio, dimensionless
(DBEP)	discounted breakeven period, years
(DCFRR)	discounted cash flow rate of return, \$/year
$\overline{\text{(DCFRR)}}$	mean discounted cash flow rate of return, \$/year
(EMIP)	equivalent maximum investment period, years
$f(x)$	frequency or relative frequency with which a particular value x occurs, dimensionless
f_{AF}	annuity future worth factor $\dfrac{i}{(1+i)^n-1}$, dimensionless
f_{AP}	annuity present worth factor $\dfrac{i(1+i)^n}{(1+i)^n-1}$, dimensionless
f_d	discount factor $\dfrac{1}{(1+i)^n}$, dimensionless
f_i	compound interest factor $(1+i)^n$, dimensionless
f_K	capitalized cost factor $\dfrac{(1+i)^n}{(1+i)^n-1}$, dimensionless
f_L	Lang factor in Equation (5.4-1), dimensionless
f_1	process piping factor in Equation (5.4-3), dimensionless
f_2	instrumentation factor in Equation (5.4-3), dimensionless
f_3	buildings factor in Equation (5.4-3), dimensionless
f_4	facilities factor in Equation (5.4-3), dimensionless

f_5	outside lines factor in Equation (5.4-3), dimensionless
f_6	engineering and construction factor in Equation (5.4-3), dimensionless
f_7	size factor in Equation (5.4-3), dimensionless
f_8	contingency factor in Equation (5.4-3), dimensionless
F	future worth of a sum of money, \$
i	interest rate of return at the cost of capital or, in general, the fractional or percentage interest rate, annual or per period, dimensionless
i'	fractional or percentage nominal annual interest rate, dimensionless
i_m	fractional interest rate per month or minimum acceptable interest rate of return on investment, dimensionless
i_r	risk rate required to guarantee the expected profit, dimensionless
i_1, i_2, i_3	interest rate on total, ownership and loan capital respectively invested in the company, dimensionless
(IRP)	interest recovery period, years
k	general constant
K	constant for a specific pattern of cash flow, dimensionless
m	number of interest payments per year, years^{-1}
(MSF)	measured survival function defined by Equation (8.6-3)
n	integer number of items, years, etc., dimensionless
N	number of men per shift, dimensionless
(NPV)	net present value of the project, \$
$\overline{(\mathrm{NPV})}$	mean net present value of the project, \$
$(\mathrm{NPV})_w$	weighted net present value of the project, \$
p	fractional probability of an event, dimensionless
P	present worth of a future sum of money F, \$, or potential gain of a contract, \$
$P_{s'}$	book value of fixed asset at the end of year n, \$
(PBP)	payback period, years
Q	capacity or size of plant or equipment
r	fractional annual decrease in fixed asset value, dimensionless
R	annual production rate or sales volume, units of production/year
$\bar{R}$	mean annual production rate or sales volume, units of production/year
R_B	breakeven production rate, units of production/year
s	service life, years
s'	particular year from start up, years
s^*	sample standard deviation of data, units of data
S	scrap or salvage value, \$
t	fractional tax rate, dimensionless
T	parameter of the logistics curve defined by Equation (7.4-13)

x	value of the independent variable, units of the variable, or yield of product per unit of raw material, dimensionless
$\bar{x}$	mean value of the independent variable, units of the variable
X	plant capacity, short ton/day
y	value of the dependent variable, units of the variable
$\bar{y}$	mean value of the dependent variable, units of the variable
Y	operating labor, manhour/ton/processing step
z	standard score $(x - \mu)/\sigma$, dimensionless
α	elasticity of demand defined by Equation (8.3-2), dimensionless
β	ratio of proceeds to disbursement, dimensionless
Δ	symbol indicating a difference of two values
ΔR_{BD}	increment of production rate R required to cover the balance sheet annual depreciation charge A_{BD}, units of production/year
ΔR_{FGE}	increment of production rate R required to cover the annual fixed general expense A_{FGE}, units of production/year
ΔR_{FME}	increment of production rate R required to cover the annual fixed manufacturing expense A_{FME}, units of production/year
η	factors as used in Equation (6.7-1)
θ	time from start of selling, years
κ	fraction of sales potential achieved, dimensionless
μ	mean value of population from which data came, units of data
σ	standard deviation of population from which data came, units of data
$\sum$	symbol indicating summation of two or more values
ϕ	capital cost factor as used in Equation (5.4-3), or symbol indicating a functional relationship between the following variables as in Equation (7.1-7), dimensionless
ψ	exponent in Equation (2.8-1) or Equation (8.3-8), dimensionless

PART ONE

Elements of Profitability Assessment

Chapter 1

Time Value of Money

Interest payable on borrowed money is the basis of modern business activity. In this chapter various types of interest are described. The consideration of annual compound interest is extended to annuities and the renewal of equipment in perpetuity.

1.1 Money and Interest

In early primitive civilizations, trade and business were based on a direct exchange of goods. As civilizations developed, money was introduced to facilitate the exchange of goods and services. These can be bought or sold for money. Money only has value when it is spent. It would be of little use to an individual marooned on a desert island. Money is only received on the understanding that it can be passed on again in exchange for something else.

A large part of business activity is based on the fact that money can be borrowed or loaned. When money is loaned there is always a risk that it may not be returned. Interest is the inducement offered to make the risk acceptable. When money is borrowed a sum of money called interest is paid for the use of the money over a period of time. Conversely when money is loaned, interest is received. The amount of a loan is known as the principal. The longer the period of time for which the principal is loaned, the greater is the total amount of interest paid. Thus the future worth F of the money is greater than its present worth P. The relationship between F and P depends on the type of interest used.

1.2 Simple Interest

When simple interest is used F and P are related by the equation

$$F = P(1 + ni) \qquad (1.2\text{-}1)$$

where

i = fractional interest rate per period
and n = number of interest periods.

Normally the interest period is taken as one year, in which case *i* is known as the effective interest rate.

Consider the figures listed in Table (1.2-1). $1,000 is invested in a small business enterprise which operates over a five-year period. It costs $300/year to run the business and the cash receipts increase from $400/year in year 1 to $800/year in year 5. Table (1.2-1) shows that the total cash receipts of $3,000

TABLE (1.2-1)

end of year	cash in	cash out	net cash flow in
0	0	1,000	-1,000
1	400	300	100
2	500	300	200
3	600	300	300
4	700	300	400
5	800	300	500
total	3,000	2,500	500

exceed the total costs of $2,500 by $500. However, Table (1.2-1) presents a very simplified picture since it assumes that $1,000 is available for investment free of interest.

The calculations are reworked in Table (1.2-2) on the basis of $1,000 being

TABLE (1.2-2)

end of year	debt excluding interest for current year	interest payable at 10%/yr	total debt	net cash flow in	reduced debt = total debt - positive net cash flow in
0	1,000	0	1,000	0	1,000
1	1,000	100	1,100	100	1,000
2	1,000	100	1,100	200	900
3	900	90	990	300	690
4	690	69	759	400	359
5	359	35.9	394.9	500	- 105.1
total	-	394.9	-	500	-

available as a simple interest loan at 10 per cent per annum. It is assumed that \$1,000 is borrowed at the end of year 0 so that no interest is payable in year 0. The amount of interest payable at the end of year 1 is 10 per cent of \$1,000 which is \$100. This increases the debt from \$1,000 to \$1,100. However, the net cash flow in during year 1 is \$100 which reduces the debt to \$1,000 at the end of year 1. Finally in year 5, the net cash flow in of \$500 exceeds the outstanding debt of \$394.9 by \$105.1. Thus on the basis of a loan of \$1,000 repayable at 10 per cent per annum simple interest, the total cash receipts exceed the total costs by \$105.1 which is significantly less than the \$500 shown in Table (1.2-1) on an interest free basis.

Even with interest included, Table (1.2-2) presents an oversimplified picture. In practice, costs tend to rise because of inflation or the falling value of money. Therefore it is most unlikely that the cost of running the business will remain constant at \$300/year.

1.3 Annual Compound Interest

More commonly, compound interest is used where F and P are related by the equation

$$F = P(1+i)^n \tag{1.3-1}$$

or

$$F = Pf_i \tag{1.3-2}$$

where

$$f_i = (1+i)^n \text{ the compound interest factor,}$$

values of which are readily available in tables similar to those in Appendix 1[1,5,9,10,12].

Figure (1.3-1) is a plot of time in years against interest rate in per cent/year when $F = 2P$ in Equation (1.3-1). The numerical values for Figure (1.3-1) are listed in Table (A1-26).

Figure (1.3-1) shows that it will take approximately eight years for money to double if compounded annually at 9 per cent/year and approximately five years for money to double if compounded annually at 15 per cent/year.

The compound interest factor can be surprisingly large for only modest interest rates. Riggs[11] questions whether the purchase of Manhattan Island in 1626 for \$24 was such an exceptional bargain since \$24 invested at a compound interest rate of 6 per cent would have grown to \$17,268,876,484 by 1976.

The present value P of a future sum of money F is given by the equation

$$P = \frac{F}{(1+i)^n} \tag{1.3-3}$$

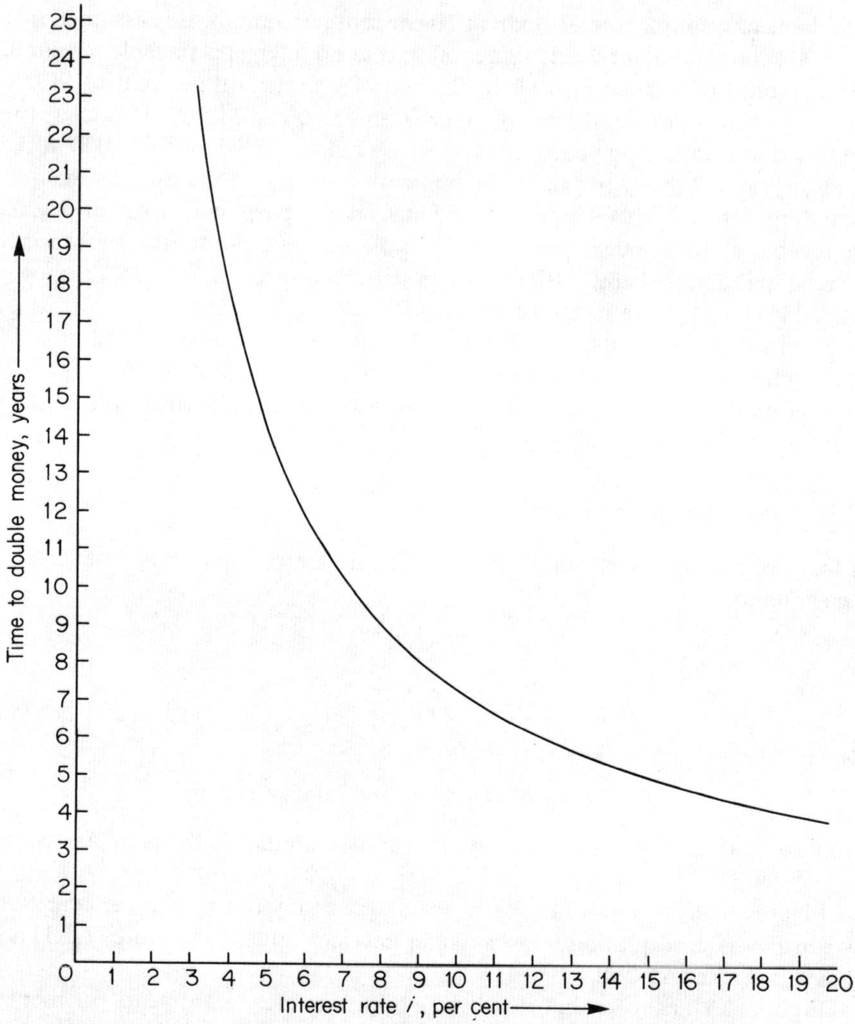

Figure (1.3-1) Time required to double a sum of money for various annual compound interest rates

or

$$P = Ff_d \tag{1.3-4}$$

where

$$f_d = \frac{1}{f_i} = \frac{1}{(1+i)^n} \text{ the discount factor,}$$

values of which are readily available in tables similar to those in Appendix 1[2, 6, 9, 10, 13].

The proof of the annual compound interest formula is as follows:

Let P = present worth

i = fractional interest rate per year

n = number of years

F = future worth

After the first year the worth is

$$F(1) = P + Pi = P(1 + i)$$

After the second year the worth is

$$\begin{aligned} F(2) &= P(1 + i) + P(1 + i)\,i \\ &= P(1 + i)^2 \end{aligned}$$

After the third year the worth is

$$\begin{aligned} F(3) &= P(1 + i)^2 + P(1 + i)^2\,i \\ &= P(1 + i)^3 \end{aligned}$$

After the nth year the worth is

$$F(n) = P(1 + i)^n$$

which is normally written as

$$F = P(1 + i)^n \tag{1.3-1}$$

1.4 Effective Annual Compound Interest Rates Equivalent to Nominal Annual Compound Interest Rates

If interest payments become due m times per year at compound interest, mn payments are required in n years. A nominal annual interest rate, i', may be defined by the equation

$$F = P\left(1 + \frac{i'}{m}\right)^{mn} \tag{1.4-1}$$

In this case the effective annual interest i is given by the equation

$$i = \left(1 + \frac{i'}{m}\right)^{m} - 1. \tag{1.4-2}$$

In the limit, such payments may be considered to be required at infinitesimally short intervals, in which case the interest is said to be compounded continuously.

Effective annual interest rates equivalent to nominal annual interest rates of 0.25 to 30 per cent are listed in Tables (A1-27), (A1-28), (A1-29), and (A1-30) for annual, monthly, daily, and continuous compounding.

Example (1.4-1)

What is the effective annual compound interest rate equivalent to a nominal annual compound interest rate of 5 per cent compounded monthly?

From Equation (1.4-2)

$$\begin{aligned} i &= \left(1 + \frac{i'}{m}\right)^m - 1 \\ &= \left(1 + \frac{0.05}{12}\right)^{12} - 1 \\ &= 0.051\,17 \text{ or } 5.117 \text{ per cent/year} \end{aligned}$$

Example (1.4-2)

What is the effective annual compound interest rate equivalent to a nominal annual compound interest rate of 5 per cent compounded daily?

From Equation (1.4-2)

$$\begin{aligned} i &= \left(1 + \frac{i'}{m}\right)^m - 1 \\ &= \left(1 + \frac{0.05}{365}\right)^{365} - 1 \\ &= 0.051\,267 \text{ or } 5.1267 \text{ per cent/year} \end{aligned}$$

1.5 Continuous Compound Interest

Expand Equation (1.4-1) by the binomial theorem to give

$$F = P\left[1 + m\cdot\left(\frac{i'}{m}\right) + \frac{m\cdot(m-1)}{1\cdot 2}\left(\frac{i'}{m}\right)^2 + \frac{m(m-1)(m-2)}{1\cdot 2\cdot 3}\left(\frac{i'}{m}\right)^3 + \dots\right]^n \tag{1.5-1}$$

As m approaches infinity the time interval between payments becomes infinitesimally small and, in the limit, Equation (1.5-1) reduces to

$$F = P\left(1 + i' + \frac{i'^2}{2!} + \frac{i'^3}{3!} + \dots\right)^n \tag{1.5-2}$$

which can also be written as

$$F = P\exp(i'n) \tag{1.5-3}$$

The same result may be obtained by writing

$$\int_P^F \frac{dF}{F} = i' \int_0^n dn \tag{1.5-4}$$

which on integration gives Equation (1.5-3).

A comparison of Equations (1.3-1) and (1.5-3) shows that the nominal interest rate i' on a continuous basis is related to the effective interest rate i on an annual basis by the equation

$$\exp(i'n) = (1+i)^n \tag{1.5-5}$$

which can also be written as

$$i = \exp(i') - 1 \tag{1.5-6}$$

or

$$i' = \log_e(1+i) = 2.303\log_{10}(1+i) \tag{1.5-7}$$

and hence

$$i' \leqslant i.$$

It is sometimes argued that continuous compound interest represents real life situations more accurately than annual compound interest. This is debatable since neither continuous nor annual compounding strictly represents the uneven cash flows in real business situations. Numerically the difference between continuous and annual compounding is very small. In practice it is probably far smaller than the errors in the estimated cash flow data. Annual compound interest has been used in the subsequent chapters in this text since this conforms more closely to current acceptable accounting practice. However it should be noted that the small difference between continuous and annual compounding may be significant when applied to large sums of money.

Example (1.5-1)

What is the effective annual compound interest rate equivalent to a nominal annual compound interest rate of 5 per cent compounded continuously?

From Equation (1.5-6)

$$\begin{aligned} i &= \exp(i') - 1 \\ &= \exp(0.05) - 1 \\ &= 0.051\,271 \text{ or } 5.1271 \text{ per cent/year} \end{aligned}$$

1.6 Monthly Compound Interest

The annual interest rate equivalent to a compound fractional interest rate of i_m per month is given by Equation (1.4-2) written in the form

$$i = (1 + i_m)^{12} - 1 \tag{1.6-1}$$

Figure (1.6-1) is a plot of equivalent interest rate per year against interest rate per month. Most people who take out loans based on what superficially

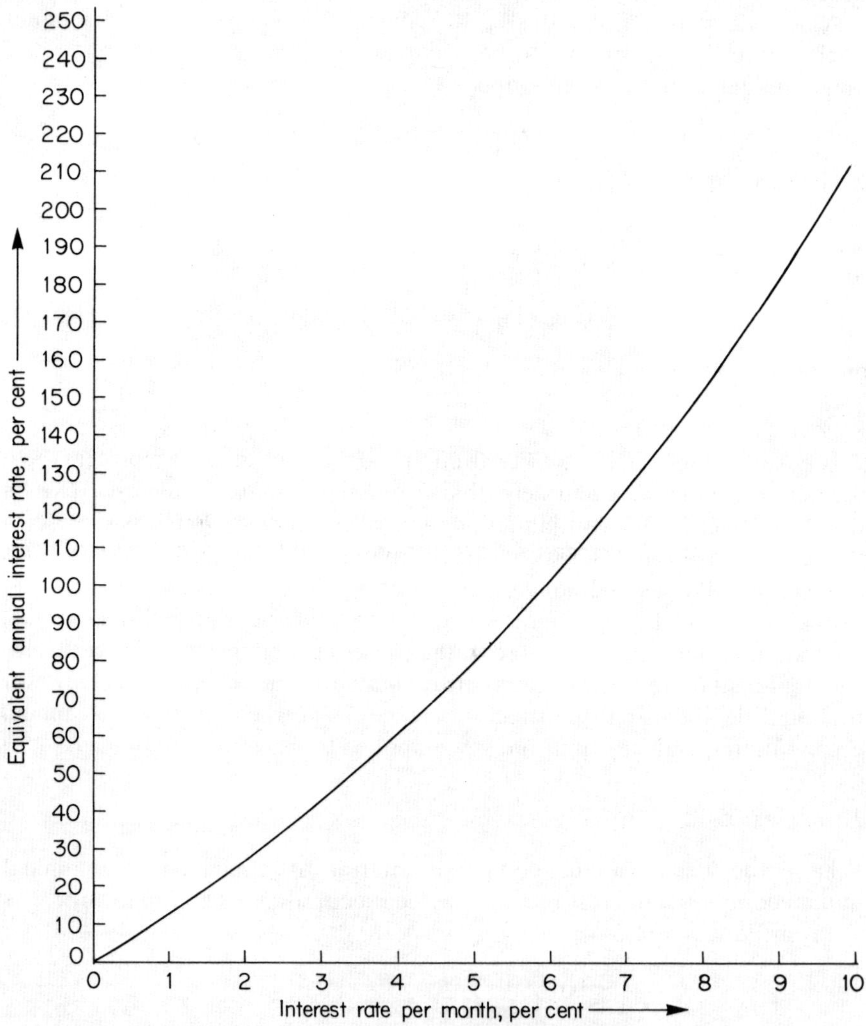

Figure (1.6-1) Equivalent annual interest rate against interest rate per month for compound interest

appears to be a reasonable interest rate per month are not fully aware of the equivalent high interest rate on an annual basis.

Example (1.6-1)

What is the annual interest rate equivalent to a compound interest rate of 3 per cent/month?

From Equation (1.6-1)

$$\begin{aligned} i &= (1 + i_m)^{12} - 1 \\ &= (1 + 0.03)^{12} - 1 \\ &= 0.426 \text{ or } 42.6 \text{ per cent/year} \end{aligned}$$

1.7 Annual Cost or Payment

A series of equal annual payments A invested at a fractional interest rate i and made at the end of each year over a period of n years may be used to build up a future sum of money F given by the equation

$$F = A\left[\frac{(1+i)^n - 1}{i}\right] \tag{1.7-1}$$

or

$$F = \frac{A}{f_{AF}} \tag{1.7-2}$$

where

$$f_{AF} = \frac{i}{(1+i)^n - 1} \text{ the annuity future worth factor}$$

values of which are readily available in tables similar to those in Appendix 1[3, 7, 9, 10, 14].

Equation (1.7-1) can be combined with Equation (1.3-3)

$$P = \frac{F}{(1+i)^n} \tag{1.3-3}$$

to give

$$P = A\left[\frac{(1+i)^n - 1}{i(1+i)^n}\right] \tag{1.7-3}$$

or

$$P = \frac{A}{f_{AP}} \tag{1.7-4}$$

where P is the present worth of the series of future equal annual payments A and

$$f_{AP} = \frac{i(1+i)^n}{(1+i)^n - 1} \text{ the annuity present worth factor}$$

values of which are readily available in tables similar to those in Appendix 1[4, 8, 9, 10, 15].

Alternatively the annual payment A required to build up a future sum of money F with a present value of P is given by the equations

$$A = Ff_{AF} \tag{1.7-5}$$

and

$$A = Pf_{AP} \tag{1.7-6}$$

It is possible to define other forms of annuity, in particular the annuity due, in which payments are made at the beginning of the year instead of at the end. In the deferred annuity, the first payment is deferred for a definite number of years. Formulae for such cases can readily be developed as follows for ordinary annuities.

Let A = annual cost or payment
i = fractional interest rate per year
n = number of years
F = future worth

The future worth of the first annual payment A is

$$F = A(1+i)^{n-1}$$

after compounding for $n-1$ years. The future worth of the second annual payment A is

$$F = A(1+i)^{n-2}$$

after compounding for $n-2$ years. Thus the combined future worth of all the payments is

$$F = A[(1+i)^{n-1} + (1+i)^{n-2} + (1+i)^{n-3} \ldots (1+i)^{n-n}]$$

where $(1+i)^{n-n} = 1$. Multiply both sides of the above equation by $(1+i)$ to give

$$F(1+i) = A[(1+i)^n + (1+i)^{n-1} + (1+i)^{n-2} \ldots (1+i)]$$

Subtract the previous equation from this to give

$$F(1+i) - F = A[(1+i)^n - 1]$$

which can be rewritten as

$$F = A\left[\frac{(1+i)^n - 1}{i}\right] \tag{1.7-1}$$

Example (1.7-1)

A man of 40 years of age plans to retire at 60 years of age. Calculate the annual payment required to give a lump sum of \$100,000 at retirement based on an annual compound interest rate of 5 per cent.

Required equation:

$$A = Ff_{\mathrm{AF}} \tag{1.7-5}$$

where the annuity future worth factor

$$f_{\mathrm{AF}} = \frac{i}{(1+i)^n - 1}$$

The annuity future worth factor for $i = 0.05$ and $n = 20$ years is

$$\begin{aligned} f_{\mathrm{AF}} &= \frac{i}{(1+i)^n - 1} \\ &= \frac{0.05}{(1+0.05)^{20} - 1} \\ &= 0.030\,24 \end{aligned}$$

The required annual payment A is given by Equation (1.7-5) to be

$$\begin{aligned} A &= Ff_{\mathrm{AF}} \\ &= (\$100{,}000)(0.030\,24) \\ &= \$3{,}024/\text{year} \end{aligned}$$

1.8 Capitalized Cost

A piece of equipment of fixed capital cost C_{FC} will have a finite life of n years. The capitalized cost of the equipment C_{K} is defined by the equation

$$(C_{\mathrm{K}} - C_{\mathrm{FC}})(1+i)^n = C_{\mathrm{K}} - S \tag{1.8-1}$$

C_{K} is in excess of C_{FC} by an amount which, when compounded at an annual interest rate i for n years, will have a future worth of C_{K} less the salvage or scrap value S. If the renewal cost of the equipment remains constant at $(C_{\mathrm{FC}} - S)$ and the interest rate remains constant at i then C_{K} is the amount of capital required to ensure that the equipment may be renewed in perpetuity.

Equation (1.8-1) may be rewritten as

$$C_K = \left[C_{FC} - \frac{S}{(1+i)^n}\right]\left[\frac{(1+i)^n}{(1+i)^n - 1}\right] \tag{1.8-2}$$

or

$$C_K = (C_{FC} - Sf_d)f_K \tag{1.8-3}$$

where

$$f_K = \frac{(1+i)^n}{(1+i)^n - 1} \quad \text{the capitalized cost factor}$$

values of which are available in tables similar to those in Appendix 1.

Example (1.8-1)

A piece of equipment has been installed at a cost of \$10,000. It is expected to have a working life of nine years with no scrap value. Calculate the capitalized cost of the equipment based on an annual compound interest rate of 6 per cent.

Required equation:

$$C_K = (C_{FC} - Sf_d)f_K \tag{1.8-3}$$

where the capitalized cost factor

$$f_K = \frac{(1+i)^n}{(1+i)^n - 1}$$

In this case $C_{FC} = \$10{,}000$
and $S = 0$

The capitalized cost factor for $i = 0.06$ and $n = 9$ years is

$$\begin{aligned} f_K &= \frac{(1+i)^n}{(1+i)^n - 1} \\ &= \frac{(1+0.06)^9}{(1+0.06)^9 - 1} \\ &= 2.450\ 37 \end{aligned}$$

The capitalized cost C_K is given by Equation (1.8-3) to be

$$\begin{aligned} C_K &= (\$10{,}000)(2.450\ 37) \\ &= \$24{,}503.7 \end{aligned}$$

References for Chapter 1

1. Baumeister, T., (Ed.), 'Standard Handbook for Mechanical Engineers', 2nd ed., p. 1–64, New York, McGraw-Hill Book Co. Inc., 1967
2. Ibid., p. 1–65
3. Ibid., p. 1–67
4. Ibid., p. 1–68
5. Perry, J. H., (Ed.), 'Chemical Business Handbook', p. 20–162, New York, McGraw–Hill Book Co. Inc., 1954
6. Ibid., p. 20–164
7. Ibid., p. 20–170
8. Ibid., p. 20–172
9. Perry, J. H., Chilton, C. H., and Kirkpatrick, S. D., (Ed.), 'Chemical Engineers' Handbook', 4th ed., p. 1–32 to 1–37, New York, McGraw–Hill Book Co. Inc., 1963
10. Perry, J. H., (Ed.), 'Engineering Manual', 2nd ed., p. 1–54 to 1–59, New York, McGraw–Hill Book Co. Inc., 1967
11. Riggs, J. L., 'Economic Decision Models for Engineers and Managers', p. 159, New York, McGraw–Hill Book Co. Inc., 1968
12. Souders, M., 'The Engineers' Companion', p. 274, New York, John Wiley and Sons, Inc., 1966
13. Ibid., p. 276
14. Ibid., p. 278
15. Ibid., p. 280

Problems for Chapter 1

(1.2-1) $1,000 is invested in a small business enterprise which operates over a five-year period. It costs $300/year to run the business and the cash receipts are $600/year in year 1 to year 5. The investment of $1,000 is available as a simple interest loan. It is assumed that the money is borrowed at the end of year 0.

Calculate the difference between the total cash receipts and the total costs over the five-year period for interest rates of 5 and 10 per cent per annum respectively.

(1.2-2) Rework the calculations in Problem (1.2-1) for a simple interest rate of 10 per cent per annum on the basis of a cash inflation of 5 per cent per annum. For year 1 take the cost of running the business as $300/year and the cash receipts as $600/year.

(1.3-1) What compound interest rates are required to make an investment of $1,000 grow to $100,000 over time periods of forty and sixty years respectively.

(1.3-2) Calculate how long it will take for money to double if compounded annually at 10 per cent/year.

(1.3-3) Annual sums of $3,000 are required at the end of one, two, three, and four years respectively. To provide these amounts, sums of money are invested now and at the end of each subsequent year for the next four years. The annual amounts invested are progressively decreased by a straight line reduction of 20 per cent each year.

Calculate the amount of the initial investment on the basis of a compound interest rate of 6 per cent/year.

(1.3-4) Write a modified form of the compound interest equation $F = P(1+i)^n$ for the case of different fractional interest rates $i_1, i_2, \ldots i_n$ in successive years.

(1.5-1) Calculate the future value of $10 after continuously compounding for fifteen years at a nominal annual interest rate of 20 per cent per year.

(1.5-2) Calculate the present value of $3,000 to be received as a single payment in twenty years' time using continuous discounting at a nominal annual interest rate of 10 per cent.

(1.6-1) Calculate the annual interest rate equivalents to compound interest rates of 1 per cent/month, and 5 per cent/month respectively.

(1.6-2) Calculate the annual interest rate equivalents to compound interest rates of 5 per cent/quarter year and 10 per cent/quarter year.

(1.7-1) The sum of $1,000 is invested at the end of each year over a period of fifteen years. Calculate the accumulated investment for compound interest rates of 4 and 8 per cent/year respectively.

(1.7-2) A sum of money is accumulated by investing a fixed annual payment at the end of each of ten years. $5,000 is withdrawn at the end of the tenth year and also at the end of each of the three subsequent years after which time the investment has been reduced to zero. Calculate the fixed annual payment on the basis of a compound interest rate of 6 per cent.

(1.8-1) A piece of equipment has been installed at a cost of $100,000. It is expected to have a working life of ten years with a scrap value of $20,000. Calculate the capitalized cost of the equipment based on an annual compound interest rate of 5 per cent.

Chapter 2

Costs and Traditional Methods of Estimating Profitability

The cash receipts from the sales of products is the main revenue of a business. For the most part, other cash flows are costs. The difference between revenue and costs is the earned income of a business. It is necessary to classify and analyse costs in order to run a business efficiently. Historical costs are costs actually incurred and these are related to past efficiency. So-called predetermined costs are costs which are expected to occur. These are the basis of standard costing and budgetary control systems. A knowledge of the variances between actual and predetermined costs facilitates the management of a business.

The day to day running of business is based largely on conventional accountancy practice. The normal accounting cost period is the calendar year. The traditional accounting method of determining profitability is to take the annual return on the invested capital. This apparently simple definition leads to much confusion since the terms can have a variety of meanings. These are discussed in this chapter together with a description of the relevant costs.

2.1 Annual Costs

Annual costs will be referred to by the letter A. The revenue A_S from the annual sales of a product minus the total annual cost or expense A_{TE} required to produce and sell the product excluding any annual provision for plant depreciation is the annual cash income A_{CI}.

$$A_{CI} = A_S - A_{TE} \tag{2.1-1}$$

The net annual cash income A_{NCI} is the annual cash income A_{CI} minus the annual amount of tax A_{IT}.

$$A_{NCI} = A_{CI} - A_{IT} \tag{2.1-2}$$

The taxable income is $(A_{CI} - A_D - A_A)$ where A_D is the annual depreciation charge and A_A is the annual amount of any other allowances. Some governments give annual tax allowances A_A to encourage companies to put in plant in otherwise unattractive areas. Neither A_D nor A_A involves any expenditure of cash since they are merely book transactions. The annual amount of tax A_{IT} is given by the equation

$$A_{IT} = (A_{CI} - A_D - A_A)\, t \tag{2.1-3}$$

where t is the fractional tax rate.

In practice the computation of the annual amount of tax A_{IT} is more complex than the method used in Equation (2.1-3). However the use of Equation (2.1-3) is justified for estimating purposes especially when the annual cash income cannot be predicted with a high degree of certainty.

Tax rates are determined by the appropriate tax authority and are subject to change. For most developed countries, the fractional tax rate t is in the region of 0.5 or 50 per cent.

The annual amount of tax A_{IT} included in Equation (2.1-2) does not necessarily correspond to the annual cash income A_{CI} in the same year. The tax payments in Equation (2.1-2) should be those actually paid in that year. In the U.S., companies pay about 80 per cent of the tax on estimated current year earnings in the same year. In the U.K., companies do not pay tax until at least nine months after the end of the accounting period which, for the most part, amounts to paying tax on the previous year's earnings. When assessing projects for foreign countries, engineers should acquaint themselves with the tax situation in that country.

In modern methods of profitability assessment, cash flows are more meaningful than profits which tend to be rather loosely defined. The net annual cash flow after tax is given by the equation

$$A_{CF} = A_{NCI} - A_{TC} \tag{2.1-4}$$

where A_{TC} is the annual expenditure of capital which is not necessarily zero after the plant has been built. For example, plant additions or modifications may be required in future years. Equations (2.1-1), (2.1-2), and (2.1-4) are illustrated diagrammatically in Figure (2.1-1).

The total annual expense A_{TE} required to produce and sell a product can be written as the sum of the annual general expense A_{GE} and the annual manufacturing cost or expense A_{ME}.

$$A_{TE} = A_{GE} + A_{ME} \tag{2.1-5}$$

The annual general expense A_{GE}[2] arises from the following items: administration, sales, shipping of product, advertising and marketing, technical service, research and development, and finance.

The terms gross annual profit A_{GP} and net annual profit A_{NP} are commonly used by accountants and businessmen. Normally both A_{GP} and A_{NP} are calculated before tax is deducted.

The gross annual profit A_{GP} is given by the equation

$$A_{GP} = A_S - A_{ME} - A_{BD} \tag{2.1-6}$$

where A_{BD} is the balance sheet annual depreciation charge which is not necessarily the same as A_D used in Equation (2.1-3) for tax purposes. For example, at the present time in the U.K., the entire fixed capital expenditure C_{FC} may be taken as a tax allowance in the first year of plant operation. In this case A_D in the first year of operation may be ten times greater than the balance sheet value A_{BD}.

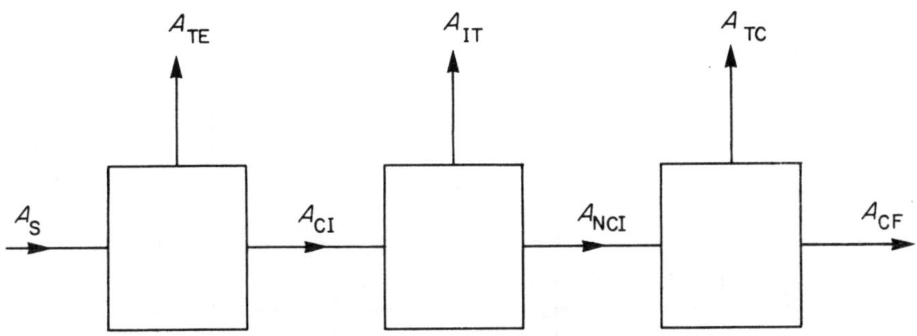

Figure (2.1-1) Annual cost and cash flows in a project

The net annual profit A_{NP} is simply A_{GP} minus the annual general expense A_{GE}.

$$A_{NP} = A_{GP} - A_{GE} \tag{2.1-7}$$

Equation (2.1-7) can also be written as

$$A_{NP} = A_{CI} - A_{BD} \tag{2.1-8}$$

The net annual profit after tax A_{NNP} can be written as

$$A_{NNP} = A_{NCI} - A_{BD} \tag{2.1-9}$$

It should be noted that A_{CI} and A_{NCI} in Equations (2.1-8) and (2.1-9) respectively are computed from actual cash flows whilst A_{BD} is merely a book transaction. This is a basic weakness in the concept of A_{NP} and A_{NNP}.

Figures (2.1-2) and (2.1-3) are diagrammatic representations of annual cash flow and annual profits respectively in a business. In these diagrams, A_{DIV} is

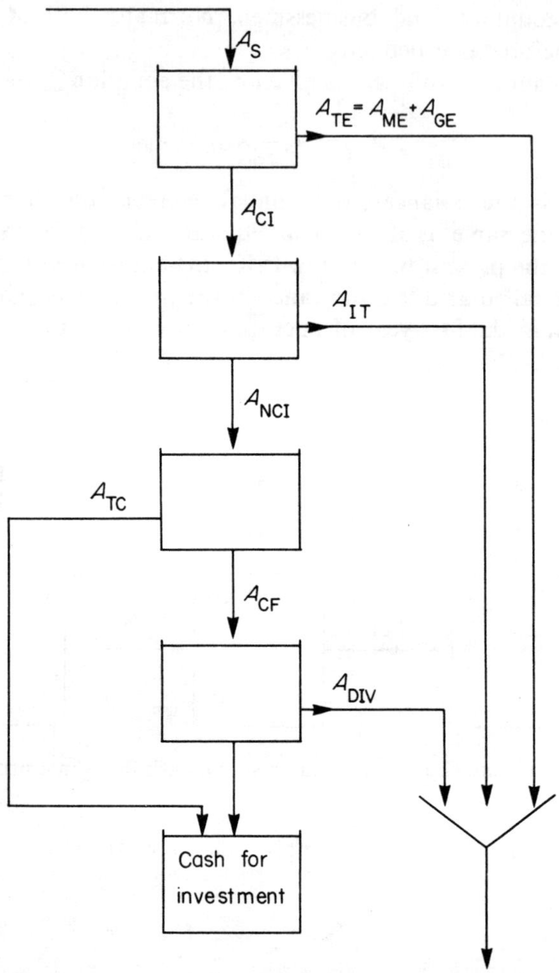

Figure (2.1-2) Diagrammatic representation of annual cash flow

the annual amount paid in dividends to the stockholders. The cash which is available for investment is that part of the revenue which remains after all costs, expenses, and cash outflows have been deducted.

The net annual cash flow A_{CF} in Equation (2.1-4) and Figure (2.1-2) excludes any provision for depreciation. A_{CF} is used in two of the more modern methods of profitability assessment; the net present value (NPV) method and the discounted cash flow rate of return (DCFRR) method. In both these methods, depreciation is inherently taken care of in the calculations which include capital recovery. These methods are described in detail in Chapter 3.

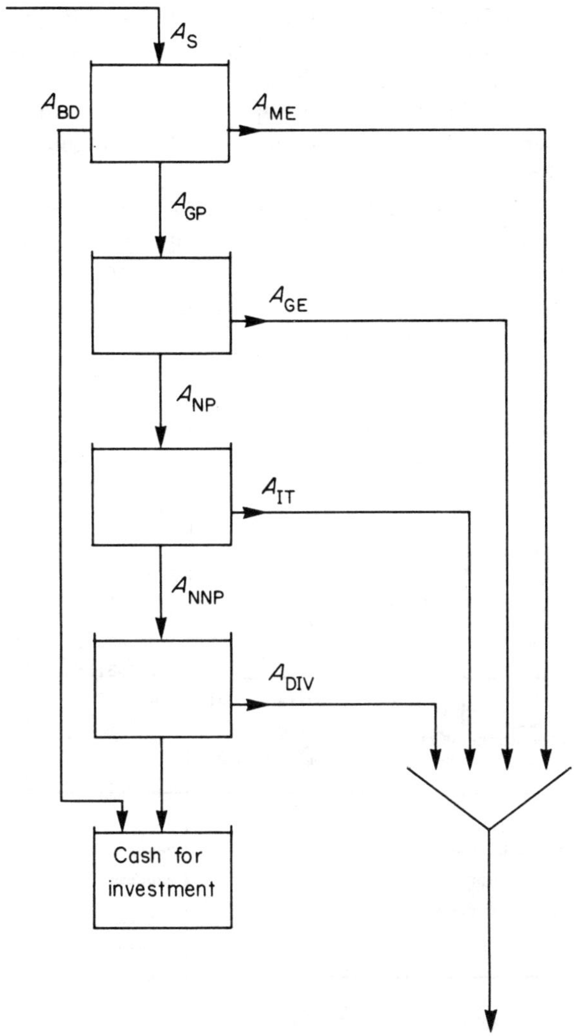

Figure (2.1-3) Diagrammatic representation of annual profits

2.2 Costs for a Manufactured Product

The annual manufacturing cost or expense A_{ME} can be written as the sum of the direct manufacturing cost or expense A_{DME} and the indirect manufacturing cost or expense A_{IME}.

$$A_{ME} = A_{DME} + A_{IME} \tag{2.2-1}$$

The direct manufacturing cost A_{DME} includes those expenses incurred directly from the production operation. These expenses arise from the following items: raw materials (including delivery), catalysts and solvents, operating labor, operating supervision, utilities, operating maintenance and repairs, operating supplies, royalties, and patents. The direct manufacturing cost is also known as the prime cost.

The indirect manufacturing cost A_{IME} includes those expenses incurred as a result of, but not directly from, the production operation. These expenses arise from the following items: payroll overhead, control laboratory, general plant overhead, packaging, and storage facilities. Other indirect costs include

TABLE (2.2-1)

Costs for a manufactured product

direct materials		prime or direct cost (variable)	manufacturing or production cost (fixed and variable)	total cost or expense
direct labor direct utilities other direct expenses	processing cost			
manufacturing overhead		indirect cost (fixed and semivariable)		
administrative expense selling and distribution expense other general overhead expenses			general expense (fixed and variable)	

those expenses which are a function of the fixed capital investment. These expenses arise from the following items: property taxes, rent, and insurance. The indirect manufacturing cost A_{IME} is often referred to as the manufacturing overhead cost.

The various items of cost for a manufactured product are listed in Table (2.2-1).

Accountants like to separate all costs into fixed and variable elements. The annual general expense A_{GE} can be written as the sum of the fixed general expense A_{FGE} and the variable general expense A_{VGE}.

$$A_{GE} = A_{FGE} + A_{VGE} \tag{2.2-2}$$

Similarly the annual manufacturing expense A_{ME} can be written as the sum of the fixed manufacturing expense A_{FME} and the variable manufacturing expense A_{VME}.

$$A_{ME} = A_{FME} + A_{VME} \tag{2.2-3}$$

2.3 Contribution and Variable Costing[13]

Equation (2.1-1) which gives the annual cash income A_{CI} can also be written in terms of Equations (2.1-5), (2.2-2), and (2.2-3) either as

$$A_{CI} = [A_S - (A_{VGE} + A_{VME})] - (A_{FGE} + A_{FME}) \tag{2.3-1}$$

or as

$$A_{CI} = A_S - A_{TVE} - A_{TFE} \tag{2.3-2}$$

where A_{TFE} and A_{TVE} are the total annual fixed expenses and the total annual variable expenses respectively.

If the annual sales volume can be taken as equal to the annual production rate R, the revenue A_S from annual sales is the product of R and the sales price c_S per unit of production.

$$A_S = Rc_S \tag{2.3-3}$$

In practice the inventory of raw materials, work in progress, and finished products at the beginning and end of the accounting year may differ. Since the annual sales volume is strictly speaking R plus the inventory at the beginning of the year minus the inventory at the end of the year, Equation (2.3-3) may be only approximately true.

For the most part, the total annual variable expense A_{TVE} can be taken as proportional to the annual production rate R and the total variable expense c_{TVE} per unit of production.

$$A_{TVE} = Rc_{TVE} \tag{2.3-4}$$

Substitute Equations (2.3-3) and (2.3-4) into Equation (2.3-2) to give

$$A_{CI} = R(c_S - c_{TVE}) - A_{TFE} \tag{2.3-5}$$

where Equation (2.3-5) gives the annual cash income A_{CI} in terms of the annual production rate R. The term $(c_S - c_{TVE})$ is called the contribution to cash income per unit of production. Sometimes the contribution is taken as the sales price minus the variable manufacturing expense per unit of production.

When inventory is valued on the basis of variable manufacturing expense, the method is known as direct, marginal, or variable costing. When inventory is valued on the basis of both variable and fixed manufacturing expenses, the method is known as full, total, or absorption costing.

Marginal costs have the advantage that they remain the same irrespective of the volume of production. However marginal costing can give misleading results when different parts of a business or plant benefit widely from assets which incur fixed costs. In this case it may be necessary to apportion fixed costs.

Although the separation of costs into fixed and variable components is popular with accountants, there are differences of opinion as to exactly which items should be included in the fixed and the variable costs respectively. Royalties and patents may be either fixed or variable costs, depending upon the way in which the agreements are written. An increasing number of companies regard labor as a fixed rather than a variable expense. Operators cannot conveniently be transferred to other duties when a plant is temporarily shut down or is operating at a reduced capacity. Similarly there are differences of opinion as to which items should be direct costs and which should be indirect costs.

Equation (2.3-5) can be combined with Equation (2.1-8) to give the equation

$$A_{NP} = R(c_S - c_{TVE}) - A_{TFE} - A_{BD} \tag{2.3-6}$$

which can also be written in the form

$$A_{NP} = R(c_S - c_{TVE}) - A_{FGE} - A_{FME} - A_{BD} \tag{2.3-7}$$

Equation (2.3-7) gives the net annual profit A_{NP} before tax in terms of the annual fixed general expense A_{FGE}, the annual fixed manufacturing expense A_{FME}, and the balance sheet annual depreciation charge A_{BD}.

The difference between the sales price c_S and the total variable cost c_{TVE} per unit of production represents a contribution to the fixed expenses A_{FGE}, A_{FME}, and A_{BD} and to the net annual profit A_{NP}. The term $(c_S - c_{TVE})$ is the contribution to net profit per unit of production and $R(c_S - c_{TVE})$ is the annual contribution for a production rate R.

2.4 Breakeven Production Rate

Equation (2.3-7) shows that the net annual profit A_{NP} is positive when $R(c_S - c_{TVE}) > (A_{FGE} + A_{FME} + A_{BD})$ and negative when $R(c_S - c_{TVE}) < (A_{FGE} + A_{FME} + A_{BD})$. The net annual profit A_{NP} is zero at an annual production rate R_B given by the equation

$$R_B = \frac{A_{FGE} + A_{FME} + A_{BD}}{c_S - c_{TVE}} \tag{2.4-1}$$

where R_B is known as the breakeven production rate. R_B can be written in terms of its component parts as follows:

$$R_B = \Delta R_{FGE} + \Delta R_{FME} + \Delta R_{BD} \tag{2.4-2}$$

where

$$\Delta R_{FGE} = \frac{A_{FGE}}{c_S - c_{TVE}} \tag{2.4-3}$$

$$\Delta R_{FME} = \frac{A_{FME}}{c_S - c_{TVE}} \tag{2.4-4}$$

and

$$\Delta R_{BD} = \frac{A_{BD}}{c_S - c_{TVE}} \tag{2.4-5}$$

ΔR_{FGE}, ΔR_{FME}, and ΔR_{BD} are the increments of production rate required to cover the annual fixed general expense A_{FGE}, the annual fixed manufacturing expense A_{FME}, and the balance sheet annual depreciation charge A_{BD} respectively.

Combine Equations (2.3-7) and (2.4-1) to give

$$A_{NP} = (R - R_B)(c_S - c_{TVE}) \tag{2.4-6}$$

Equation (2.4-6) shows that above the breakeven production rate R_B, the contribution is all net profit.

Equation (2.3-7) is diagrammatically illustrated in Figure (2.4-1). A decrease in selling price c_S will decrease the slope of the line in Figure (2.4-1)

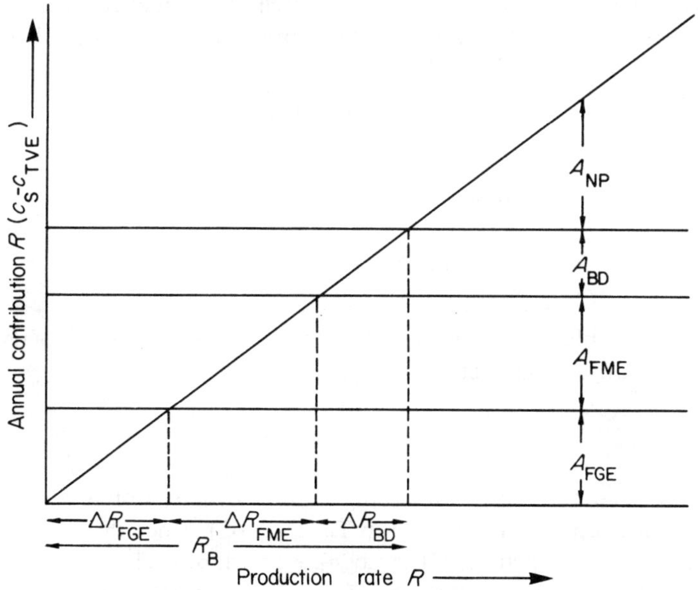

Figure (2.4-1) Annual contribution against production rate

TABLE (2.4-1)

Effect of production rate on net profit

	\$	\$	\$
selling price per lb c_S	0.10	0.10	0.10
total variable expense per lb c_{TVE} including materials	0.09	0.09	0.09
annual production rate lb/yr R	10,000,000	20,000,000	30,000,000
$R(c_S - c_{TVE})$	100,000	200,000	300,000
total annual fixed expense A_{TFE}	50,000	50,000	50,000
annual depreciation charge A_{BD}	50,000	50,000	50,000
net annual profit A_{NP}	0	100,000	200,000
net profit per lb	0	0.005	0.0067

and increase the required breakeven production rate R_B. The effect of production rate on net profit is also illustrated in Table (2.4-1).

A consideration of contribution is extremely helpful to management in analysing cost data. Because of the fixed components in net profit, a solution which maximizes contribution also maximizes profit. This is useful when considering whether to add or delete a particular product from a company's product range. The contribution to sales price ratio (CSR) is also used to analyse this kind of problem where

$$(\text{CSR}) = \frac{c_S - c_{TVE}}{c_S} \tag{2.4-7}$$

which can also be written as

$$(\text{CSR}) = 1 - \frac{c_{TVE}}{c_S} \tag{2.4-8}$$

The most profitable product is the one with the highest (CSR). This parameter is useful for ranking products.

Example 2.4-1

A company is committed to producing a range of five similar products. The present production pattern is given in Table (2.4-2). Since the manufacturing process is similar in each case it is possible to adapt each of the production lines to produce the given quantity of any of the other products. Compare the present cash flow pattern with that obtainable from the most profitable

TABLE (2.4-2)

product	A	B	C	D	E
units/year	1,000	2,000	3,000	5,000	10,000
direct materials cost, $/unit	6.00	6.00	7.30	5.80	6.80
direct labor cost, $/unit	3.00	3.00	2.50	2.50	2.00
variable overhead cost, $/unit	1.00	1.40	3.10	4.20	1.70
fixed overhead cost, $/unit	5.00	4.50	4.20	2.50	1.20
sales price, $/unit	14.00	14.50	17.00	15.00	12.00

use of the existing equipment. Assume that the fixed overhead costs relate to the production line and not to the product made.

The profitability calculations for the present method of working are given in Table (2.4-3) from which it will be seen that the products are produced at rates ranked according to profit per unit. This results in a profit to sales ratio of $900/$289,000 = 0.31 per cent.

TABLE (2.4-3)

product	A	B	C	D	E	total $/year
units/year	1,000	2,000	3,000	5,000	10,000	
direct materials cost, $/unit	6.00	6.00	7.30	5.80	6.80	136,900
direct labor cost, $/unit	3.00	3.00	2.50	2.50	2.00	49,000
variable overhead cost, $/unit	1.00	1.40	3.10	4.20	1.70	51,100
fixed overhead cost, $/unit	5.00	4.50	4.20	2.50	1.20	51,100
manufacturing cost, $/unit	15.00	14.90	17.10	15.00	11.70	288,100
selling price, $/unit	14.00	14.50	17.00	15.00	12.00	289,000
profit (loss), $/unit	(1.00)	(0.40)	(0.10)	0.00	0.30	900
total variable cost, $/unit	10.00	10.40	12.90	12.50	10.50	
contribution, $/unit	4.00	4.10	4.10	2.50	1.50	
(CSR)	0.286	0.283	0.241	0.167	0.125	
profitability ranking	1	2	3	4	5	

The profitability calculations for highest margin are given in Table (2.4-4) where the products are produced at rates ranked according to contribution to sales ratio (CSR). This results in a profit to sales ratio of $28,200/$305,500 = 9.23 per cent with the capital tied up in manufactured stock reduced by $10,800/$288,100 = 3.75 per cent.

It would be advisable to boost the sales of products A and B at the expense of D and E, possibly by increasing the price of the latter. Product C is marginal and a slight increase in production rate or price, or a lowering of costs, could make it profitable.

TABLE (2.4-4)

product	E	D	C	B	A	total $/year
units/year	1,000	2,000	3,000	5,000	10,000	
direct materials cost, $/unit	6.80	5.80	7.30	6.00	6.00	130,300
direct labor cost, $/unit	2.00	2.50	2.50	3.00	3.00	59,500
variable overhead cost, $/unit	1.70	4.20	3.10	1.40	1.00	36,400
fixed overhead cost, $/unit	5.00	4.50	4.20	2.50	1.20	51,100
manufacturing cost, $/unit	15.50	17.00	17.10	12.90	11.20	277,300
selling price, $/unit	12.00	15.00	17.00	14.50	14.00	305,500
profit (loss), $/unit	(3.50)	(2.00)	(0.10)	1.60	2.80	28,200
total variable cost, $/unit	10.50	12.50	12.90	10.40	10.00	
contribution, $/unit	1.50	2.50	4.10	4.10	4.00	
(CSR)	0.125	0.167	0.241	0.283	0.286	
profitability ranking	5	4	3	2	1	

2.5 Capital Cost

The total capital cost C_{TC} of a project consists of the fixed capital cost C_{FC} plus the working capital cost C_{WC} plus the cost of land and other non-depreciable costs C_L.

$$C_{TC} = C_{FC} + C_{WC} + C_L \tag{2.5-1}$$

The project may be a complete plant, an addition to an existing plant, or a modification of an existing plant.

Table (2.5-1) shows an estimated profit and loss statement for a new chemical showing the rate of return on total capital employed C_{TC}.

Fixed capital cost:[1, 3, 10] The fixed capital cost C_{FC} includes the following items:

major process equipment (i.e. reactors, tanks, pumps, filters, distillation columns, etc.),
installation of major process equipment,
process piping,
insulation,
instrumentation,
auxiliary facilities (i.e. power substations, transformers, boiler house, fire control equipment, etc.),
outside lines (i.e. piping external to buildings plus supports and posts for overhead piping, electric feeders from power substations),
land and site improvements,
buildings and structures,

TABLE (2.5-1)

Profit and loss statement for a mature year

Basis: new chemical product - 5 million lb/year

		$	¢/lb	% sales revenue
revenue from annual sales A_S		1,000,000	20.00	100.00
raw materials	442,000		8.84	44.2
catalysts and solvents	34,400		0.69	3.4
operating labor	51,000		1.02	5.1
operating supervision	10,000		0.20	1.0
utilities	11,000		0.22	1.1
operating maintenance	10,600		0.21	1.1
operating supplies	2,000		0.04	0.2
royalties and patents	5,000		0.10	0.5
direct manufacturing expense, A_{DME}	566,000	566,000	11.32	56.6
payroll overhead	14,000		0.28	1.4
central laboratory	5,000		0.10	0.5
general plant overhead	26,000		0.52	2.6
packaging and storage	11,000		0.22	1.1
property taxes	7,000		0.14	0.7
insurance	3,000		0.06	0.3
indirect manufacturing expense, A_{IME}	66,000	66,000	1.32	6.6
total manufacturing expense excluding depreciation, A_{ME}		632,000	12.64	63.2
depreciation, A_{BD}		34,000	0.68	3.4
administration	37,000		0.74	3.7
sales and shipping	62,000		1.24	6.2
advertising and marketing	20,000		0.40	2.0
technical service	5,000		0.10	0.5
research and development	30,000		0.60	3.0
	154,000	154,000	3.08	15.4
total cost or expense, A_{TE}		820,000	16.40	82.0

	$
net annual profit, A_{NP}	180,000
less taxes @ 50.0%	90,000
net annual profit after tax, A_{NNP}	90,000
total capital, C_{TC}	495,000
includes fixed capital, C_{FC}	350,000
and working capital, C_{WC}	145,000

$$\text{after tax rate of return, } i = \frac{A_{NNP}}{C_{TC}}$$

$$= 18.2\%$$

engineering and construction (design and engineering fees plus supervision of plant erection),

contractors' fees.

Some companies make an allowance for the escalation of equipment prices, unforeseen engineering and process design charges.

Working capital cost: The working capital cost C_{WC} of a process or business normally includes the following items:

raw materials for plant start up,
raw material, work in progress, and finished product inventories,
cost of handling and transportation of materials to and from store,
cost of inventory control, warehouse, associated insurance, security arrangements, etc.,
money to carry accounts receivable (i.e. credit extended to customers), less accounts payable (i.e. credit extended by suppliers),
money to meet payrolls when starting up,
readily available cash for emergencies,
any additional cash required to operate the process or business.

Since working capital is completely recoverable at any time, in theory if not in practice, no tax allowance is made for depreciation. The same is also true of the value of the land occupied by the plant.

The working capital may vary from a very small fraction of the total capital cost to almost the whole of the invested capital depending on the process and the industry. For example in jewelry store operations the fixed capital is very small in comparison with the working capital. In the process industries, land costs are normally a small fraction of the total investment while the working capital is likely to be of the order of 10 to 20 per cent of the value of the fixed capital investment.

Bechtel[4] gave the following three methods for estimating the required working capital:

(1) Compute inventory costs on the basis of one month's supply of raw material, one month's supply of semifinished material (based on raw material plus one half the conversion cost) and one month's supply of finished material. Add accounts receivable valued as one month's sales. Also add one month's operating cash.

(2) Take 30 per cent of annual sales.

(3) Take 15 per cent of the fixed capital investment.

The three methods are listed in order of decreasing accuracy. However, where seasonal markets exist, method (1) is subject to error. Bechtel[4] cited a project in which the rate of return was 32.5 per cent excluding working capital. The rate of return with working capital included was 27.0 per cent using method (1), 25.8 per cent using method (2), and 28.5 per cent using method (3).

It is common in accountancy to regard the working capital of a business as the current assets minus the current liabilities. Inadequate working capital may result in underusage of fixed assets. An increase in credit to customers in order to stimulate sales tends to increase the working capital required. Too much expansion may lead to overtrading and finally bankruptcy.

The working capital required is a function of the inventory turnover and sales cycle. These are inversely proportional to each other. Thus for an inventory turnover of twelve times per year, the sales cycle is one month. The higher the inventory turnover, the lower the ratio of required working capital to sales. However, if sales decrease, additional working capital would be required to launch or increase an advertising campaign.

2.6 Depreciation[12]

The term depreciation is used in a number of different contexts. The most common of these are as:

(1) a cost of operation
(2) a tax allowance
(3) a means of building up a fund to finance plant replacement
(4) a measure of falling value

In the first case, depreciation is considered to be a manufacturing cost in the same way as labor cost or raw materials cost. However, it is more difficult to estimate a depreciation cost per unit of product than it is a labor or a raw materials cost. In the net present value (NPV) and discounted cash flow rate of return (DCFRR) methods of measuring profitability, which are discussed in Chapter 3, depreciation as a cost of operation is implicitly accounted for. (NPV) and (DCFRR) give measures of return after a project has generated sufficient money to recover the original investment.

The depreciation cost is a major cost of running a car, as is the case with any other piece of equipment. It is not possible to calculate this cost without first making an estimate of the life of the car and either its scrap or used value. The depreciation cost can be estimated either on the basis of time or usage. On the basis of time, the same depreciation cost can be taken for each year of the car's life. Alternatively a higher depreciation cost can be taken in the earlier years to offset the higher maintenance costs required in the later years of the car. An additional consideration is whether depreciation should be based on the historical cost of the car, i.e. the price actually paid for it. The alternative is to base depreciation on an adjusted or revalued cost to account for the fact that in a time of inflation an equivalent new car will cost more. Considerations such as these apply to the depreciation of process plant.

In the second case, the annual taxable income is reduced by an annual depreciation charge or allowance which reduces the annual amount of tax payable. The annual depreciation charge is merely a book transaction and does not involve any expenditure of cash. The method of determining the annual depreciation charge must be agreed with the appropriate tax authority within the context of the existing tax laws.

In the third case, depreciation is considered as a means of providing for plant replacement. However, in the rapidly changing modern processing industries, it is doubtful if many plants will ever be replaced since the processes are likely to have become obsolete during operation. Furthermore, management must be free to invest its available capital in the currently most profitable projects. However, management may wish to regard a proportion of retained profits as a fund to finance new capital projects. For the most part these are likely to differ substantially from the projects which originally generated the profits.

A plant may become obsolete before the end of its estimated life. In general a plant should be scrapped when an alternative process becomes more profitable to operate. The risk of premature obsolescence is increasing in modern industry. Companies should have reserves to take care of technological obsolescence of fixed assets in addition to normal depreciation.

In the fourth case, a plant or a piece of equipment has a limited useful life. The primary reason for the decrease in value is the decrease in future life and the consequent decrease in the number of years for which income will be earned. At the end of its life, the equipment may be worth nothing or it may have a salvage or scrap value S. Thus a plant of fixed capital cost C_{FC} depreciates in value during its useful life of s years by an amount $(C_{FC} - S)$. The useful life of s years is taken from the start up of the plant.

On the basis of straight line depreciation, the average annual amount of depreciation A_D is given by the equation

$$A_D = \frac{(C_{FC} - S)}{s} \tag{2.6-1}$$

Estimated values for the useful life s of common pieces of equipment are widely available. However, it is more difficult to predict the life of a plant. This may be a function of climatic conditions in addition to wear and tear.

The book value after the first year, P_1 is given by the equation

$$P_1 = C_{FC} - A_D \tag{2.6-2}$$

The book value at the end of a particular year s' is given by the equation

$$P_{s'} = C_{FC} - s' A_D \tag{2.6-3}$$

The principal significance of a particular depreciation rate is for tax purposes. The annual depreciation A_D is subtracted from the annual profit before the latter is taxed. The basis for depreciation in a particular case is a matter for agreement between the taxation authority and the company within the context of the existing tax laws.

Two other commonly used methods of computing depreciation are the declining balance method, also known as the fixed percentage method, and the sum of years digits method.

On the basis of declining balance or fixed percentage depreciation the book value at the end of the first year is given by the equation

$$P_1 = C_{FC}(1 - r) \tag{2.6-4}$$

where r is a fraction to be agreed with the taxation authority.

The book value at the end of a particular year s' is given by the equation

$$P_{s'} = C_{FC}(1 - r)^{s'} \tag{2.6-5}$$

When the fraction r is chosen to be $2/s$, i.e. twice the reciprocal of the service life s, the method is called the double declining balance method.

The declining balance method of depreciation allows equipment or plant to be depreciated by a greater amount during the early years than during the later years. The method does not allow equipment or plant to be depreciated to a zero value at the end of the service life.

On the basis of sum of years digits depreciation, the annual amount of depreciation for a particular year s' is given by the equation

$$A_{Ds'} = \frac{s - s' + 1}{1 + 2 + 3 + \ldots + s}(C_{FC} - S) \tag{2.6-6}$$

for a plant of fixed capital cost C_{FC} and scrap value S.

Equation (2.6-6) can also be written in the form

$$A_{Ds'} = \frac{2(s - s' + 1)}{s(s + 1)}(C_{FC} - S) \tag{2.6-7}$$

It can be shown that the book value at the end of a particular year s' is given by the equation

$$P_{s'} = \frac{(s - s')(s - s' + 1)(C_{FC} - S)}{s(s + 1)} + S \tag{2.6-8}$$

The sum of years digits depreciation also allows equipment or plant to be depreciated by a greater amount during the early years than during the later years. This method is not allowed in the U.K.

A fourth method of computing depreciation which is now seldom used is the sinking fund method. In this method, the annual depreciation A_D is the same for each year of the life of the equipment or plant. The series of equal amounts of depreciation A_D invested at a fractional interest rate i and made at the end of each year over the life of the equipment or plant of s years are used to build up a future sum of money equal to $(C_{FC} - S)$. The latter is the fixed capital cost of the equipment or plant C_{FC} minus its salvage or scrap value S and is the total amount of depreciation during its useful life of s years. The equation relating $(C_{FC} - S)$ and A_S is simply the annual cost or payment equation written either as

$$C_{FC} - S = A_D\left[\frac{(1+i)^s - 1}{i}\right] \tag{2.6-9}$$

or as

$$C_{FC} - S = \frac{A_D}{f_{AF}} \tag{2.6-10}$$

where

$$f_{AF} = \frac{i}{(1+i)^s - 1} \text{ the annuity future worth factor}$$

values of which are readily available in tables similar to those in Appendix 1.

In the sinking fund method of depreciation, the effect of interest is to make the annual decrease of the book value of the equipment or plant less in the early than in the later years.

Some of the above methods of computing depreciation are not allowed by the taxation authorities in certain countries. When calculating depreciation, it is necessary to obtain details of the methods and rates permitted by the appropriate authority, and to use the information provided. In order to stimulate investment in certain countries, a government may allow one hundred per cent depreciation in the first year. This is currently the case in the U.K.

Example (2.6-1)

Calculate the annual depreciation charge A_D to be allowed on the basis of:

(a) straight line depreciation over ten years
(b) double declining depreciation
(c) sum of the years digit depreciation over ten years for a plant with fixed capital cost $C_{FC} = \$200,000$ and estimated scrap value $S = \$10,000$

(a) *With straight line depreciation*

Required equation:

$$A_D = \frac{(C_{FC} - S)}{s} \tag{2.6-1}$$

Substitute $C_{FC} = \$200,000$, $S = \$10,000$ and the depreciable life $s = 10$ years into Equation (2.6-1) to give

$$A_D = \frac{(C_{FC} - S)}{s}$$

$$= \frac{(\$200{,}000 - \$10{,}000)}{10 \text{ years}}$$

$$= \$19{,}000/\text{year}$$

in each of the ten years.

(b) *With double declining depreciation*

Required equation:

$$P_{s'} = C_{FC}(1 - r)^{s'} \tag{2.6-5}$$

Double declining depreciation is a special case of declining balance depreciation in which the annual fractional rate of decline r is defined as $r = 2/s$. In the present case

$$r = \frac{2}{10 \text{ years}} = 0.2/\text{year}$$

The annual depreciation charge in year s' is

$$A_D = P_{s'-1} - P_{s'} = C_{FC}\, r(1 - r)^{s'-1}$$

The depreciation in year 1 is therefore

$$A_{D1} = (\$200{,}000)(0.2)(0.8)^0 = \$40{,}000$$

The depreciation in year 2 is

$$A_{D2} = (\$200{,}000)(0.2)(0.8)^1 = (\$40{,}000)(0.8) = \$32{,}000$$

The depreciation in year 3 is

$$A_{D3} = (\$200{,}000)(0.2)(0.8)^2 = (\$32{,}000)(0.8) = \$25{,}600$$

The calculation is continued in the same way until the sum of the annual depreciation allowances totals $(C_{FC} - S) = \$190{,}000$. This requires the calculated value for year 10 to be increased from \$5,369 to \$16,843 in order to write off the debt in ten years.

(c) *With sum of the years digits depreciation*

Required equation:

$$A_{Ds'} = \frac{2(s - s' + 1)}{s(s + 1)}(C_{FC} - S) \tag{2.6-7}$$

From Equation (2.6-7) the depreciation in year 1 is

$$A_{Ds'} = \frac{2(s - s' + 1)}{s(s+1)}(C_{FC} - S)$$
$$= \frac{2(10 - 1 + 1)}{10(11)}(\$200{,}000 - \$10{,}000)$$
$$= (11 - 1)(\$3{,}454.5)$$
$$= \$34{,}545$$

Similarly for year 2

$$A_{D2} = (11 - 2)(\$3{,}454.5)$$
$$= \$31{,}091$$

The results of the above calculations are presented in Table (2.15-1).

2.7 Cost Indexes[11]

A quotation for a piece of equipment or a job of work is given at a particular point in time. Since most costs tend to increase it is necessary to have some basis for comparing costs at one time with those at another. Various cost indexes are used for this purpose. A typical cost index is the Marshall and Stevens equipment cost index for the U.S. process industry, values of which are published regularly in 'Chemical Engineering'. The Marshall and Stevens equipment cost index has a base value of 100 in 1926, a value of 206 in 1956 and a value of 252 in 1966. Thus if a plant costs \$1,000,000 in 1956 it would have cost

$$\$1{,}000{,}000 \times \frac{252}{206} = \$1{,}223{,}000 \text{ in } 1966.$$

Cost indexes can be very useful if used intelligently. However, they only give average costs and may be misleading when used for specific items. Furthermore, different indexes in the same field can predict costs which differ significantly.

2.8 Cost Scaling[7,8]

Let the cost of a piece of equipment or plant of size or capacity Q_1 be C_1. The cost C_2 of a similar piece of equipment or plant of size or capacity Q_2 can be calculated from the equation

$$C_2 = C_1 \left(\frac{Q_2}{Q_1}\right)^{\psi} \tag{2.8-1}$$

where the value of the exponent ψ depends on the type of equipment or plant[5,6]. For many types of equipment $\psi = 0.6$ and Equation (2.8-1) is commonly referred to as the six tenths factor rule. However, this rule should only be used in the absence of available cost data for the particular size of equipment required. For complete process plants the exponent in Equation (2.8-1) is usually taken to be $\psi = 0.7$. However, in the case of process plants where the capacity is increased by duplicating a number of pieces of equipment the exponent will be higher and may even approach a value of 1.0. Highly instrumentated and continuous processes scale up on a lower power than 0.7.

For many processes, labor hours can be scaled up using an exponent of 0.25 in Equation (2.8-1)[9]. For batch processes the exponent may be higher.

2.9 Cost of Money

Capital for new installations may be obtained in one of the following ways:

(1) loans from banks
(2) issue by the company of common stock (equity capital), preferred stock, and bonds or debentures
(3) out of net cash flow arising from undistributed profits and depreciation

Interest on loans, preferred stock, and bonds is paid at a fixed interest rate. The interest on common stock varies according to the prosperity of the company.

Traditionally a relatively high interest rate is paid on common stock since the holder is liable to lose the whole of his capital. A relatively low interest rate is paid on bonds since the holder usually has a prior claim on the assets of the company. The holder of preferred stock is in an intermediate position with some chance of losing his capital. In recent years low interest rates have been paid on many common stocks. Their attraction has been the relatively high probability of increasing capital value.

Interest payable on loans and bonds is regarded as a business expense. Thus every dollar spent on interest for loans and bonds costs the company only $\$(1 - t)$ where t is the fractional tax rate. In contrast interest on both common and preferred stock must be paid out of net profits remaining after payment of tax.

In general, the cost of capital should be set at a level which gives stockholders the rate of return obtainable from comparable investments outside the company. New issues of common stock should give a yield at least as great as that obtained from existing common stock in the company. Usually a company will finance its projects by issuing a mixture of new common stock and fixed interest bonds or loans. The cost of the new finance is obtained by calculating the weighted average return which must be paid on the various types of capital. Thus the true cost of capital for a firm is the marginal cost of obtaining new finance.

Suppose that the capital structure of a company is made up of an amount C_B of loans or bonds and an amount C_O of ownership capital. If the net annual cash income after deduction of tax is A_{NCI}, then the fractional rate of interest i_1 on the total capital is

$$i_1 = \frac{A_{NCI}}{C_O + C_B} \tag{2.9-1}$$

or

$$A_{NCI} = i_1(C_O + C_B) \tag{2.9-2}$$

The fractional rate of interest i_2 earned on the ownership capital will be

$$i_2 = \frac{A_{NCI} - i_3(1-t)\,C_B}{C_O} \tag{2.9-3}$$

where i_3 is the fractional interest rate payable on the loan capital and t is the fractional tax rate. Combine Equations (2.9-2) and (2.9-3) and write

$$i_2 = \frac{i_1(C_O + C_B) - i_3(1-t)\,C_B}{C_O} \tag{2.9-4}$$

or

$$i_2 = i_1 + \frac{C_B}{C_O}[i_1 - i_3(1-t)] \tag{2.9-5}$$

The ratio C_B/C_O is known as the 'gearing ratio' or leverage and, for many companies, lies between zero and 1.0. The calculation becomes more complex if taxation of capital gains and stockholders' dividends are considered.

Clearly, no common stock holders will be satisfied if management decisions result in a lower rate of return on their investments. They will try to recover their capital by selling their equity stock, thus reducing the quoted stock market prices. This, in turn, will increase the effective yield of a given dividend payment.

In practice, the dividend yield depends on the composite returns from all activities of the company. These may include unprofitable as well as profitable activities. They also include social and welfare activities which involve expenditure and earn no income. Failures and non-productive facilities lower the average yield earned by a firm. Hence, any new activity should promise a better than average yield on the equity capital.

2.10 Rate of Return on Invested Capital

The traditional rate of return methods of estimating profitability are based on the equation

$$\text{per cent rate of return} = \frac{\text{annual return}}{\text{invested capital}} \times 100 \qquad (2.10\text{-}1)$$

These methods are still widely employed by accountants in spite of the development of more modern methods for estimating profitability. The most common of the modern methods are described in Chapter 3.

Although the traditional methods based on Equation (2.10-1) have the advantage of simplicity they can give very misleading results.

The annual return in Equation (2.10-1) can either be the annual cash income A_{CI} given by Equation (2.1-1), the net annual cash income A_{NCI} given by Equation (2.1-2), the gross annual profit A_{GP} given by Equation (2.1-6), the net annual profit A_{NP} given by Equation (2.1-7), or the net annual profit after tax A_{NNP} given by Equation (2.1-9). The values of A_{GP}, A_{NP}, and A_{NNP} all depend on the value of the balance sheet annual depreciation charge A_{BD}. Since A_{BD} is arbitrarily chosen, A_{GP}, A_{NP}, and A_{NNP} can be made high or low depending on company policy.

The invested capital in Equation (2.10-1) can either be the original total capital cost or value, the depreciated capital value, the average capital value over the life of the plant, or the current capital replacement value. The depreciated capital value depends on the arbitrarily chosen method of depreciation. The total capital cost includes the working capital C_{WC} and this in turn depends on the valuation of the inventory.

Since annual return and invested capital have so many meanings it is necessary to define the terms precisely before making use of Equation (2.10-1).

The traditional rate of return methods have the disadvantage that they do not take into account the period before the project generates positive net cash flows. This is in contrast to the modern methods for estimating profitability such as the net present value (NPV) method and the discounted cash flow rate of return (DCFRR) method described in Chapter 3. The traditional rate of return methods have the additional disadvantage that they do not take into account the time value of money.

2.11 Rate of Return on Original Investment

The rate of return on the original total capital investment C_{TC} can be taken on the basis of net annual profit before tax A_{NP}, the net annual profit after tax A_{NNP}, the annual cash income before tax A_{CI}, or the net annual cash income after tax A_{NCI}.

In the first case the fractional interest rate of return on C_{TC} is

$$i = \frac{A_{NP}}{C_{TC}} \tag{2.11-1}$$

which can also be written in terms of Equation (2.1-8) as

$$i = \frac{A_{CI}}{C_{TC}} - \frac{A_{BD}}{C_{TC}} \tag{2.11-2}$$

where A_{BD} is the balance sheet annual depreciation charge.

In the second case the fractional interest rate of return on C_{TC} is

$$i = \frac{A_{NNP}}{C_{TC}} \tag{2.11-3}$$

which can also be written in terms of Equation (2.1-9) as

$$i = \frac{A_{NCI}}{C_{TC}} - \frac{A_{BD}}{C_{TC}} \tag{2.11-4}$$

In the third case the fractional interest rate of return on C_{TC} is

$$i = \frac{A_{CI}}{C_{TC}} \tag{2.11-5}$$

In the fourth case the fractional interest rate of return on C_{TC} is

$$i = \frac{A_{NCI}}{C_{TC}} \tag{2.11-6}$$

The main disadvantage of using Equations (2.11-1), (2.11-2), (2.11-3), and (2.11-4) is that the fractional depreciation rate A_{BD}/C_{TC} is arbitrarily assessed. Its value will affect the fractional rate of return considerably and may lead to erroneous conclusions when making comparison between different companies. This is particularly true when making international comparisons.

The fractional rate of return based on net annual cash income after tax A_{NCI} given by Equation (2.11-6) is recommended in preference to the other equations. It is then quite easy to deduct any particular value of the fractional depreciation rate A_{BD}/C_{TC} from the value of i given by Equation (2.11-6) in order to get the fractional interest rate of return based on net annual profit after tax A_{NNP}.

In Equation (2.11-6), i can either be taken on the basis of the net annual cash income A_{NCI} for a particular year or on the basis of an average net annual cash income over the length of life of the project.

2.12 Rate of Return on Depreciated Investment

This can also be done on the basis of A_{NP}, A_{NNP}, A_{CI}, or A_{NCI}.

In the second case the fractional interest rate of return on the depreciated total capital investment for a particular year is

$$i = \frac{A_{NNP}}{P_{s'} + C_{WC} + C_L} \tag{2.12-1}$$

where $P_{s'}$ is the book value of the fixed capital investment at the end of a particular year s'.

Equation (2.12-1) can be written in terms of Equation (2.1-9) as

$$i = \frac{A_{NCI} - A_{BD}}{P_{s'} + C_{WC} + C_L} \tag{2.12-2}$$

In the fourth case the fractional interest rate of return on the depreciated total investment for a particular year is

$$i = \frac{A_{NCI}}{P_{s'} + C_{WC} + C_L} \tag{2.12-3}$$

In Equations (2.12-1), (2.12-2), and (2.12-3), the book value $P_{s'}$ for a particular year can be calculated either by the straight line method, the declining balance method, or the sum of years digits method. On the basis of straight line depreciation, the average annual amount of depreciation A_{BD} is given by the equation

$$A_{BD} = \frac{(C_{FC} - S)}{s} \tag{2.12-4}$$

and the book value at the end of a particular year s' is given by the equation

$$P_{s'} = C_{FC} - s' A_{BD} \tag{2.12-5}$$

2.13 Rate of Return on Average Investment

This can also be done on the basis of A_{NP}, A_{NNP}, A_{CI}, or A_{NCI}.

In the second case the fractional interest rate of return on the average total capital investment for a particular year is

$$i = \frac{2A_{NNP}}{C_{FC} + S + 2C_{WC} + 2C_L} \tag{2.13-1}$$

which can be written in terms of Equation (2.1-9) as

$$i = \frac{2A_{NCI} - 2A_{BD}}{C_{FC} + S + 2C_{WC} + 2C_L} \tag{2.13-2}$$

If i is taken on the basis of average values for A_{NNP} and A_{NCI} over the length of life of the project, an average value for the working capital C_{WC} must be used.

In the fourth case the fractional interest rate of return on the average total capital investment for a particular year is

$$i = \frac{2A_{NCI}}{C_{FC} + S + 2C_{WC} + 2C_L} \tag{2.13-3}$$

The last two methods are based on the cost of land and other non-depreciable costs C_L not changing. This is unrealistic since the value of land has a tendency to rise. In such circumstances the accountancy principle of conservatism requires that the lowest valuation be adopted.

2.14 Payback Period

Another traditional method of measuring profitability is the payback period. This is not really a measure of profitability but of the time it takes for the cash flows to recoup the original fixed capital expenditure.

The net annual cash flow after tax is given by the equation

$$A_{CF} = A_{NCI} - A_{TC} \tag{2.1-4}$$

where A_{TC} is the annual expenditure of capital which is not necessarily zero after the plant has been built. The payback period (PBP) is the time taken for the cumulative net cash flow taken from the start up of the plant to equal the depreciable fixed capital investment ($C_{FC} - S$). It is the value of s' which satisfies the equation

$$\sum_{s'=0}^{s'=(PBP)} A_{CF} = C_{FC} - S \tag{2.14-1}$$

The payback period (PBP) method takes no account of cash flows or profits received after the breakeven point has been reached. The method is based on the premise that the earlier the fixed capital is recovered the better the project. However, this approach can be misleading.

Consider projects A and B with net annual cash flows listed in Table (2.14-1). Both projects have initial fixed capital expenditures of \$100,000. On the basis of payback period, project A is the most desirable since the fixed capital expenditure is recovered in three years compared with five years for project B. However, project B runs for seven years with a cumulative net cash flow of \$110,000. This is obviously more profitable than project A which runs for only four years with a cumulative net cash flow of only \$10,000.

TABLE (2.14-1)

year	A_{CF} for project A	A_{CF} for project B
0	-100,000	-100,000
1	50,000	0
2	30,000	10,000
3	20,000	20,000
4	10,000	30,000
5	0	40,000
6	0	50,000
7	0	60,000
ΣA_{CF}	10,000	110,000
(PBP)	3 years	5 years

Example (2.14-1)

Calculate:

(a) the net annual cash income and net annual profit after tax rate of return on the original investment
(b) the net annual cash income rate of return on the depreciated investment
(c) the net annual cash income rate of return on the average investment
(d) the payback period (PBP)

for a project described by the following data:

(i) cash flow information given in first two columns of Table (2.14-2)
(ii) fixed capital cost $C_{FC} = \$1{,}000{,}000$
(iii) estimated salvage value of plant items $S = \$200{,}000$
(iv) working capital $C_{WC} = \$100{,}000$
(v) cost of land $C_L = \$50{,}000$
(vi) straight line depreciation over ten years

(a) *Net annual cash income rate of return on original investment*

Required equations:

$$A_{CF} = A_{NCI} - A_{TC} \tag{2.1-4}$$

TABLE (2.14-2)

year	A_{CF}, $	A_{NCI}, $	rate of return on original capital investment, per cent/year	rate of return on depreciated capital investment, per cent/year	rate of return on average capital investment, per cent/year
0	- 16,000				
1	- 48,000				
2	- 96,000				
3	-1,200,000				
4	- 240,000				
5	+ 160,000	160,000	13.91	14.95	21.33
6	+ 240,000	240,000	20.87	24.24	32.00
7	+ 320,000	320,000	27.83	35.16	42.67
8	+ 320,000	320,000	27.83	38.55	42.67
9	+ 290,000	290,000	25.22	38.67	38.67
10	+ 260,000	260,000	22.61	38.81	34.67
11	+ 220,000	220,000	19.13	37.29	29.33
12	+ 190,000	190,000	16.52	37.25	25.33
13	+ 190,000	190,000	16.52	44.19	25.33
14	+ 370,000	20,000*	1.74	5.71	2.67
Av			19.22	31.48	29.47

* From Equation (2.1-4)

$$A_{NCI} = A_{CF} + A_{TC} = \$370{,}000/\text{year} + (-\$200{,}000-\$100{,}000-\$50{,}000)/\text{year}$$

$$= \$20{,}000/\text{year}$$

$$C_{TC} = C_{FC} + C_{WC} + C_L \tag{2.5-1}$$

$$i = \frac{A_{NCI}}{C_{TC}} \tag{2.11-6}$$

The fractional interest rate of return i, given by Equation (2.11-6), applies only for situations in which the process has a positive net cash flow. In the present case this first occurs in the fifth year of the project, which is the first year of productive operation. For this year the net cash flow after tax is

\$160,000. Equation (2.5-1) gives the total capital cost C_{TC}. In the present case

$$C_{FC} = \$1{,}000{,}000$$
$$C_{WC} = \$100{,}000$$
$$C_{L} = \$50{,}000$$

hence

$$\begin{aligned} C_{TC} &= C_{FC} + C_{WC} + C_{L} \\ &= \$1{,}000{,}000 + \$100{,}000 + \$50{,}000 \\ &= \$1{,}150{,}000 \end{aligned}$$

From Equation (2.1-4) the net annual cash income for the fifth year is

$$\begin{aligned} A_{NCI} &= A_{CF} + A_{TC} \\ &= \$160{,}000/\text{year} + \$0/\text{year} \\ &= \$160{,}000/\text{year} \end{aligned}$$

The annual capital expenditure A_{TC} is zero in each year after start up except for the last year of operation at the end of which the working capital, the cost of land the the salvage value are recovered and $A_{TC} = -\$200{,}000 - \$100{,}000 - \$50{,}000 = -\$350{,}000$ in year 14.

From Equation (2.11-6) the net annual cash income rate of return on the original capital investment for the fifth year is

$$\begin{aligned} i &= \frac{A_{NCI}}{C_{TC}} \\ &= \frac{\$160{,}000/\text{year}}{\$1{,}150{,}000} \\ &= 0.1391/\text{year} \\ &= 13.91 \text{ per cent/year} \end{aligned}$$

Values for subsequent years are calculated in the same way and listed in Table (2.14-2).

(b) *Net annual cash income rate of return on depreciated capital investment*

Required equations:

$$A_{CF} = A_{NCI} - A_{TC} \qquad (2.1\text{-}4)$$

$$A_{BD} = \frac{(C_{FC} - S)}{s} \qquad (2.12\text{-}4)$$

$$P_{s'} = C_{\mathrm{FC}} - s' A_{\mathrm{BD}} \tag{2.12-5}$$

$$i = \frac{A_{\mathrm{NCI}}}{P_{s'} + C_{\mathrm{WC}} + C_{\mathrm{L}}} \tag{2.12-3}$$

The annual rate of straight line depreciation of the plant items from \$1,000,000, at start up, to \$200,000, at the end of ten years of productive life, is given by Equation (2.12-4) to be

$$\begin{aligned} A_{\mathrm{BD}} &= \frac{(C_{\mathrm{FC}} - S)}{s} \\ &= \frac{\$1{,}000{,}000 - \$200{,}000}{10 \text{ years}} \\ &= \$80{,}000/\text{year} \end{aligned}$$

As in part (a), $C_{\mathrm{FC}} = \$1{,}000{,}000$, $C_{\mathrm{WC}} = \$100{,}000$, $C_{\mathrm{L}} = \$50{,}000$, and $A_{\mathrm{NCI}} = \$160{,}000/\text{year}$ for year 5. In the fifth year the net cash flow after tax is positive for the first time so that Equation (2.12-3) applies from the fifth year onward. The fifth year is also the first year after plant start up, so that $s' = 1$ year. For year 5 the book value $P_{s'}$ is given by Equation (2.12-5) to be

$$\begin{aligned} P_{s'} &= C_{\mathrm{FC}} - s' A_{\mathrm{BD}} \\ &= \$1{,}000{,}000 - (1 \text{ year})(\$80{,}000/\text{year}) \\ &= \$920{,}000 \end{aligned}$$

From Equation (2.12-3) the net annual cash income rate of return on the depreciated capital investment is

$$\begin{aligned} i &= \frac{A_{\mathrm{NCI}}}{P_{s'} + C_{\mathrm{WC}} + C_{\mathrm{L}}} \\ &= \frac{\$160{,}000/\text{year}}{\$920{,}000 + \$100{,}000 + \$50{,}000} \\ &= 0.1495/\text{year} \\ &= 14.95 \text{ per cent/year} \end{aligned}$$

Values for subsequent years are calculated in the same way and listed in Table (2.14-2).

(c) *Net annual cash income rate of return on average capital investment*

Required equations:

$$A_{\mathrm{CF}} = A_{\mathrm{NCI}} - A_{\mathrm{TC}} \tag{2.1-4}$$

$$i = \frac{2A_{\mathrm{NCI}}}{C_{\mathrm{FC}} + S + 2C_{\mathrm{WC}} + 2C_{\mathrm{L}}} \tag{2.13-3}$$

As in part (b), $C_{FC} = \$1{,}000{,}000$, $C_{WC} = \$100{,}000$, $C_L = \$50{,}000$, and $A_{NCI} = \$160{,}000$/year for year 5. From Equation (2.13-3) the net annual cash income rate of return on the average capital investment for the first year of profitable working, year 5, is

$$\begin{aligned} i &= \frac{2A_{NCI}}{C_{FC} + S + 2C_{WC} + 2C_L} \\ &= \frac{2(\$160{,}000/\text{year})}{\$1{,}000{,}000 + \$200{,}000 + 2(\$100{,}000) + 2(\$50{,}000)} \\ &= 0.2133/\text{year} \\ &= 21.33 \text{ per cent/year} \end{aligned}$$

Values for subsequent years are calculated in the same way and listed in Table (2.14-2).

(d) *Payback period* (PBP)

Required equations:

$$A_{BD} = \frac{(C_{FC} - S)}{s} \tag{2.12-4}$$

$$\sum_{s'=0}^{s'=(PBP)} A_{CF} = C_{FC} - S \tag{2.14-1}$$

Payback period is usually measured as the time from the start of production to recovery of the capital investment.

The fixed capital cost $C_{FC} = \$1{,}000{,}000$, the salvage value $s = \$200{,}000$, and the annual cash flows, A_{CF}, are listed in Table (2.14-2). Starting from the beginning of year 5, the start up year, as $s' = 0$, values for A_{CF} and $\sum A_{CF}$ are listed in Table (2.14-3).

The payback period, (PBP), is the time from start up until $\sum A_{CF} = C_{FC} - S = \$1{,}000{,}000 - \$200{,}000 = \$800{,}000$, and this occurs between years 7 and 8.

TABLE (2.14-3)

year	s'	A_{CF}	ΣA_{CF}
5	1	+160,000	+160,000
6	2	+240,000	+400,000
7	3	+320,000	+720,000
8	4	+320,000	+1,040,000

Straight line interpolation gives the time from year 7 to be

$$\frac{\$800{,}000 - \$720{,}000}{\$1{,}040{,}000 - \$720{,}000} = 0.25 \text{ years}$$

Hence

$$(\text{PBP}) = 3 \text{ years} + 0.25 \text{ years} = 3.25 \text{ years}$$

The project will break even 7.25 years from the start of the project.

(a) *Net annual profit after tax rate of return on original capital investment*

Required equations:

$$i = \frac{A_{\text{NNP}}}{C_{\text{TC}}} \tag{2.11-3}$$

$$i = \frac{A_{\text{NCI}}}{C_{\text{TC}}} - \frac{A_{\text{BD}}}{C_{\text{TC}}} \tag{2.11-4}$$

The annual rate of straight line depreciation over a ten-year period is

$$A_{\text{BD}} = \$80{,}000/\text{year}$$

The original total capital investment

$$C_{\text{TC}} = \$1{,}150{,}000$$

In this case the fractional depreciation rate

$$\begin{aligned} \frac{A_{\text{BD}}}{C_{\text{TC}}} &= \frac{\$80{,}000/\text{year}}{\$1{,}150{,}000} \\ &= 0.0696 \\ &= 6.96 \text{ per cent/year} \end{aligned}$$

From Equation (2.11-4) the average rate of return on the original total capital investment on the basis of net annual profit after tax A_{NNP} is

$$\begin{aligned} i &= \frac{A_{\text{NCI}}}{C_{\text{TC}}} - \frac{A_{\text{BD}}}{C_{\text{TC}}} \\ &= (19.22 - 6.96) \text{ per cent/year} \\ &= 12.3 \text{ per cent/year} \end{aligned}$$

for straight line depreciation over a ten-year period.

2.15 Effect of Depreciation Method on Annual Profit

The net annual profit after tax and the corresponding rate of return on the original investment are very much affected by the method chosen to compute the annual amount of depreciation even if the net annual cash income A_{NCI} remains constant.

Example (2.15-1)

Calculate the net annual profit after tax A_{NNP} and the corresponding rate of return on the original investment on the basis of

(a) straight line depreciation over ten years
(b) double declining depreciation
(c) sum of years digits depreciation

for a project described by the following data:

(i) net annual cash income after tax $A_{NCI} = \$50,000$ in each of ten years
(ii) fixed capital cost $C_{FC} = \$200,000$
(iii) estimated salvage value of plant items $S = \$10,000$
(iv) working capital $C_{WC} = \$100,000$
(v) cost of land $C_L = \$20,000$
(vi) values for balance sheet annual depreciation A_{BD} calculated for the methods given are listed in Table (2.15-1)

Required equations:

$$C_{TC} = C_{FC} + C_{WC} + C_L \tag{2.5-1}$$

$$i = \frac{A_{NCI}}{C_{TC}} \tag{2.11-6}$$

$$A_{NNP} = A_{NCI} - A_{BD} \tag{2.1-9}$$

$$i = \frac{A_{NNP}}{C_{TC}} \tag{2.11-3}$$

Equation (2.5-1) gives the total capital cost C_{TC}. In the present case

$$C_{FC} = \$200,000$$
$$C_{WC} = \$100,000$$
$$C_L = \$20,000$$

hence

$$\begin{aligned} C_{TC} &= C_{FC} + C_{WC} + C_L \\ &= \$200,000 + \$100,000 + \$20,000 \\ &= \$320,000 \end{aligned}$$

TABLE (2.15-1)

end of year	straight line depreciation			double declining depreciation			sum of years digits depreciation		
	A_{BD}	$\frac{A_{BD}}{C_{TC}}$	i	A_{BD}	$\frac{A_{BD}}{C_{TC}}$	i	A_{BD}	$\frac{A_{BD}}{C_{TC}}$	i
1	19,000	0.0594	0.0969	40,000	0.1250	0.0313	34,545	0.1080	0.0483
2	19,000	0.0594	0.0969	32,000	0.1000	0.0563	31,091	0.0972	0.0591
3	19,000	0.0594	0.0969	25,600	0.0800	0.0763	27,636	0.0864	0.0699
4	19,000	0.0594	0.0969	20,480	0.0640	0.0923	24,182	0.0756	0.0807
5	19,000	0.0594	0.0969	16,384	0.0512	0.1051	20,727	0.0648	0.0915
6	19,000	0.0594	0.0969	13,107	0.0410	0.1153	17,273	0.0540	0.1023
7	19,000	0.0594	0.0969	10,486	0.0328	0.1235	13,818	0.0432	0.1131
8	19,000	0.0594	0.0969	8,389	0.0262	0.1301	10,364	0.0324	0.1239
9	19,000	0.0594	0.0969	6,711	0.0210	0.1353	6,909	0.0216	0.1347
10	19,000	0.0594	0.0969	16,843	0.0526	0.1037	3,455	0.0108	0.1455

From Equation (2.11-6) the net annual cash income rate of return on the original capital investment in each year is

$$i = \frac{A_{\text{NCI}}}{C_{\text{TC}}} = \frac{\$50{,}000/\text{year}}{\$320{,}000} = 0.1563/\text{year} = 15.63 \text{ per cent/year}$$

(a) *A_{NNP} and rate of return for straight line depreciation*

From Equation (2.1-9) and the depreciation data in Table (2.15-1) the net annual profit after tax for each year is

$$A_{\text{NNP}} = A_{\text{NCI}} - A_{\text{BD}} = (\$50{,}000 - \$19{,}000)/\text{year} = \$31{,}000/\text{year}$$

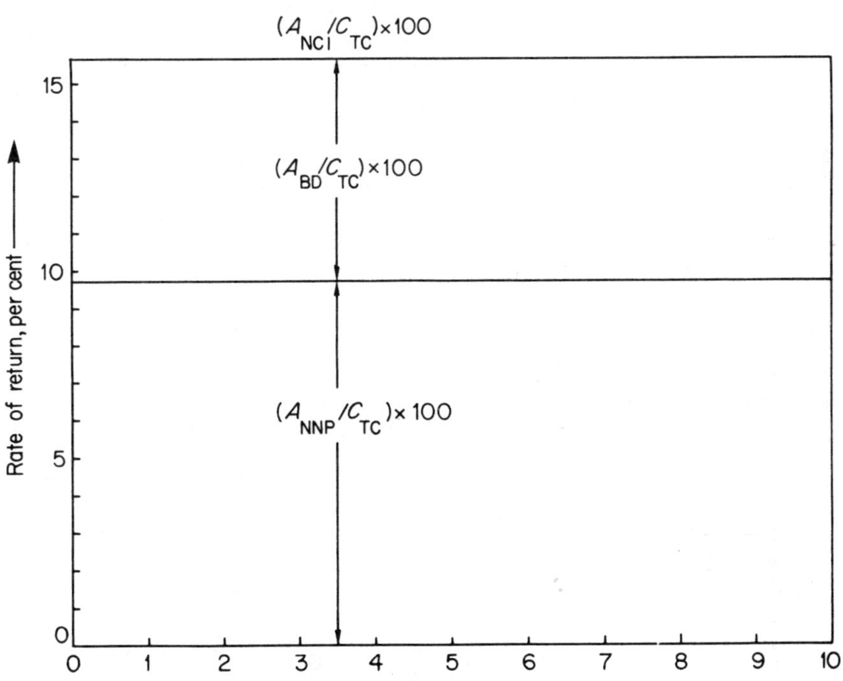

Figure (2.15-1) Rate of return against time for straight line depreciation

From Equation (2.11-3) the net annual profit after tax rate of return on the original capital investment in each year is

$$\begin{aligned} i &= \frac{A_{NNP}}{C_{TC}} \\ &= \frac{\$31,000/\text{year}}{\$320,000} \\ &= 0.0969/\text{year} \\ &= 9.69 \text{ per cent/year} \end{aligned}$$

The rate of return data are plotted in Figure (2.15-1).

(b) and (c) *A_{NNP} and rate of return for double declining balance and sum of years digits depreciation*

The net annual profit after tax and rate of return data for each year are calculated using Equations (2.1-9) and (2.11-3) and the depreciation data in Table (2.15-1). These are tabulated in Table (2.15-1) and plotted in Figures

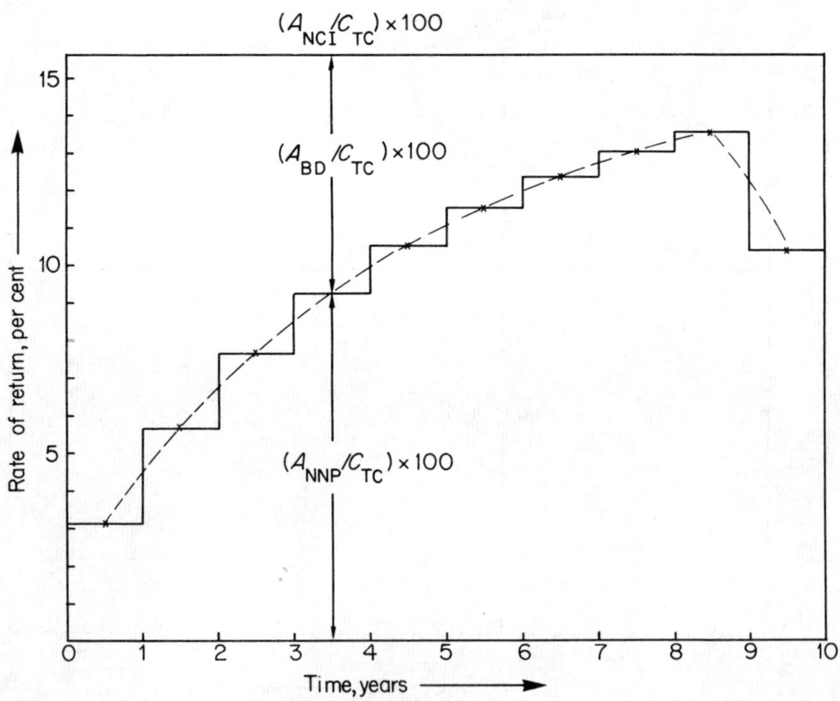

Figure (2.15-2) Rate of return against time for double declining depreciation

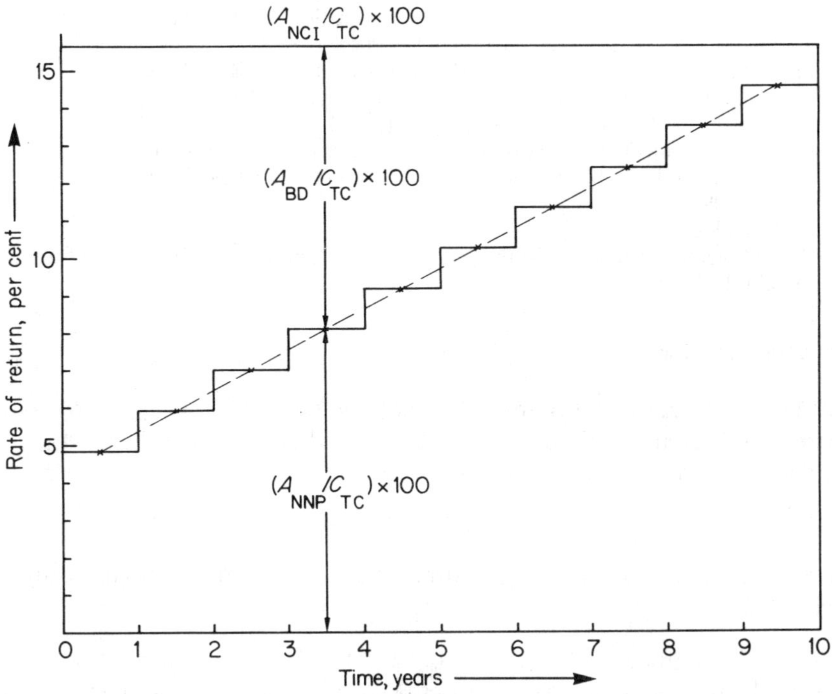

Figure (2.15-3) Rate of return against time for sum of years digits depreciation

(2.15-2) and (2.15-3) for double declining and sum of years digits depreciation respectively.

Figures (2.15-2) and (2.15-3) show that for both double declining balance and sum of years digits depreciation the net annual profit after tax rate of return increases with time for a constant net annual cash income A_{NCI}. This is in contrast to the constant net annual profit after tax rate of return for straight line depreciation which is illustrated in Figure (2.15-1).

It is clear that to state the net annual profit after tax rate of return without being quite specific about the basis of the inherent depreciation is misleading and uninformative.

References for Chapter 2

1. Aries, R. S., and Newton, R. D., 'Chemical Engineering Cost Estimation', p. 1, New York, McGraw–Hill Book Co., Inc., 1955
2. Ibid., p. 185
3. Bauman, H. C., 'Fundamentals of Cost Engineering in the Chemical Industry', p. 27, New York, Reinhold Publishing Corporation, 1964.
4. Bechtel, L. R., *Chem. Eng.*, **67**, No. 4 (1960)

5. 'Capital Cost Estimation', London, The Institution of Chemical Engineers, 1969
6. Hackney, J. W., *Chem. Eng.*, **67**, No. 5 (1960)
7. Holland, F. A., and Brinkerhoff, R., *Brit. Chem. Eng.*, **8**, 384 (1964)
8. Holland, F. A., and Brinkerhoff, R., *Chem. Eng.*, **70**, No. 3 (1963)
9. O'Connell, F. P., *Chem. Eng.*, **69**, No. 4 (1962)
10. Peters, M. S., and Timmerhaus, K. D., 'Plant Design and Economics for Chemical Engineers', 2nd ed., p. 96, New York, McGraw–Hill Book Co. Inc., 1968
11. Ibid., p. 99
12. Ibid., p. 218
13. Wright, M. G., 'Financial Management', p. 92, London, McGraw–Hill Publishing Co. Ltd., 1970

Problems for Chapter 2

(2.1-1) In certain circumstances, the net annual cash flow A_{CF} after tax is related to the annual cash income A_{CI}, the annual depreciation charge A_D, and the fractional tax rate t by the equation

$$A_{CF} = A_{CI}(1 - t) + A_D t$$

Discuss the limitations of this equation and the assumptions involved in its derivation.

(2.3-1) The annual cash income A_{CI} is related to the annual production rate R, the total annual fixed expenses A_{TFE} and the contribution $(c_S - c_{TVE})$ by the equation

$$A_{CI} = R(c_S - c_{TVE}) - A_{TFE} \tag{2.3-15}$$

Plot A_{CI} against R for the following data:

$$A_{TFE} = \$150{,}000/\text{year}$$
$$c_S - c_{TVE} = 1\,¢/\text{lb}$$
$$R_{max} = 30{,}000{,}000\ \text{lb/year}$$

Discuss the significance of the plot.

(2.4-1) A company is committed to producing a range of six products, details of which are given in the following table.

product	A	B	C	D	E	F
units/year	2,000	3,000	10,000	15,000	20,000	50,00
direct materials cost, \$/unit	5.94	7.40	7.00	6.92	7.98	8.75
direct labor cost, \$/unit	3.20	3.20	3.20	1.60	1.60	1.00
variable overhead cost, \$/unit	0.74	1.16	3.44	1.86	4.59	1.72
fixed overhead cost, \$/unit	5.33	3.74	3.60	1.52	1.58	0.53
sales price, \$/unit	14.11	14.70	17.00	11.80	15.75	12.20

It is possible to adapt any of the production lines to produce the present number of units of any of the products. Compare the present cash flow pattern with the best production schedule which could be obtained from the existing equipment using the contribution to sales ratio (CSR) as the measure of profitability. Assume that the fixed overhead costs relate to the production line and not to the product made.

(2.6-1) A piece of equipment has a fixed capital cost of $120,000, a useful life of ten years and a scrap value after ten years of $20,000. Tabulate the annual amount of depreciation and the book value at the end of each year for the equipment on the basis of

(a) straight line depreciation
(b) double declining depreciation
(c) sum of years digits depreciation

Plot the book value against time for each of the three methods.

(2.9-1) A company has an issued capital of 28,000 shares of common stock, each having a par value of $100 and paying a current dividend of 10 per cent per annum. Long term finance consists of $2,000,000 with annual interest charges of 5 per cent. Suppose that there are no retained earnings, and that earnings after tax for the year are expected to be $400,000 but may only reach $150,000. Calculate the annual rates of interest on total capital and on ownership capital for the two possibilities. Assume that the fractional tax rate for the company $t = 0.5$ but ignore the effects of taxation on the stockholders' capital and earnings.

Chapter 3

Comparative Profitability Based on the Time Value of Money

Since money can be invested to earn interest, a sum of money received now has a greater present value than if received at some time in the future. Modern methods of estimating profitability based on the time value of money are described in this chapter. The most common are the net present value (NPV) and the discounted cash flow rate of return (DCFRR) methods. Although both methods have the same basis they can give different orders of ranking when comparing a number of projects. In general it is better to make an overall assessment rather than base a decision on a single criterion of profitability.

(NPV) and (DCFRR) estimates are based on cash flow forecasts. The longer the time period involved, the less likely are these cash forecasts to be correct. There is great difficulty in forecasting sales and costs for any period longer than say four or five years. No profitability estimate is better than the available data. The more information that is available, the greater is the probability that a management decision will be correct.

The (NPV) and (DCFRR) estimates in this chapter are based on the simplifying assumption that the cash flows in a particular year take place at the end of that year. In practice cash flows generally take place at random times throughout any particular year. Normally the error introduced by this assumption is far less than errors inherent in the accuracy of the predicted cash flow data. However this problem can always be taken care of by using a cash flow period of less than one year.

The (NPV) and (DCFRR) methods of estimating profitability have the advantage that they do not depend on arbitrarily chosen methods of estimating depreciation as an operating cost. This is because the methods inherently make provision for the recovery of capital expenditure.

3.1 Cash Flow

In this chapter, the cash flow referred to is the net annual cash flow A_{CF} after tax given by Equation (2.1-4).

$$A_{CF} = A_{NCI} - A_{TC} \qquad (2.1\text{-}4)$$

where A_{NCI} is the net annual cash income and A_{TC} is the annual capital expenditure which is not necessarily zero after the plant has been built.

Equation (2.1-4) can also be written in terms of Equation (2.1-2) as

$$A_{CF} = A_{CI} - A_{IT} - A_{TC} \tag{3.1-1}$$

The total capital cost C_{TC} of a project consists of the fixed capital cost C_{FC} plus the working capital cost C_{WC} plus the cost of land and other non-depreciable costs C_L.

$$C_{TC} = C_{FC} + C_{WC} + C_L \tag{2.5-1}$$

Consider a project in which

$$C_{FC} = \$1{,}000{,}000$$
$$C_{WC} = \$90{,}000$$

and

$$C_L = \$10{,}000$$

From Equation (2.5-1) the total capital cost for this project $C_{TC} = \$1{,}100{,}000$.

If all this capital expenditure occurs in year 0 of the project then $A_{TC} = \$1{,}100{,}000$ in year 0 and $-A_{TC} = -\$1{,}100{,}000$. From Equation (2.1-4) it is seen that any capital expenditure makes a negative contribution to the net annual cash flow A_{CF}.

Consider a project in which the fixed capital expenditure is spread over two years according to the following pattern:

$$C_{FC} = C_{FC0} + C_{FC1}$$

in year 0, $\quad C_{FC0} = \$400{,}000$

$\quad C_L = \$10{,}000$

in year 1, $\quad C_{FC1} = \$600{,}000$

$\quad C_{WC} = \$90{,}000$

In year 0, $\quad A_{TC} = \$410{,}000$

and in year 1, $A_{TC} = \$690{,}000$

In the final year of the project the working capital and the land are recovered which in this case cost a total of \$100,000. Thus in the final year of the project $A_{TC} = -\$100{,}000$ and $-A_{TC} = +\$100{,}000$. From Equation (2.1-4) it is seen that any capital recovery makes a positive contribution to the net annual cash flow A_{CF}. In the same way government investment grants also provide a positive contribution to the net annual cash flow A_{CF}.

During the development and construction stages of a project A_{NCI} is zero in Equation (2.1-4). For this period the cash flow is negative and is given by

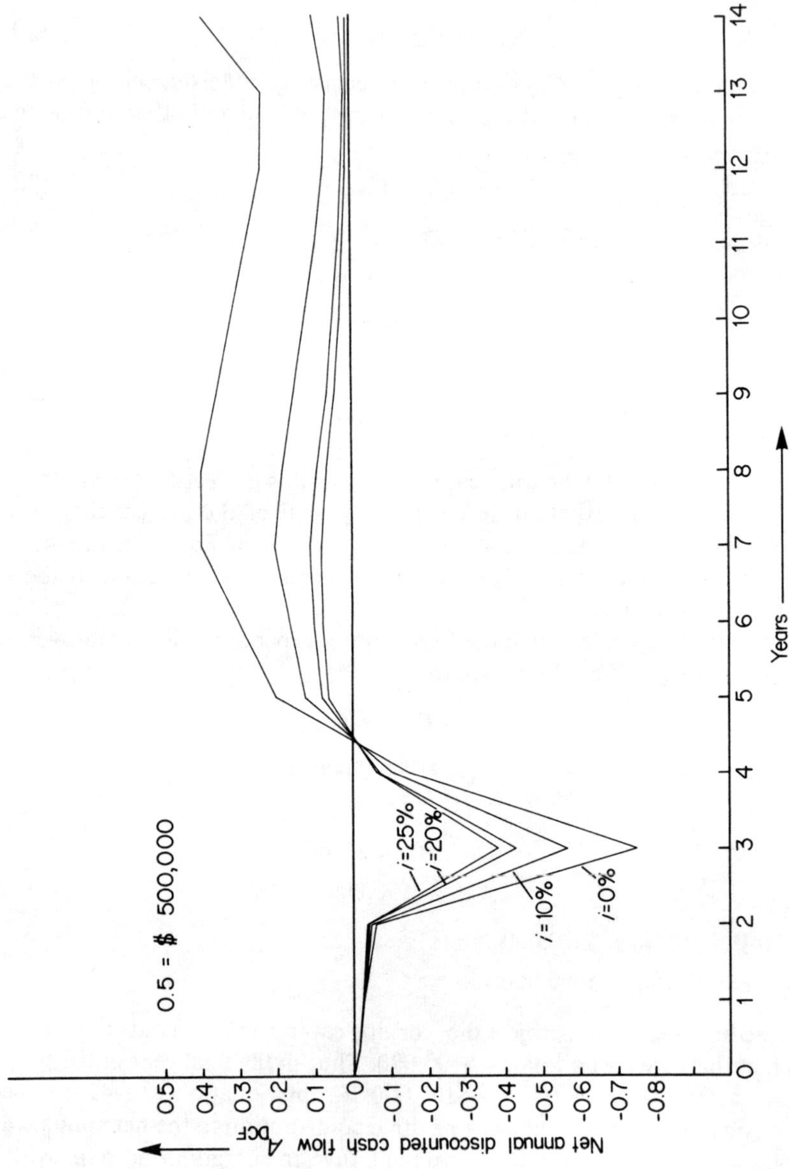

Figure (3.1-1) Net annual discounted cash flow against time

the equation

$$A_{CF} = -A_{TC} \tag{3.1-2}$$

Figure (3.1-1) shows the cash flow stages in a project. The expenditure during the research and development stage is normally relatively small. It will usually include some preliminary process design and a market survey. Once the decision to go ahead with the project has been taken, detailed process engineering design will commence and the rate of expenditure starts to increase. The rate is increased still further when equipment is purchased and construction gets under way. There is no return on the investment until the plant is started up. Even during start up there is some additional expenditure. Once the plant is operating smoothly an inflow of cash is established. During the early stages of a project there may be a tax credit due to the existence of expenses without corresponding income.

3.2 Discounted Cash Flow

The present value P of a future sum of money F is given by Equation (1.3-4)

$$P = Ff_d \tag{1.3-4}$$

where $f_d = 1/(1+i)^n$ the discount factor, values of which are readily available in tables similar to those in Appendix 1. Table (A1-10) shows that \$90,909 invested at an annual interest rate of 10 per cent becomes \$100,000 after 1 year. Similarly \$38,554 invested at an annual compound interest rate of 10 per cent becomes \$100,000 after 10 years.

Thus cash flow in the early years of a project has a greater value than the same amount of cash flow in the later years of a project. It therefore pays to receive money as soon as possible and to delay paying out money for as long as possible. Time is taken into account by using the annual discounted cash flow A_{DCF} which is related to the annual cash flow A_{CF} and the discount factor f_d by the equation

$$A_{DCF} = A_{CF} f_d \tag{3.2-1}$$

Thus at the end of year 1

$$A_{DCF1} = \frac{A_{CF1}}{(1+i)}$$

at the end of year 2

$$A_{DCF2} = \frac{A_{CF2}}{(1+i)^2}$$

and at the end of year n

$$A_{DCFn} = \frac{A_{CFn}}{(1+i)^n}$$

TABLE (3.2-1)

year	A_{CF}	ΣA_{CF}	discounted at 10%			discounted at 20%			discounted at 25%		
			f_d	A_{DCF}	ΣA_{DCF}	f_d	A_{DCF}	ΣA_{DCF}	f_d	A_{DCF}	ΣA_{DCF}
0	-10,000	- 10,000	1.00000	- 10,000	- 10,000	1.00000	- 10,000	- 10,000	1.00000	- 10,000	- 10,000
1	-30,000	- 40,000	0.90909	- 27,273	- 37,273	0.83333	- 25,000	- 35,000	0.80000	- 24,000	- 34,000
2	-60,000	- 100,000	0.82645	- 49,587	- 86,860	0.69444	- 41,666	- 76,666	0.64000	- 38,400	- 72,400
3	-750,000	- 850,000	0.75131	-563,483	-650,343	0.57870	-434,025	-510,691	0.51200	-384,000	-456,400
4	-150,000	-1,000,000	0.68301	-102,452	-752,795	0.48225	- 72,338	-583,029	0.40960	- 61,440	-517,840
5	+200,000	- 800,000	0.62092	+124,184	-628,611	0.40188	+ 80,376	-502,653	0.32768	+ 65,536	-452,304
6	+300,000	- 500,000	0.56447	+169,341	-459,270	0.33490	+100,470	-402,183	0.26214	+ 78,642	-373,662
7	+400,000	- 100,000	0.51316	+205,264	-254,006	0.27908	+111,632	-290,551	0.20972	+ 83,888	-289,774
8	+400,000	+ 300,000	0.46651	+186,604	- 67,402	0.23257	+ 93,028	-197,523	0.16777	+ 67,108	-222,666
9	+360,000	+ 660,000	0.42410	+152,676	+ 85,274	0.19381	+ 69,772	-127,751	0.13422	+ 48,319	-174,347
10	+320,000	+ 980,000	0.38554	+123,373	+208,647	0.16151	+ 51,683	- 76,068	0.10737	+ 34,358	-139,989
11	+280,000	+1,260,000	0.35049	+ 98,137	+306,784	0.13459	+ 37,685	- 38,383	0.08590	+ 24,052	-115,937
12	+240,000	+1,500,000	0.31863	+ 76,471	+383,255	0.11216	+ 26,918	- 11,465	0.06872	+ 16,493	- 99,444
13	+240,000	+1,740,000	0.28966	+ 69,518	+452,773	0.09346	+ 22,430	+ 10,965	0.05498	+ 13,195	- 86,249
14	+400,000	+2,140,000	0.26333	+105,332	+558,105	0.07789	+ 31,156	+ 42,121	0.04398	+ 17,592	- 68,657

The sum of the annual discounted cash flows over n years $\sum A_{DCF}$ is known as the net present value (NPV) of the project.

$$(NPV) = \sum A_{DCF} \quad (3.2\text{-}2)$$

The value of (NPV) is of course directly dependent on the choice of the fractional interest rate i. An interest rate can be chosen to make (NPV) = 0 after a chosen number of years. This value of i is given by the equation

$$(NPV) = \sum A_{DCF} = 0 \quad (3.2\text{-}3)$$

and may be found either graphically or by an iterative trial and error procedure. The value of i given by Equation (3.2-3) is known as the discounted cash flow rate of return (DCFRR). It is also called by other names which include: the profitability index, the true rate of return, the investor's rate of return, and the interest rate of return.

The main advantage of (DCFRR) over (NPV) is that it is independent of the zero or base year chosen. In contrast the value of (NPV) varies according to the zero year chosen.

Figure (3.1-1) shows the cash flow stages in a project together with their discounted cash flow values for the data given in Table (3.2-1). In addition to cash flow and discounted cash flow curves it is also instructive to plot cumulative cash flow and cumulative discounted cash flow curves. These are shown in Figure (3.2-1) for the data given in Table (3.2-1).

The cost of capital[3, 5] is also the interest rate at which money can be invested instead of putting it at risk in a manufacturing process. Consider the process data listed in Table (3.2-1) and plotted in Figure (3.2-1). If the cost of capital is 10 per cent then the appropriate cumulative discounted cash flow curve in Figure (3.2-1) is abcdef. Up to point e or 8.49 years the capital is at risk. Point e is the discounted breakeven point (DBEP). At this point the manufacturing process has produced the same return as an equivalent amount of capital invested at a compound interest rate of 10 per cent. Beyond the breakeven point e on Figure (3.2-1) the capital is no longer at risk and any cash flow above the horizontal base line $\sum A_{DCF} = 0$ is in excess of the return on an equivalent amount of capital invested at a compound interest rate of 10 per cent. Thus the greater the area above the horizontal base line $\sum A_{DCF} = 0$, the more profitable the process.

When net present value (NPV) and discounted cash flow rate of return (DCFRR) are computed, depreciation is not considered as a separate factor. It is simply used as an allowance in Equation (2.1-3) to reduce the annual amount of tax A_{IT}.

$$A_{IT} = (A_{CI} - A_D - A_A)\,t \quad (2.1\text{-}3)$$

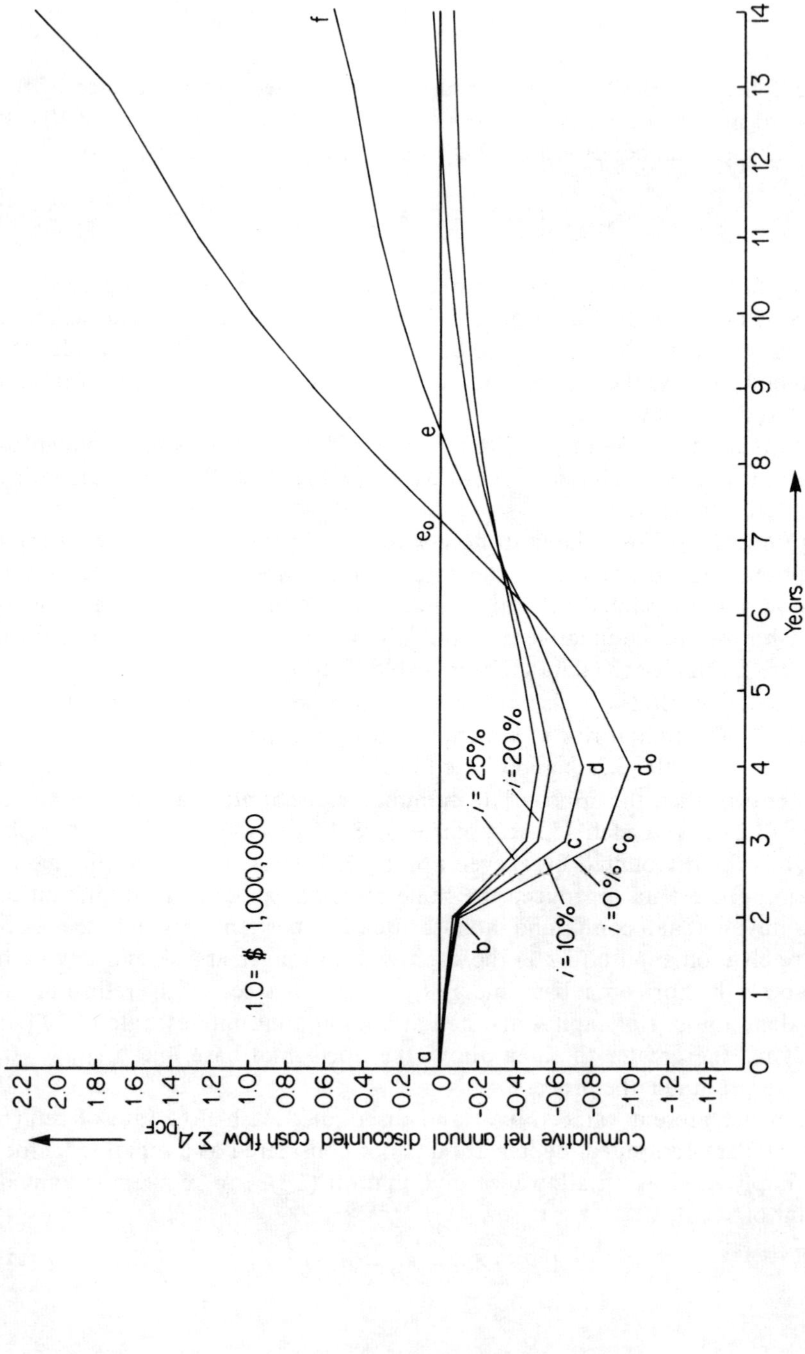

Figure (3.2-1) Cumulative net annual discounted cash flow against time

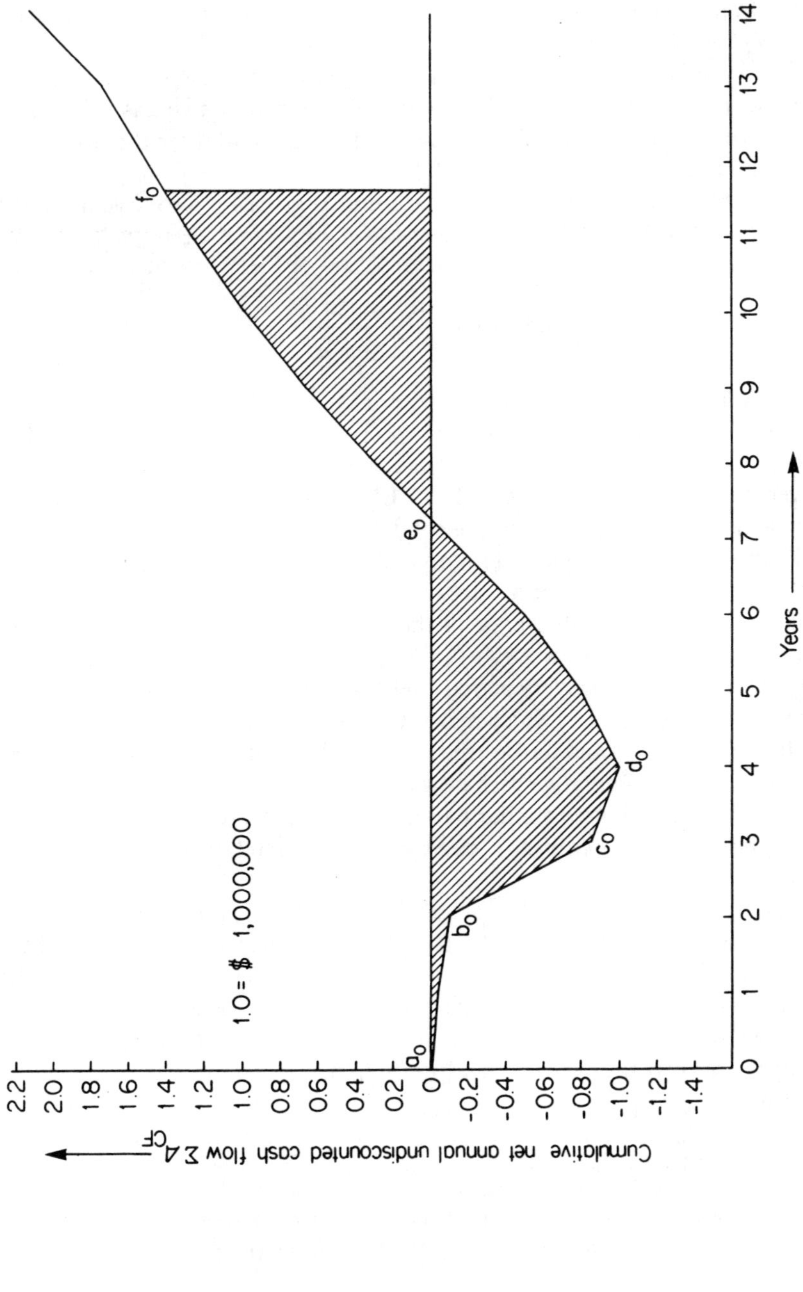

Figure (3.2-2) Cumulative net annual undiscounted cash flow against time

A (DCFRR) of say 15 per cent implies that 15 per cent per year will be earned on the investment in addition to which the project generates sufficient money to repay the original investment. Frequently depreciation is considered as the means of recovering the original investment. This is done implicitly in the case of (NPV) and (DCFRR) calculations.

It is normally not possible to make a comprehensive assessment of profitability with a single number. The shape of the cumulative cash flow and cumulative discounted cash flow curves both before and after the breakeven point is an important factor.

Allen[2] accounted for the shape of the cumulative cash flow curve up to the breakeven point (shown as e_0 in Figure (3.2-1)) by using a parameter known as the equivalent maximum investment period (EMIP) which is defined as follows:

$$(\text{EMIP}) = \frac{\text{Area } (a_0 \text{ to } e_0)}{-\sum A_{\text{CFmax}}} \tag{3.2-4}$$

where the area (a_0 to e_0) refers to the area below the horizontal base line $\sum A_{\text{CF}} = 0$ on the cumulative cash flow curve shown in Figure (3.2-2). The sum $-\sum A_{\text{CFmax}}$ is the maximum cumulative expenditure on the project which is given by point d_0 in Figure (3.2-2). (EMIP) is a time in years. It is 'the equivalent period during which the total project debt would be outstanding if it were all incurred at one instant and all repaid at one instant'. Clearly the shorter the (EMIP) the more attractive the project.

Allen[2] accounted for the shape of the cumulative cash flow curve beyond the breakeven point (shown as e_0 in Figure (3.2-1)) by using a parameter known as the interest recovery period (IRP). This is the time period graphically illustrated in Figure (3.2-2) which makes the area (e_0 to f_0) above the horizontal base line $\sum A_{\text{CF}} = 0$ equal to the area (a_0 to e_0) below the horizontal base line $\sum A_{\text{CF}} = 0$ on the cumulative cash flow curve.

Sinclair[6] has considered similar parameters to the (EMIP) and (IRP) based not on the cumulative cash flow curve but on a cumulative discounted cash flow curve.

Consideration of the cash flow stages in Figure (3.2-1) illustrates the factors which can affect the (EMIP) and (IRP). If the required capital investment is increased, it is necessary to increase the rate of income after start up for the (EMIP) to remain the same. This is also the case if the research and development stage were prolonged. Clearly in order to have the (EMIP) small it is necessary to keep the research and development, design, and construction stages short.

3.3 Profitability[4,7]

An investment in a manufacturing process must earn more than the cost of capital in order for it to be worthwhile. The larger the additional earnings, the more profitable the venture and the greater the justification for putting the capital at risk. A profitability estimate is an attempt to quantify the desirability of taking this risk. The ways of assessing profitability so far considered are:

(1) Discounted cash flow rate of return (DCFRR).
(2) Net present value (NPV) based on a particular discount rate.
(3) Equivalent maximum investment period (EMIP).
(4) Interest recovery period (IRP).
(5) Discounted breakeven point (DBEP).
(6) Rate of return on original investment.
(7) Rate of return on depreciated investment.
(8) Rate of return on average investment.
(9) Payback period (PBP).
(10) Capitalized cost C_K.

The ten methods named in this section for assessing profitability are not the only ones available. Abrams[1] has listed twenty methods. However, the assessment of the profitability of a project using all twenty methods tends to lead to confusion.

An intelligent consideration of the cumulative cash flow and cumulative discounted cash flow curves together with experience and good judgment is the best way of assessing the financial merit of a project. A useful additional piece of information is the capital rate of return ratio (CRR) given by Equation (3.3-1).

$$(\text{CRR}) = \frac{(\text{NPV})}{-\sum A_{\text{CFmax}}} \tag{3.3-1}$$

Example (3.3-1)

Calculate

(a) net present value (NPV) with straight line depreciation and 10 per cent discount factor

(b) (NPV) with straight line depreciation and 20 per cent discount factor

(c) (NPV) with double declining depreciation and 10 per cent discount factor

(d) (NPV) with sum of years digits depreciation and 10 per cent discount factor

(e) (NPV) with straight line depreciation and 10 per cent discount factor and income tax delayed for one year

(f) the discounted cash flow rate of return (DCFRR) with straight line depreciation for a project described by the following data:

(i) revenue A_S from annual sales and total annual expense A_{TE} over a ten-year period given in the first three columns of Table (3.3-1a)
(ii) fixed capital investment $C_{FC} = \$1{,}000{,}000$
(iii) zero salvage value of plant items
(iv) working capital $C_{WC} = \$90{,}000$
(v) cost of land $C_L = \$10{,}000$
(vi) no tax allowances other than depreciation, i.e. $A_A = 0$
(vii) fractional tax rate $t = 0.50$

(a) and (b) (NPV) *with straight line depreciation*

Required equations:

$$A_{CI} = A_S - A_{TE} \tag{2.1-1}$$

$$A_{NCI} = A_{CI} - A_{IT} \tag{2.1-2}$$

$$A_{IT} = (A_{CI} - A_D - A_A)\,t \tag{2.1-3}$$

$$A_{CF} = A_{NCI} - A_{TC} \tag{2.1-4}$$

$$C_{TC} = C_{FC} + C_{WC} + C_L \tag{2.5-1}$$

$$A_D = \frac{(C_{FC} - S)}{s} \tag{2.6-1}$$

$$A_{DCF} = A_{CF}\, f_d \tag{3.2-1}$$

$$(\text{NPV}) = \sum A_{DCF} \tag{3.2-2}$$

Equation (2.5-1) gives the total capital cost C_{TC}. In the present case

$$C_{FC} = \$1{,}000{,}000$$
$$C_{WC} = \$90{,}000$$
$$C_L = \$10{,}000$$

hence

$$\begin{aligned} C_{TC} &= C_{FC} + C_{WC} + C_L \\ &= \$1{,}000{,}000 + \$90{,}000 + \$10{,}000 \\ &= \$1{,}100{,}000 \end{aligned}$$

The annual rate of straight line depreciation of the fixed capital investment from \$1,000,000, at start up, to zero value at the end of ten years of productive

TABLE (3.3-1a)

Annual cash flows with straight line depreciation and 10 per cent discount factor

year	before tax			depreciation charge plus other allowances	taxable income	when t=0.5 amount of tax	net capital expenditure	after tax			
	revenue	total expense	cash income					net cash flow	discount factor at i=10%	discounted net cash flow	net present value (NPV)
	A_S	A_{TE}	A_{CI}	A_D+A_A	$A_{CI}-A_D-A_A$	$A_{IT} = (A_{CI}-A_D-A_A)t$	A_{TC}	$A_{CF} = A_{CI}-A_{IT}-A_{TC}$	f_d	A_{DCF}	$= \Sigma A_{DCF}$
0	0	0	0	0	0	0	+1,100,000	-1,100,000	1.0000	-1,100,000	-1,100,000
1	400,000	100,000	300,000	100,000	200,000	100,000	0	200,000	0.90909	181,820	- 918,180
2	500,000	100,000	400,000	100,000	300,000	150,000	0	250,000	0.82645	206,610	- 711,570
3	500,000	110,000	390,000	100,000	290,000	145,000	0	245,000	0.75131	184,070	- 527,500
4	500,000	120,000	380,000	100,000	280,000	140,000	0	240,000	0.68301	163,920	- 363,580
5	520,000	130,000	390,000	100,000	290,000	145,000	0	245,000	0.62092	152,120	- 211,460
6	520,000	130,000	390,000	100,000	290,000	145,000	0	245,000	0.56447	138,300	- 73,160
7	520,000	140,000	380,000	100,000	280,000	140,000	0	240,000	0.51316	123,160	+ 50,000
8	390,000	140,000	250,000	100,000	150,000	75,000	0	175,000	0.46651	81,640	+ 131,640
9	350,000	150,000	200,000	100,000	100,000	50,000	0	150,000	0.42410	63,610	+ 195,250
10	280,000	160,000	120,000	100,000	20,000	10,000	- 100,000	210,000	0.38554	80,960	+ 276,210

life is given by Equation (2.6-1) to be

$$A_D = \frac{(C_{FC} - S)}{s}$$
$$= \frac{\$1{,}000{,}000 - \$0}{10 \text{ years}}$$
$$= \$100{,}000/\text{year}$$

The annual cash income A_{CI} for year 1 when $A_S = \$400{,}000$/year and $A_{TE} = \$100{,}000$/year, is given by Equation (2.1-1) to be

$$A_{CI} = A_S - A_{TE}$$
$$= \$400{,}000/\text{year} - \$100{,}000/\text{year}$$
$$= \$300{,}000/\text{year}$$

Values for subsequent years are calculated in the same way and listed in Tables (3.3-1a), (3.3-1b), (3.3-1c), (3.3-1d), and (3.3-1e).

The annual amount of tax A_{IT} for year 1 when $A_{CI} = \$300{,}000$/year, $A_D = \$100{,}000$/year, $A_A = \$0$/year, and $t = 0.5$, is given by Equation (2.1-3) to be

$$A_{IT} = (A_{CI} - A_D - A_A)\,t$$
$$= [(\$300{,}000 - \$100{,}000 - \$0)/\text{year}](0.5)$$
$$= \$100{,}000/\text{year}$$

Values for subsequent years are calculated in the same way and listed in Tables (3.3-1a) and (3.3-1b).

The net annual cash flow A_{CF} after tax for year 0 when $A_{CI} = \$0$/year, $A_{IT} = \$0$/year, and $A_{TC} = \$1{,}100{,}000$/year, is given by Equation (2.1-4) to be

$$A_{CF} = A_{NCI} - A_{TC}$$
$$= \$0/\text{year} - \$1{,}100{,}000/\text{year}$$
$$= -\$1{,}100{,}000/\text{year}$$

The net annual cash flow A_{CF} after tax for year 1 when $A_{CI} = \$300{,}000$/year, $A_{IT} = \$100{,}000$/year, and $A_{TC} = \$0$/year, is given by Equation (2.1-4) to be

$$A_{CF} = A_{NCI} - A_{TC}$$
$$= \$200{,}000/\text{year} - \$0/\text{year}$$
$$= \$200{,}000/\text{year}$$

Values for the years up to and including year 9 are calculated in the same way and listed in Tables (3.3-1a) and (3.3-1b).

TABLE (3.3-1b)

Annual cash flows with straight line depreciation and 20 per cent discount factor

year	before tax			depreciation charge plus other allowances	taxable income	when t=0.5 amount of tax	net capital expenditure	after tax			
	revenue	total expense	cash income					net cash flow	discount factor at i=20%	discounted net cash flow	net present value (NPV)
	A_S	A_{TE}	A_{CI}	A_D+A_A	$A_{CI}-A_D-A_A$	$A_{IT} = (A_{CI}-A_D-A_A)t$	A_{TC}	$A_{CF} = A_{CI}-A_{IT}-A_{TC}$	f_d	A_{DCF}	$= \Sigma A_{DCF}$
0	0	0	0	0	0	0	+ 1,100,000	- 1,100,000	1.00000	-1,100,000	-1,100,000
1	400,000	100,000	300,000	100,000	200,000	100,000	0	200,000	0.83333	166,670	- 933,330
2	500,000	100,000	400,000	100,000	300,000	150,000	0	250,000	0.69444	173,610	- 759,720
3	500,000	110,000	390,000	100,000	290,000	145,000	0	245,000	0.57870	141,780	- 617,940
4	500,000	120,000	380,000	100,000	280,000	140,000	0	240,000	0.48225	115,740	- 502,200
5	520,000	130,000	390,000	100,000	290,000	145,000	0	245,000	0.40188	98,460	- 403,740
6	520,000	130,000	390,000	100,000	290,000	145,000	0	245,000	0.33490	82,050	- 321,690
7	520,000	140,000	380,000	100,000	280,000	140,000	0	240,000	0.27908	66,980	- 254,710
8	390,000	140,000	250,000	100,000	150,000	75,000	0	175,000	0.23257	40,700	- 214,010
9	350,000	150,000	200,000	100,000	100,000	50,000	0	150,000	0.19381	29,070	- 184,940
10	280,000	160,000	120,000	100,000	20,000	10,000	- 100,000	210,000	0.16151	33,920	- 151,020

TABLE (3.3-1c)

Annual cash flows with double declining depreciation and 10 per cent discount factor

year	before tax: revenue A_S	before tax: total expense A_{TE}	before tax: cash income A_{CI}	depreciation charge plus other allowances A_D+A_A	taxable income $A_{CI}-A_D-A_A$	when t = 0.5 amount of tax A_{IT} = $(A_{CI}-A_D-A_A)t$	net capital expenditure A_{TC}	after tax: net cash flow A_{CF} = $A_{CI}-A_{IT}-A_{TC}$	after tax: discount factor at i=10% f_d	after tax: discounted net cash flow A_{DCF}	after tax: net present value (NPV) = ΣA_{DCF}
0	0	0	0	0	0	0	+1,100,000	-1,100,000	1.00000	-1,100,000	-1,100,000
1	400,000	100,000	300,000	200,000	100,000	50,000	0	250,000	0.90909	227,270	- 872,730
2	500,000	100,000	400,000	160,000	240,000	120,000	0	280,000	0.82645	231,410	- 641,320
3	500,000	110,000	390,000	128,000	262,000	131,000	0	259,000	0.75131	194,590	- 446,730
4	500,000	120,000	380,000	102,400	277,600	138,800	0	241,200	0.68301	164,740	- 281,990
5	520,000	130,000	390,000	81,920	308,080	154,040	0	235,960	0.62092	146,510	- 135,480
6	520,000	130,000	390,000	65,536	324,464	162,232	0	227,768	0.56447	128,570	- 6,910
7	520,000	140,000	380,000	52,429	327,571	163,786	0	216,214	0.51316	110,950	+ 104,040
8	390,000	140,000	250,000	41,943	208,057	104,028	0	145,972	0.46651	68,100	+ 172,140
9	350,000	150,000	200,000	33,554	166,446	83,223	0	116,777	0.42410	49,530	+ 221,670
10	280,000	160,000	120,000	26,844	93,156	46,578	- 100,000	173,422	0.38554	66,860	+ 288,530

TABLE (3.3-1d)

Annual cash flows with sum of years digits depreciation and 10 per cent discount factor

year	before tax			depreciation charge plus other allowances	taxable income	when $t = 0.5$ amount of tax	net capital expenditure	after tax			
	revenue	total expense	cash income			$A_{IT} =$		net cash flow $A_{CF} =$	discount factor at i=10%	discounted net cash flow	net present value (NPV)
	A_S	A_{TE}	A_{CI}	$A_D + A_A$	$A_{CI} - A_D - A_A$	$(A_{CI} - A_D - A_A)t$	A_{TC}	$A_{CI} - A_{IT} - A_{TC}$	f_d	A_{DCF}	$= \Sigma A_{DCF}$
0	0	0	0	0	0	0	+1,100,000	-1,100,000	1.00000	-1,100,000	-1,100,000
1	400,000	100,000	300,000	181,818	118,182	59,091	0	240,909	0.90909	219,010	- 880,990
2	500,000	100,000	400,000	163,637	236,363	118,182	0	281,818	0.82645	232,910	- 648,080
3	500,000	110,000	390,000	145,455	244,545	122,273	0	267,727	0.75131	201,150	- 446,930
4	500,000	120,000	380,000	127,272	252,728	126,364	0	253,636	0.68301	173,240	- 273,690
5	520,000	130,000	390,000	109,090	280,910	140,455	0	249,545	0.62092	154,950	- 118,740
6	520,000	130,000	390,000	90,909	299,091	149,545	0	240,455	0.56447	135,730	+ 16,990
7	520,000	140,000	380,000	72,727	307,273	153,637	0	226,363	0.51316	116,160	+ 133,150
8	390,000	140,000	250,000	54,545	195,455	97,727	0	152,273	0.46651	71,040	+ 204,190
9	350,000	150,000	200,000	36,364	163,636	81,818	0	118,182	0.42410	50,120	+ 254,310
10	280,000	160,000	120,000	18,182	101,818	50,909	- 100,000	169,091	0.38554	65,190	+ 319,500

TABLE (3.3-1e)

Annual cash flows with straight line depreciation and 10 per cent discount factor and income tax delayed for one year

year	before tax			depreciation charge plus other allowances	taxable income	when t = 0.5 amount of tax	net capital expenditure	after tax			
	revenue	total expense	cash income					net cash flow	discount factor at i=10 %	discounted net cash flow	net present value (NPV)
	A_S	A_{TE}	A_{CI}	A_D+A_A	$A_{CI}-A_D-A_A$	A_{IT} = $(A_{CI}-A_D-A_A)t$	A_{TC}	A_{CF} = $A_{CI}-A_{IT}-A_{TC}$	f_d	A_{DCF}	$= \Sigma A_{DCF}$
0	0	0	0	0	0	0	+1,100,000	-1,100,000	1.00000	-1,100,000	-1,100,000
1	400,000	100,000	300,000	100,000	200,000	0	0	300,000	0.90909	272,730	- 827,270
2	500,000	100,000	400,000	100,000	300,000	100,000	0	300,000	0.82645	247,940	- 579,330
3	500,000	110,000	390,000	100,000	290,000	150,000	0	240,000	0.75131	180,310	- 399,020
4	500,000	120,000	380,000	100,000	280,000	145,000	0	235,000	0.68301	160,510	- 238,510
5	520,000	130,000	390,000	100,000	290,000	140,000	0	250,000	0.62092	155,230	- 83,280
6	520,000	130,000	390,000	100,000	290,000	145,000	0	245,000	0.56447	138,300	+ 55,020
7	520,000	140,000	380,000	100,000	280,000	145,000	0	235,000	0.51316	120,590	+ 175,610
8	390,000	140,000	250,000	100,000	150,000	140,000	0	110,000	0.46651	51,320	+ 226,930
9	350,000	150,000	200,000	100,000	100,000	75,000	0	125,000	0.42410	53,010	+ 279,940
10	280,000	160,000	120,000	100,000	20,000	50,000	- 100,000	170,000	0.38554	65,540	+ 345,480
			0	0	0	10,000	0	- 10,000	0.35049	- 3,500	+ 341,980

At the end of year 10, the working capital $C_{WC} = \$90{,}000$, and the cost of land $C_L = \$10{,}000$, are recovered so that the annual expenditure of capital A_{TC} in year 10 is $-\$100{,}000$/year.

The net annual cash flow A_{CF} after tax for year 10 when $A_{CI} = \$120{,}000$/year, $A_{IT} = \$10{,}000$/year, and $A_{TC} = \$100{,}000$/year, is given by Equation (2.1-4) to be

$$\begin{aligned} A_{CF} &= A_{NCI} - A_{TC} \\ &= \$110{,}000/\text{year} + \$100{,}000/\text{year} \\ &= \$210{,}000/\text{year} \end{aligned}$$

The net annual discounted cash flow A_{DCF} for year 1 when $A_{CF} = \$200{,}000$/year and $f_d = 0.909\,09$ for $i = 10$ per cent, is given by Equation (3.2-1) to be

$$\begin{aligned} A_{DCF} &= A_{CF} f_d \\ &= (\$200{,}000/\text{year})(0.909\,09) \\ &= \$181{,}820/\text{year} \end{aligned}$$

Values for subsequent years are calculated in the same way and listed in Table (3.3-1a).

The same procedure is used in Table (3.3-1b) although in this case the discount factors f_d are for $i = 20$ per cent.

The net present value (NPV) for year 10 is given by Equation (3.2-2) to be

$$\begin{aligned} (\text{NPV}) &= \sum A_{DCF} \\ &= \$276{,}210 \\ &\qquad \text{for } i = 10 \text{ per cent} \\ \text{and} \quad &= -\$151{,}020 \\ &\qquad \text{for } i = 20 \text{ per cent} \end{aligned}$$

These values are found by summing the values of A_{DCF} in Tables (3.3-1a) and (3.3-1b) respectively.

(c) (NPV) *with double declining depreciation*

Required equations:

as in parts (a) and (b) but with Equation (2.6-1) replaced by Equation (2.6-5)

$$P_{s'} = C_{FC}(1 - r)^{s'} \tag{2.6-5}$$

where $r = 2/s$. Since $s = 10$ years, $r = 2/s = 0.2$ and $(1 - r) = 0.8$.

The book value $P_{s'}$ for year 0 when $C_{FC} = \$1{,}000{,}000$ is given by Equation

(2.6-5) to be

$$\begin{aligned} P_{s'} &= C_{FC}(1-r)^{s'} \\ &= P_0 = (\$1{,}000{,}000)(0.8)^0 \\ &= \$1{,}000{,}000 \end{aligned}$$

The book value $P_{s'}$ for year 1 is given by Equation (2.6-5) to be

$$\begin{aligned} P_{s'} &= C_{FC}(1-r)^{s'} \\ &= P_1 = (\$1{,}000{,}000)(0.8)^1 \\ &= \$800{,}000 \end{aligned}$$

and for year 2 to be

$$\begin{aligned} P_2 &= (\$1{,}000{,}000)(0.8)^2 \\ &= \$640{,}000 \end{aligned}$$

Values for subsequent years are calculated in the same way.

The annual amount of depreciation for year 1 is

$$\begin{aligned} A_{D1} &= P_0 - P_1 \\ &= \$1{,}000{,}000 - \$800{,}000 \\ &= \$200{,}000/\text{year} \end{aligned}$$

The annual amount of depreciation for year 2 is

$$\begin{aligned} A_{D2} &= P_1 - P_2 \\ &= \$800{,}000 - \$640{,}000 \\ &= \$160{,}000/\text{year} \end{aligned}$$

Values for subsequent years are calculated in the same way and listed in Table (3.3-1c).

All other calculations follow the same procedure as for parts (a) and (b) and the results are listed in Table (3.3-1c).

The net present value (NPV) for year 10 is given by Equation (3.2-2) to be

$$\begin{aligned} (\text{NPV}) &= \sum A_{DCF} \\ &= \$288{,}530 \\ &\qquad \text{for } i = 10 \text{ per cent} \end{aligned}$$

(d) (NPV) *with sum of years depreciation*

Required equations:

as in parts (a) and (b) but with Equation (2.4-1) replaced by Equation

(2.6-7).

$$A_{Ds'} = \frac{2(s - s' + 1)}{s(s+1)}(C_{FC} - S) \tag{2.6-7}$$

The annual amount of depreciation for year 1 when $C_{FC} = \$1{,}000{,}000$ and $S = \$0$ is given by Equation (2.6-7) to be

$$\begin{aligned} A_{Ds'} &= \frac{2(s - s' + 1)}{s(s+1)}(C_{FC} - S) \\ = A_{D1} &= \frac{(2)(10)}{(10)(11)}(\$1{,}000{,}000 - \$0) \\ &= \$181{,}818 \end{aligned}$$

Values for subsequent years are calculated in the same way and listed in Table (3.3-1d).

All other calculations follow the same procedure as for parts (a) and (b) and the results are listed in Table (3.3-1d).

The net present value (NPV) for year 10 is given by Equation (3.2-2) to be

$$\begin{aligned} (\text{NPV}) &= \sum A_{DCF} \\ &= \$319{,}500 \\ &\qquad \text{for } i = 10 \text{ per cent} \end{aligned}$$

(e) (NPV) *with straight line depreciation and income tax delayed for one year*

The equations and the calculations follow the same procedure as for parts (a) and (b) although the annual amount of tax A_{IT} is calculated for a particular year and then deducted from the annual cash income A_{CI} for the following year. The results are listed in Table (3.3-1e).

The net present value (NPV) for year 11 is given by Equation (3.2-2) to be

$$\begin{aligned} (\text{NPV}) &= \sum A_{DCF} \\ &= \$341{,}980 \\ &\qquad \text{for } i = 10 \text{ per cent} \end{aligned}$$

(f) (DCFRR) *with straight line depreciation*

$$\begin{aligned} (\text{NPV}) &= \$276{,}210 \quad \text{for } i = 10 \text{ per cent} \\ (\text{NPV}) &= -\$151{,}020 \quad \text{for } i = 20 \text{ per cent} \end{aligned}$$

from Tables (3.3-1a) and (3.3-1b) respectively.

The discounted cash flow rate of return (DCFRR) can readily be obtained by interpolation to be

$$(\text{DCFRR}) = 0.1000 + \frac{(\$276{,}210)(0.20 - 0.10)}{\$276{,}210 - (-\$151{,}020)}$$
$$= 0.164$$
$$= 16.4 \text{ per cent}$$

It is clear that double declining depreciation is more advantageous than straight line depreciation and that sum of years digits depreciation is more advantageous than double declining depreciation. However, a significant advantage is obtained by delaying the payment of tax for one year even with straight line depreciation.

This example is a simplified one. The cost of the working capital is assumed to be paid for in year 0 and returned in year 10. In practice the working capital increases with production rate. Thus there may be an annual expenditure A_{TC} on working capital in a number of years subsequent to year 0.

3.4 Comparison of Projects

An important function of management is to decide if, and when, to start or stop certain projects. Frequently this involves comparing an existing process with a newly developed one. Although not all the factors involved are economic, for the most part economic factors tend to be dominant.

There is no single economic criterion which can take the place of good judgment. The various criteria used can be classified roughly under the headings of time, capital and interest.

Comparisons on the basis of time: These can be summarized with reference to the cumulative cash flow curves in Figures (3.2-1) and (3.2-2) as follows:

(1) the duration of the project

(2) the breakeven point (BEP) shown as e_0

(3) the discounted breakeven point (DBEP) shown as e (in this case for a discount factor of 10 per cent)

(4) the equivalent maximum investment period

$$(\text{EMIP}) = \frac{\text{Area } (a_0 \text{ to } e_0)}{-\sum A_{\text{CFmax}}} \tag{3.2-4}$$

where $-\sum A_{\text{CFmax}}$ is given by point d_0

(5) the interest recovery period (IRP) which makes the area (e_0 to f_0) equal to the area (a_0 to e_0)

(6) the payback period (PBP) which is the value of s' which satisfies the

equation

$$\sum_{s'=0}^{s'=(\mathrm{PBP})} A_{\mathrm{CF}} = C_{\mathrm{FC}} - S \tag{2.14-1}$$

where $(C_{\mathrm{FC}} - S)$ is the depreciable fixed capital investment

Comparisons on the basis of capital: These can be summarized as follows:

(1) the maximum cumulative expenditure on the project, $-\sum A_{\mathrm{CFmax}}$ given by point $\mathrm{d_0}$

(2) the maximum discounted cumulative expenditure on the project, $-\sum A_{\mathrm{DCFmax}}$ given by point d (in this case for a discount factor of 10 per cent)

(3) the cumulative net annual cash flow $\sum A_{\mathrm{CF}}$

(4) the cumulative net annual discounted cash flow $\sum A_{\mathrm{DCF}}$ or net present value (NPV) where

$$(\mathrm{NPV}) = \sum A_{\mathrm{DCF}} \tag{3.2-2}$$

(5) the capitalized cost C_{K} where

$$C_{\mathrm{K}} = \left[C_{\mathrm{FC}} - \frac{S}{(1+i)^n}\right]\left[\frac{(1+i)^n}{(1+i)^n - 1}\right] \tag{1.8-2}$$

Comparisons on the basis of interest: These can be summarized as follows:

(1) the discounted cash flow rate of return (DCFRR) which is the fractional interest rate i which satisfies the equation

$$(\mathrm{NPV}) = \sum A_{\mathrm{DCF}} = 0 \tag{3.2-3}$$

(2) those based on the equation

$$\text{per cent of return} = \frac{\text{annual return}}{\text{invested capital}} \times 100 \tag{2.10-1}$$

The rate of return can be calculated either on the basis of net annual profit before tax A_{NP}, the net annual profit after tax A_{NNP}, the annual cash income before tax A_{CI}, or the net annual cash income after tax A_{NCI}. In addition the rate of return can be calculated either on the basis of the original total capital investment C_{TC}, the depreciated total capital investment in any particular year, or the average total capital investment over the life of the project.

The most common of the modern methods of estimating profitability are the discounted cash flow rate of return (DCFRR) method and the net present value (NPV) method.

Since (DCFRR) is a single percentage it has the advantage of being readily understood. (NPV) has the disadvantage of being a sum of money and additional information is needed before its significance can be appreciated. However, when a company is considering investment in a portfolio of projects, individual (NPV)s have the advantage that they can be added together. This cannot be done with (DCFRR)s.

An (NPV) or (DCFRR) estimation will be no better than the accuracy of the predicted cash flows over the life of the project. Clearly one is likely to predict cash flows more accurately for two or three years ahead than for say nine or ten years ahead. However, since the cash flows in the later years are discounted to a greater extent than for the earlier years the latter have less effect on the overall estimation. Nevertheless the difficulty of predicting cash flows in later years and the inherent lack of confidence in these predictions is a serious disadvantage of the (DCFRR) method. In this respect (NPV)s are more useful since they are calculated for each year of a project. Thus a project with a favorable (NPV) in the early years is a good-looking project.

One way of overcoming this particular disadvantage of the (DCFRR) method is to make estimates of the times to reach certain values of (DCFRR). For example, how many years will it take to reach (DCFRR)s of 10, 15, 20 per cent/year etc? Although (DCFRR) trial and error calculations are tedious if done manually, computer programs are readily available and widely used for (NPV) and (DCFRR) calculations.

It is possible for some projects to reach a stage when repairs, replacements, etc., can exceed net earnings in a particular year. In this case the cumulative discounted cash flow $\sum A_{DCF}$ or (NPV) against time curve can have a genuine maximum. The (DCFRR) method has the disadvantage that no negative cash flow can appear after the first year of positive cash flow unless special evaluation techniques are employed.

(DCFRR) estimates are liable to misuse if a company uses a particular (DCFRR) value as a cut off point. Estimators may calculate the cash flows required to ensure that particular (DCFRR) value and then persuade various people in the company that these projected cash flows are possible.

It is important when computing (NPV) and (DCFRR) not to consider the past in profitability estimations. Good money should never follow bad. Money should not continue to be put into a project if a more profitable project exists even though this may involve scrapping expensive plant.

When considering future projects top management will most likely require the discounted cash flow rate of return (DCFRR). However, the estimators should also supply top management with the following information:

(1) the cumulative discounted cash flow or (NPV) curve for a discount rate of 10 per cent/year

(2) the maximum net outlay, $-\sum A_{CFmax}$

(3) the discounted breakeven point (DBEP)

(4) a plot of capital return ratio (CRR) against time over the life of the project for a discount rate of say 10 per cent/year

(5) the number of years to reach discounted cash flow rates of return (DCFRR) of say 10 and 15 per cent/year respectively

The various interest measures should be evaluated regularly and plotted against time while the project is actually running. These data help management to take decisions such as when to terminate the project.

Example (3.4-1)

The research department of company A developed a product on which a feasibility study and a market survey were carried out. It is company policy to treat such expenditures as overhead charges. The results of the studies were promising and \$100,000 was spent on a design study in year 0. It is company policy to treat such expenditure as part of the fixed capital cost of any project which is completed and as overhead if the project is terminated. In year 1 a site was purchased for \$10,000 and \$640,000 was spent on plant and its erection. In year 2 the plant was commissioned and \$100,000 working capital provided. The costs of completion, commissioning and of the original promotional drive to launch the project exceeded the revenue from the process for year 2 by \$100,000. The company agreed with the tax authority that \$10,000 of this deficit was part of the fixed capital cost while the remaining \$90,000 could be treated as a negative cash income allowable for tax purposes. It was further agreed with the tax authority that, for the purpose of evaluating the allowable depreciation charge, the whole of the \$750,000 depreciable capital cost could be written off against plant earnings over an estimated working life of ten years, any difference to be adjusted in the last year of operation. The annual cash income A_{CI} of the process for years 3, 4, 5, 6 and 7 was \$500,000. In the meantime the research department had developed an improved replacement product and the management negotiated an agreement to licence the existing process to company B with the condition that the existing plant would be phased out over a period of three years. The annual cash incomes A_{CI} to company A for those years were \$400,000, \$300,000, and \$190,000 respectively. Additionally, in the last year there was recovery of the cost of land and working capital and also \$100,000 received as the salvage value of the plant.

Company B on completing the agreement purchased a site for \$10,000 and paid \$750,000 for a package deal plant, including a know how payment, in year 0. The plant was commissioned in year 1 with the provision of \$100,000 working capital but promotional and other costs exceeded revenue by \$40,000. The negative annual cash income was agreed with the tax authority to be allowable for tax purposes. The cash income from the process in years 2, 3, 4, 5 and 6 were \$350,000, \$350,000, \$500,000, \$500,000, and \$500,000 respectively. In year 7 the influence of the replacement product produced by company A was felt and the annual cash incomes A_{CI} for years 7, 8, 9, and 10 were \$500,000, \$400,000, \$200,000, and \$40,000 respectively. Additionally in the last year there was recovery of the cost of land and working capital and also \$100,000 received as the salvage value of the plant. The arrangement for writing off the depreciable capital investment was the same as for company A.

Calculate the various measures of profitability for projects A and B assuming a cost of capital of 10 per cent and a tax rate of 50 per cent. For the purpose of calculating the traditional return on investment measures use the net annual profit before tax but after depreciation A_{NP}. It may be assumed that the annual depreciation charge A_{BD} as shown in the balance sheets of the companies is the same as the total allowable charge for tax purposes $(A_D + A_A)$ and that the companies can take advantage of any tax concessions in the year in which they arise.

Required equations:

$$C_K = (C_{FC} - Sf_d)\, f_K \tag{1.8-3}$$

$$A_{NP} \doteq A_{CI} - A_{BD} \tag{2.1-8}$$

together with equations used in Examples (2.14-1) and (3.3-1).

The definitions and methods required for calculating the traditional measures of profitability are given in Example (2.14-1). The only difference is that in this example the net annual profit A_{NP} is to be used in place of the net annual cash income A_{NCI}.

The definitions and methods required for the modern discounted measures of profitability are given in Example (3.3-1). Profitabilities by the less usual modern methods are calculated from the definitions given in section 3.2.

The \$100,000 salvage value of the plant received in excess of the agreed value of zero will be treated by the tax authority as a negative capital allowance A_A while the agreed depreciation A_D of the \$750,000 fixed capital investment C_{FC} is an allowable expense from the year of start up of the plant. The data for the annual tax allowances $(A_D + A_A)$ for each project is entered in Table (3.4-1a). The net annual profit A_{NP} is the annual cash income A_{CI} less the balance sheet annual depreciation charge A_{BD} which in the present instance is the same as $(A_D + A_A)$. The remaining entries in Table (3.4-1a) are calculated in the same way as those in Table (3.3-1a).

It will be noted that the following information is identical for each project; duration = 10 years, total cash income $\sum A_{CI}$ = \$3,300,000, total tax allowances $\sum (A_D + A_A)$ = \$650,000, total net profit $\sum A_{NP}$ = \$2,650,000, total tax paid $\sum A_{IT}$ = \$1,325,000, total income after tax $\sum A_{NCI}$ = \$1,975,000, total capital outlay $\sum A_{TCmax}$ = \$860,000, total after tax cash flow $\sum A_{CF}$ = \$1,325,000. It follows that the projects differ mainly in the timing of the cash flows. The respective net present values (NPV) for projects A and B at a cost of capital of 10 per cent are, from Table (3.4-1a), \$430,227 and \$437,938.

TABLE (3.4-1a)

	year	A_{CI}	$A_D + A_A$	A_{NP}	t=0.5 A_{IT}	A_{NCI}	A_{TC}	A_{CF}	ΣA_{CF}	i=10% A_{DCF}	ΣA_{DCF}
project A	0	0	0	0	0	0	100,000	-100,000	- 100,000	-100,000	-100,000
	1	0	0	0	0	0	650,000	-650,000	- 750,000	-590,909	-690,909
	2	- 90,000	+75,000	-165,000	- 82,500	- 7,500	110,000	-117,500	- 867,500	- 97,108	-788,017
	3	+500,000	+75,000	+425,000	+212,500	+287,500	0	+287,500	- 580,000	+216,002	-572,015
	4	+500,000	+75,000	+425,000	+212,500	+287,500	0	+287,500	- 292,500	+196,365	-375,650
	5	+500,000	+75,000	+425,000	+212,500	+287,500	0	+287,500	- 5,000	+178,515	-197,135
	6	+500,000	+75,000	+425,000	+212,500	+287,500	0	+287,500	+ 282,500	+162,285	- 34.850
	7	+500,000	+75,000	+425,000	+212,500	+287,500	0	+287,500	+ 570,000	+147,534	+112,684
	8	+400,000	+75,000	+325,000	+162,500	+237,500	0	+237,500	+ 807,500	+110,796	+223,480
	9	+300,000	+75,000	+225,000	+112,500	+187,500	0	+187,500	+ 995,000	+ 79,519	+302,999
	10	+190,000	+50,000	+140,000	+ 70,000	+120,000	-210,000	+330,000	+1,325,000	+127,228	+430,227

	year	A_{CI}	$A_D + A_A$	A_{NP}	t=0.5 A_{IT}	A_{NCI}	A_{TC}	A_{CF}	ΣA_{CF}	i=10% A_{DCF}	ΣA_{DCF}
project B	0	0	0	0	0	0	+760,000	-760,000	- 760,000	-760,000	-760,000
	1	- 40,000	+75,000	-115,000	- 57,500	+ 17,500	+100,000	- 82,500	- 842,500	- 75,000	-835,000
	2	+350,000	+75,000	+275,000	+137,500	+212,500	0	+212,500	- 630,000	+175,621	-659,379
	3	+350,000	+75,000	+275,000	+137,500	+212,500	0	+212,500	- 417,500	+159,653	-499,726
	4	+500,000	+75,000	+425,000	+212,500	+287,500	0	+287,500	- 130,000	+196,365	-303,361
	5	+500,000	+75,000	+425,000	+212,500	+287,500	0	+287,500	+ 157,500	+178,515	-124,846
	6	+500,000	+75,000	+425,000	+212,500	+287,500	0	+287,500	+ 445,000	+162,285	+ 37,439
	7	+500,000	+75,000	+425,000	+212,500	+287,500	0	+287,500	+ 732,500	+147,534	+184,973
	8	+400,000	+75,000	+325,000	+162,500	+237,500	0	+237,500	+ 970,000	+110,796	+295,769
	9	+200,000	+75,000	+125,000	+ 62,500	+137,500	0	+137,500	+1,107,500	+ 58,314	+354,083
	10	+ 40,000	-25,000	+ 65,000	+ 32,500	+ 7,500	-210,000	+217,500	+1,325,000	+ 83,855	+437,938

Values of the various measures of profitability are listed in Table (3.4-1b). Note that the payback period (PBP) is measured from the time of plant start up while traditional return on investment measures consider only those years in which the measure, in this case net annual profit A_{NP}, is positive.

TABLE (3.4-1b)

Comparison of the profitabilities of projects A and B

	project A	project B
duration of project	10 years	10 years
earning life of project	9 years	10 years
breakeven point, undiscounted (BEP)	5.02 years	4.45 years
breakeven point, discounted (DBEP)	6.24 years	5.77 years
equivalent maximum investment period (EMIP)	2.93 years	2.81 years
interest recovery period (IRP)	9.37 years	8.57 years
payback period (PBP)	2.67 years	3.07 years
maximum net outlay, undiscounted $-A_{CFmax}$	\$867,500	\$842,500
maximum net outlay, discounted at 10 per cent $-A_{DCFmax}$	\$788,017	\$835,000
maximum return, undiscounted	\$1,325,000	\$1,325,000
maximum return, discounted at 10 per cent (NPV)	\$430,227	\$434,938
capitalized cost C_K	\$1,228,700	\$1,157,800
average rate of return on original investment	40.92%/year	35.72%/year
average rate of return on depreciated investment	80.52%/year	64.88%/year
average rate of return on average capital investment	65.77%/year	54.84%/year
discounted cash flow rate of return (DCFRR)	20.68%/year	19.68%/year
capital rate of return ratio (CRR)	49.56%	51.62%

As an alternative to graphical methods note that the cash flow curves are defined by line segments. The area between the curve and the axis may readily be calculated by formulas for the area under a polygon. Also the point at which the line segment crosses the zero cash flow axis may be obtained with sufficient accuracy by linear interpolation.

The plot of capital return ratio (CRR) against time can be obtained from the $\sum A_{DCF}$ column of Table (3.4-1a) by dividing each annual entry by $-\sum A_{CFmax}$. The value of (CRR) for the final year of each project is the only one listed in Table (3.4-1b).

Example 3.4-2

A process has been in operation for eight years. A recently developed machine could replace an existing machine in the process. The process could run without the existing machine but an additional \$1,000 per year would have to be spent in maintenance. In addition, the absence of the machine would result in significantly increased environmental discomfort for the operators which is regarded as socially unacceptable. The new machine would give a lower spoilage rate and lead to additional savings on maintenance. Management has the following three choices:

(a) retain the existing machine
(b) purchase the new machine
(c) lease the new machine

Evaluate the merits of the three alternatives on the basis of the following information:

(1) There are six further years of life for the process which will cease to operate at the end of year 14.

(2) The existing machine was purchased eight years ago for \$10,000; straight line depreciation was allowed over a ten-year period with a scrap value S of \$200.

(3) The existing machine is expected to continue to earn a marginal income of \$1,000 per year but will required a major overhaul in year 12 costing \$2,000.

(4) The new machine would cost \$15,000; 25 per cent of this expenditure is given as a government grant in the first year of operation; straight line depreciation is allowed on the remaining 75 per cent of the expenditure over a ten-year period with a scrap value S of \$250.

(5) The new machine is expected to save an additional \$2,800 per year because of reduced spoilage and maintenance; thus the new machine would earn a marginal income of \$3,800/year.

(6) The new machine could be leased for a prepayment of \$900, five annual payments of \$2,700 and a final payment of \$1,800.

(7) The tax rate is 50 per cent; a negative taxable income may be assumed in any year in which the tax allowances exceed the cash income since in practice this is absorbed in the economy of the entire plant.

(8) Cost of capital is 10 per cent/year.

Also evaluate the merits of the three alternatives if the process were unexpectedly terminated at the end of year 11.

(a) *Retain the existing machine*

Required equations:

$$A_{\text{NCI}} = A_{\text{CI}} - A_{\text{IT}} \tag{2.1-2}$$

$$A_{CF} = A_{NCI} - A_{TC} \tag{2.1-4}$$

$$A_{IT} = (A_{CI} - A_D - A_A)\, t \tag{2.1-3}$$

$$A_D = \frac{(C_{FC} - S)}{s} \tag{2.6-1}$$

$$A_{DCF} = A_{CF} f_d \tag{3.2-1}$$

$$(\text{NPV}) = \sum A_{DCF} \tag{3.2-2}$$

$$(\text{NPV}) = \sum A_{DCF} = 0 \tag{3.2-3}$$

where in this case $i = (\text{DCFRR})$.

The annual rate of straight line depreciation of the existing machine from \$10,000, at start up, to \$200 at the end of ten years is given by Equation (2.6-1) to be

$$\begin{aligned} A_D &= \frac{(C_{FC} - S)}{s} \\ &= \frac{\$10{,}000 - \$200}{10 \text{ years}} \\ &= \$980/\text{year} \end{aligned}$$

Thus the cumulative depreciation to the end of year 8 is

$$(8 \text{ years})(\$980/\text{year}) = \$7{,}840$$

The book value $P_{s'}$ at the end of year 8 is therefore

$$\$10{,}000 - \$7{,}840 = \$2{,}160$$

Other book values are calculated in the same way and listed in Table (3.4-2a).

The annual amount of tax A_{IT} for year 1 when $A_{CI} = \$1{,}000/\text{year}$, $A_D = \$980/\text{year}$, $A_A = \$0/\text{year}$, and $t = 0.5$ is given by Equation (2.1-3) to be

$$\begin{aligned} A_{IT} &= (A_{CI} - A_D - A_A)\, t \\ &= [(\$1{,}000 - \$980 - \$0)/\text{year}]\,(0.5) \\ &= \$10/\text{year} \end{aligned}$$

Values for subsequent years are calculated in the same way and listed in Table (3.4-2a).

The net annual cash flow A_{CF} after tax for year 0 when $A_{CI} = \$0/\text{year}$, $A_{IT} = \$0/\text{year}$, and $A_{TC} = \$10{,}000/\text{year}$, is given by Equation (2.1-2) to be

$$\begin{aligned} A_{CF} &= A_{NCI} - A_{TC} \\ &= \$0/\text{year} - \$10{,}000/\text{year} \\ &= -\$10{,}000/\text{year} \end{aligned}$$

TABLE (3.4-2a)

Annual cash flows for option (a): retain the existing machine

year	book value of machine	cash income from machine before tax	depreciation charge plus other allowances	taxable income	when t= 0.5 amount of tax A_{IT} =	net capital expenditure	after tax				
							net cash flow A_{CF} =	net cash flow adjusted at i = 10%	discount factor at i = 10%	discounted net cash flow	net present value (NPV)
	P_s'	A_{CI}	$A_D + A_A$	$A_{CI}-A_D-A_A$	$(A_{CI}-A_D-A_A)t$	A_{TC}	$A_{CI}-A_{IT}-A_{TC}$		f_d	A_{DCF}	$= \Sigma A_{DCF}$
0	10,000	0	0	0	0	10,000	- 10,000	- 10,000	1.00000	-10,000.0	-10,000.0
1	9,020	1,000	980	20	10	0	990	990	0.90909	900.0	- 9,100.0
2	8,040	1,000	980	20	10	0	990	990	0.82645	818.2	- 8,281.8
3	7,060	1,000	980	20	10	0	990	990	0.75131	743.8	- 7,538.0
4	6,080	1,000	980	20	10	0	990	990	0.68301	676.2	- 6,861.8
5	5,100	1,000	980	20	10	0	990	990	0.62092	614.7	- 6,247.1
6	4,120	1,000	980	20	10	0	990	990	0.56447	558.8	- 5,688.3
7	3,140	1,000	980	20	10	0	990	990	0.51316	508.0	- 5,180.3
8	2,160	1,000	980	20	10	0	990	990	0.46651	461.8	- 4,718.5
9	1,180	1,000	980	20	10	0	990	990	0.42410	419.9	- 4,298.6
10	200	1,000	980	20	10	0	990	990	0.38554	381.7	- 3,916.9
11	200	1,000	0	1,000	500	0	500	45	0.35049	175.2	-3,741.7
12	200	- 1,000	0	- 1,000	- 500	0	- 500	0	0.31863	- 159.3	-3,901.0
13	200	1,000	0	1,000	500	0	500	500	0.28966	144.8	-3,756.2
14	200	1,000	0	1,000	500	- 200	700	700	0.26333	184.3	-3,571.9

The net annual cash flow A_{CF} after tax for year 1 when $A_{CI} = \$1{,}000$/year, $A_{IT} = \$10$/year, and $A_{TC} = \$0$/year, is given by Equation (2.1-4) to be

$$\begin{aligned} A_{CF} &= A_{NCI} - A_{TC} \\ &= \$990/\text{year} - \$0/\text{year} \\ &= \$990/\text{year} \end{aligned}$$

Values for subsequent years are calculated in the same way and listed in Table (3.4-2a).

After year 10 the existing machine is fully depreciated and the depreciation allowance is zero.

In year 12 the existing machine is overhauled at a cost of \$2,000 resulting in a negative annual cash income

$$\begin{aligned} A_{CI} &= \$1{,}000/\text{year} - \$2{,}000/\text{year} \\ &= -\$1{,}000/\text{year} \end{aligned}$$

At the end of year 14 the salvage value S of the existing machine is \$200. This is recovered so that the annual expenditure of capital A_{TC} in year 14 is −\$200/year.

The net annual discounted cash flow A_{DCF} for year 1 when $A_{CF} = \$990$/year and $f_d = 0.909\ 09$ for $i = 10$ per cent, is given by Equation (3.2-1) to be

$$\begin{aligned} A_{DCF} &= A_{CF} f_d \\ &= (\$990/\text{year})(0.909\ 09) \\ &= \$900/\text{year} \end{aligned}$$

Values for subsequent years are calculated in the same way and listed in Table (3.4-2a).

The net present value (NPV) for year 14 is given by Equation (3.2-2) to be

$$\begin{aligned} (\text{NPV}) &= \sum A_{DCF} \\ &= -\$3{,}571.9 \\ &\quad \text{for } i = 10 \text{ per cent} \end{aligned}$$

This value is found by summing the values of A_{DCF} in Table (3.4-2a).

The value of (NPV) is of course directly dependent on the choice of the fractional interest rate i. An interest rate can be chosen to make (NPV) = 0. This value of i is given by Equation (3.2-3)

$$\sum A_{DCF} = 0$$

and is shown by an iterative procedure to be 1.76 per cent. Thus the discounted cash flow rate of return (DCFRR) = 1.76 per cent.

Although this value is low, the presence of the machine avoids a significant amount of environmental discomfort for the operators. It can therefore be regarded as a socially necessary part of the process.

The discounted cash flow rate of return (DCFRR) cannot be obtained unambiguously if a negative value of the net annual cash flow A_{CF} follows the first positive value of A_{CF}. This happens in year 12 in Table (3.4-2a). An adjustment can be made to prevent this. This is done by nominally borrowing from the positive net annual cash flow A_{CF} in an adjacent year. The loan is discounted at the cost of capital which in this case is assumed to be 10 per cent.

The sum of \$455 borrowed in year 11 would have grown to \$500 in year 12 with an interest rate of 10 per cent. Thus the amount of A_{CF} left in year 11 would be \$500 – \$455 = \$45. The adjusted values of A_{CF} are listed in Table (3.4-2a).

Strictly speaking the discounting should be done at the (DCFRR) as in Table (3.4-2e).

(b) *Purchase the new machine*

Required equations:

as in part (a)

The calculations for the first seven years are the same as in part (a).

As listed in Table (3.4-2b), the book value $P_{s'}$ of the original machine at the end of year 8 is \$2,160 which is \$1,960 more than the salvage value S of \$200. The difference of \$1,960 is the balancing allowance which is given as a tax allowance in the following year, i.e. year 9.

The new machine is purchased in year 8 for \$15,000; 25 per cent of this expenditure, i.e., \$3,750, is given as a government grant in the first year of operation, i.e. year 9. Thus the net cost of the new machine is \$11,250. The annual rate of straight line depreciation from \$11,250 to \$250 at the end of ten years is given by Equation (2.6-1) to be

$$A_D = \frac{(C_{FC} - S)}{s}$$

$$= \frac{\$11{,}250 - \$250}{10 \text{ years}}$$

$$= \$1{,}100/\text{year}$$

In year 8 the new machine is purchased for \$15,000 and the existing machine is sold for the scrap value of \$200. Thus the net capital outlay in year 8 is \$14,800.

The net annual cash flow A_{CF} after tax for year 8 when $A_{CI} = \$1{,}000/\text{year}$, $A_{IT} = \$10/\text{year}$, and $A_{TC} = (\$15{,}000 - \$200)/\text{year} = \$14{,}800/\text{year}$, is given by

TABLE (3.4-2b)

Annual cash flows for option (b): purchase the new machine

year	book value of machine	cash income from machine before tax	depreciation charge plus other allowances	taxable income	when t= 0.5 amount of tax A_{IT} =	net capital expenditure	after tax: net cash flow A_{CF} =	after tax: net cash flow adjusted at i = 10%	after tax: discount factor at i = 10%	after tax: discounted net cash flow	after tax: net present value (NPV)
	P_s'	A_{CI}	$A_D + A_A$	$A_{CI}-A_D-A_A$	$(A_{CI}-A_D-A_A)t$	A_{TC}	$A_{CI}-A_{IT}-A_{TC}$		f_d	A_{DCF}	$= \Sigma A_{DCF}$
0	10,000	0	0	0	0	+ 10,000	- 10,000	- 10,000	1.00000	-10,000.0	-10,000.0
1	9,020	1,000	980	20	10	0	990	990	0.90909	900.0	- 9,100.0
2	8,040	1,000	980	20	10	0	990	990	0.82645	818.2	- 8,281.8
3	7,060	1,000	980	20	10	0	990	990	0.75131	743.8	- 7,538.0
4	6,080	1,000	980	20	10	0	990	990	0.68301	676.2	- 6,861.8
5	5,100	1,000	980	20	10	0	990	0	0.62092	614.7	- 6,247.1
6	4,120	1,000	980	20	10	0	990	0	0.56447	558.8	- 5,688.3
7	3,140	1,000	980	20	10	0	990	0	0.51316	508.0	- 5,180.3
8	2,160 / 15,000	1,000	980	20	10	14,800	- 13,810	0	0.46651	- 6,442.5	-11,622.8
9	10,150	3,800	3,060	740	370	- 3,750	7,180	0	0.42410	3,045.0	- 8.577.8
10	9,050	3,800	1,100	2,700	1,350	0	2,450	0	0.38554	944.6	- 7,633.2
11	7,950	3,800	1,100	2,700	1,350	0	2,450	249	0.35049	858.7	- 6,774.5
12	6,850	3,800	1,100	2,700	1,350	0	2,450	2,450	0.31863	780.6	- 5,993.9
13	5,750	3,800	1,100	2,700	1,350	0	2,450	2,450	0.28966	709.7	- 5,284.2
14	4,650	3,800	1,100	2,700	1,350	- 250	2,700	2,700	0.26333	711.0	- 4,573.2
15	0	0	4,400	- 4,400	- 2,200	0	2,200	2,200	0.23939	526.7	- 4,046.5

Equation (2.1-4) to be

$$
\begin{aligned}
A_{\mathrm{CF}} &= A_{\mathrm{NCI}} - A_{\mathrm{TC}} \\
&= \$990/\text{year} - \$14{,}800/\text{year} \\
&= -\$13{,}810/\text{year}
\end{aligned}
$$

In year 9 the depreciation allowance

$$A_{\mathrm{D}} = \$1{,}100/\text{year}$$

In year 9 the balancing allowance resulting from the sale of the existing machine

$$A_{\mathrm{A}} = \$1{,}960/\text{year}$$

Thus for year 9 the depreciation plus the balancing allowance

$$A_{\mathrm{D}} + A_{\mathrm{A}} = \$3{,}060/\text{year}$$

The annual amount of tax A_{IT} for year 9 when $A_{\mathrm{CI}} = \$3{,}800/\text{year}$, $A_{\mathrm{D}} = \$1{,}100/\text{year}$, $A_{\mathrm{A}} = \$1{,}960/\text{year}$ and $t = 0.5$ is given by Equation (2.1-3) to be

$$
\begin{aligned}
A_{\mathrm{IT}} &= (A_{\mathrm{CI}} - A_{\mathrm{D}} - A_{\mathrm{A}})\,t \\
&= [(\$3{,}800 - \$1{,}100 - \$1{,}960)/\text{year}](0.5) \\
&= \$370/\text{year}
\end{aligned}
$$

Values for subsequent years are calculated in the same way and listed in Table (3.4-2b).

The net annual cash flow A_{CF} after tax for year 9 when $A_{\mathrm{CI}} = \$3{,}800/\text{year}$, $A_{\mathrm{IT}} = \$370/\text{year}$, and $A_{\mathrm{TC}} = -\$3{,}750/\text{year}$ (25 per cent of \$15,000 given as a government grant) is given by Equation (2.1-4) to be

$$
\begin{aligned}
A_{\mathrm{CF}} &= A_{\mathrm{NCI}} - A_{\mathrm{TC}} \\
&= \$3{,}430/\text{year} + \$3{,}750/\text{year} \\
&= \$7{,}180/\text{year}
\end{aligned}
$$

Values for subsequent years are calculated in the same way and listed in Table (3.4-2b).

As listed in Table (3.4-2b), the book value $P_{s'}$ of the new machine at the end of year 14 is \$4,650 which is \$4,400 more than the salvage value S of \$250. The difference of \$4,400 is the balancing allowance which is given as a tax allowance in the following year, i.e. year 15.

The annual amount of tax A_{IT} for year 15 (after the process has been closed down) when $A_{\mathrm{CI}} = \$0/\text{year}$, $A_{\mathrm{D}} = \$0/\text{year}$, $A_{\mathrm{A}} = \$4{,}400/\text{year}$ (balancing allowance), and $t = 0.5$, is given by Equation (2.1-3) to be

$$\begin{aligned} A_{IT} &= (A_{CI} - A_D - A_A)\,t \\ &= [(\$0 - \$0 - \$4{,}400)/\text{year}](0.5) \\ &= -\$2{,}200/\text{year} \end{aligned}$$

The net annual cash flow A_{CF} after tax for year 15 when $A_{CI} = \$0$/year, $A_{IT} = -\$2{,}200$/year, and $A_{TC} = \$0$/year, is given by Equation (2.1-4) to be

$$\begin{aligned} A_{CF} &= A_{NCI} - A_{TC} \\ &= \$2{,}200/\text{year} - \$0/\text{year} \\ &= \$2{,}200/\text{year} \end{aligned}$$

The net annual discounted cash flow A_{DCF} for each year is calculated as in part (a) and the values are listed in Table (3.4-2b).

The net present value (NPV) for year 15 is given by Equation (3.2-2) to be

$$\begin{aligned} (\text{NPV}) &= \sum A_{DCF} \\ &= -\$4{,}046.5 \\ &\quad \text{for } i = 10 \text{ per cent} \end{aligned}$$

This value is found by summing the values of A_{DCF} in Table (3.4-2b).

Using the same iterative procedure as in part (a), the discounted cash flow rate of return (DCFRR) is found to be 3.48 per cent.

(c) *Lease the new machine*

Required equations:

as in part (a)

The calculations for the first seven years are the same as in part (a).

The annual cash income A_{CI} before tax for year 8 is \$100/year, i.e. the marginal income of \$1,000/year for the existing machine minus the lease prepayment of \$900 for the new machine.

The annual cash income A_{CI} before tax for year 9 is \$1,100/year, i.e. the marginal income of \$3,800/year for the new machine minus the first annual payment of \$2,700/year on the lease.

Since the existing machine is sold and the new machine leased in year 8, there is no depreciation allowance in year 9 or in any subsequent years.

In year 9 the balancing allowance resulting from the sale of the existing machine

$$A_A = \$1{,}960/\text{year}$$

TABLE (3.4-2c)

Annual cash flows for option (c): lease the new machine

year	book value of machine	cash income from machine before tax	depreciation charge plus other allowances	taxable income	when t= 0.5 amount of tax A_{IT} =	net capital expenditure	after tax				
							net cash flow A_{CF} =	net cash flow adjusted at i = 10%	discount factor at i = 10%	discounted net cash flow	net present value (NPV)
	P_s'	A_{CI}	$A_D + A_A$	$A_{CI}-A_D-A_A$	$(A_{CI}-A_D-A_A)t$	A_{TC}	$A_{CI}-A_{IT}-A_{TC}$		f_d	A_{DCF}	$= \Sigma A_{DCF}$
0	10,000	0	0	0	0	10,000	- 10,000	- 10,000	1,00000	-10,000.0	- 10,000.0
1	9,020	1,000	980	20	10	0	990	990	0.90909	900.0	- 9,100.0
2	8,040	1,000	980	20	10	0	990	990	0.82645	818.2	- 8,281.8
3	7,060	1,000	980	20	10	0	990	990	0.75131	743.8	- 7,538.0
4	6,080	1,000	980	20	10	0	990	990	0.68301	676.2	- 6,861.8
5	5,100	1,000	980	20	10	0	990	990	0.62092	614.7	- 6,247.1
6	4,120	1,000	980	20	10	0	990	990	0.56447	558.8	- 5,688.3
7	3,140	1,000	980	20	10	0	990	990	0.51316	508.0	- 5,180.3
8	2,160	100	980	- 880	- 440	- 200	+ 740	740	0.46651	345.2	- 4,835.1
9	0	1,100	1,960	- 860	- 430	0	1,530	1,530	0.42410	648.9	- 4,186.2
10	0	1,100	0	1,100	550	0	550	550	0.38554	212.0	- 3,974.2
11	0	1,100	0	1,100	550	0	550	550	0.35049	192.8	- 3,781.4
12	0	1,100	0	1,100	550	0	550	550	0.31863	175.2	- 3,606.2
13	0	1,100	0	1,100	550	0	550	550	0.28966	159.3	- 3,446.9
14	0	2,000	0	2,000	1,000	0	1,000	1,000	0.26333	263.3	- 3,183.6

The annual amount of tax A_{IT} for year 8 when $A_{CI} = \$100/\text{year}$, $A_D = \$980/\text{year}$, $A_A = \$0/\text{year}$, and $t = 0.5$, is given by Equation (2.1-3) to be

$$\begin{aligned} A_{IT} &= (A_{CI} - A_D - A_A)t \\ &= [(\$100 - \$980 - \$0)/\text{year}](0.5) \\ &= -\$440/\text{year} \end{aligned}$$

The annual amount of tax A_{IT} for year 9 when $A_{CI} = \$1{,}100/\text{year}$, $A_D = \$0/\text{year}$, $A_A = \$1{,}960/\text{year}$, and $t = 0.5$, is given by Equation (2.1-3) to be

$$\begin{aligned} A_{IT} &= (A_{CI} - A_D - A_A)t \\ &= [(\$1{,}100 - \$0 - \$1{,}960)/\text{year}](0.5) \\ &= -\$430/\text{year} \end{aligned}$$

Values for subsequent years are calculated in the same way and listed in Table (3.4-2c).

The net annual cash flow A_{CF} after tax for year 8 when $A_{CI} = \$100/\text{year}$, $A_{IT} = -\$440/\text{year}$, and $A_{TC} = -\$200/\text{year}$ (the recovered scrap value of the existing machine), is given by Equation (2.1-4) to be

$$\begin{aligned} A_{CF} &= A_{NCI} - A_{TC} \\ &= \$540/\text{year} + \$200/\text{year} \\ &= \$740/\text{year} \end{aligned}$$

The net annual cash flow A_{CF} after tax for year 9 when $A_{CI} = \$1{,}100/\text{year}$, $A_{IT} = -\$430/\text{year}$, and $A_{TC} = \$0/\text{year}$, is given by Equation (2.1-4) to be

$$\begin{aligned} A_{CF} &= A_{NCI} - A_{TC} \\ &= \$1{,}530/\text{year} + \$0/\text{year} \\ &= \$1{,}530/\text{year} \end{aligned}$$

Values for subsequent years are calculated in the same way and listed in Table (3.4-2c).

The annual cash income A_{CI} before tax for year 14 is \$2,000/year, i.e. the marginal income of \$3,800/year for the new machine minus the final payment of \$1,800 on the lease.

The net annual discounted cash flow A_{DCF} for each year is calculated as in part (a) and the values are listed in Table (3.4-2c).

The net present value (NPV) for year 14 is given by Equation (3.2-2) to be

$$\begin{aligned} (\text{NPV}) &= \sum A_{DCF} \\ &= -\$3{,}183.6 \\ &\quad \text{for } i = 10 \text{ per cent} \end{aligned}$$

This value is found by summing the values of A_{DCF} in Table (3.4-2c).

Using the same iterative procedure as in part (a), the discounted cash flow rate of return (DCFRR) is found to be 3.24 per cent.

Comparison of alternatives (a), (b), and (c)

The results of the (NPV) and (DCFRR) calculations for alternatives (a), (b), and (c) are listed in Table (3.4-2d). The (NPV) calculations show that it is more profitable to lease the new machine than to keep the existing machine

TABLE (3.4-2d)

Comparison of options on basis of (NPV) and (DCFRR)

option	for termination at end of year 14		for termination at end of year 11	
	(NPV)	(DCFRR)	(NPV)	(DCFRR)
a	-$3,571.9	1.76%	-$3,671.6	1.25%
b	-$4,046.5	3.48%	-$5,460.2	-2.38%
c	-$3,183.6	3.24%	-$4,839.6	-5.70%

running. They also show that it is more profitable to retain the existing machine than to buy the new machine.

However, if it were necessary to terminate the process at the end of year 11, the (NPV) values listed in Table (3.4-2d) show that it is more profitable to retain the existing machine.

For option (a) the (NPV) for year 11 has been recalculated on the basis of the recovery of the scrap value of the existing machine, i.e. $200 in year 11 instead of year 14.

For option (b) the (NPV) for year 12 (based on termination of the process at the end of year 11) has been recalculated on the following basis:

(i) recovery of the scrap value of the new machine, i.e. $250 in year 11 instead of year 14,

(ii) a balancing allowance of $7,950 – $250 = $7,700 in year 12 which is the book value $P_{s'}$ of the new machine in year 11 minus the scrap value of the new machine.

For option (c) the (NPV) for year 11 has been recalculated on the basis of a continuing commitment to pay the lease for the new machine with no income after year 11.

Incremental comparison of alternatives (a) and (c)

The (NPV) calculations show that alternatives (a) and (c) are both significantly more attractive than alternative (b).

On the basis of (NPV), alternative (c) has a marginal advantage over alternative (a) provided the process continues to operate until the end of year 14. However, if the process were to terminate prematurely at the end of year 11, alternative (a) would have a significant advantage over alternative (c) Alternative (a), which is to retain the existing machine, involves the least amount of risk. It is hardly worth while choosing alternative (c), which is to lease the new machine. The small advantage in (NPV) is more than outweighed by the increased risk. This is illustrated by the (DCFRR) values listed in Table (3.4-2d).

However, it is possible to make alternative (c) look a far better prospect than alternative (a) by doing incremental (DCFRR) calculations, the results of which are shown in Table (3.4-2e). This is because of the very low scrap value of the existing machine and the costly overhaul which is required in year 12.

In Table (3.4-2e) the incremental net annual cash flow ΔA_{CF} for year 8, when $A_{CF} = \$740/\text{year}$ for alternative (c) and $A_{CF} = \$990/\text{year}$ for alternative (a), is

$$\begin{aligned}\Delta A_{CF} &= \$740/\text{year} - \$990/\text{year} \\ &= -\$250/\text{year}\end{aligned}$$

Values for subsequent years are calculated in the same way and listed in Table (3.4-2e).

The incremental net annual cash flow ΔA_{DCF} for each year is calculated as in part (a) and the values are listed in Table (3.4-2e). The values of ΔA_{DCF} are adjusted as already described in part (a) to avoid a negative value following the first positive value of ΔA_{DCF}.

In Table (3.4-2e) the discounting is done from year 8 and not from year 0 as in Tables (3.4-2a), (3.4-2b), and (3.4-2c). In Table (3.4-2e) trials are done for $i = 100$ per cent and $i = 95$ per cent. Since both these interest rates give negative values for the incremental (NPV) in year 14, the interest rate required to make (NPV) $= 0$ is found by extrapolation to be $i = 93.9$ per cent. This is the discounted cash flow rate of return (DCFRR) for alternative (c) over alternative (a) based on the decision year 8 using incremental net annual cash flows.

Although the (DCFRR) obtained using the incremental method emphasizes the advantage of leasing the new machine, this involves a definite commitment to pay a total of $16,200 over six years whether the new machine produces or

TABLE (3.4-2e)

Incremental cash flows for leasing the new machine over retaining the present machine

year	incremental net cash flow ΔA_{CF}	ΔA_{CF} adjusted at i=100%	discount factor at i=100% f_d	(NPV) of ΔA_{CF} at i=100% $= \Sigma A_{DCF}$	ΔA_{CF} adjusted at i = 95%	discount factor at i = 95% f_d	(NPV) of ΔA_{CF} at i =95% $= \Sigma A_{DCF}$	ΔA_{CF} adjusted at i=93.9%	discount factor at i = 93.9% f_d	(NPV) of ΔA_{CF} at i=93.9% $= \Sigma A_{DCF}$
8	- 250	- 250	1.00000	- 250.0	- 250	1.00000	- 250.0	- 250	1.00000	- 250.0
9	540	320	0.50000	- 90.0	314	0.51282	- 89.0	313	0.51573	- 88.6
10	- 440	0	0.25000	- 90.0	0	0.26298	- 89.0	0	0.26598	- 88.6
11	50	50	0.12500	- 83.8	50	0.13486	- 82.2	50	0.13717	- 81.7
12	1,050	1,050	0.06250	- 18.1	1,050	0.06916	- 9.6	1,050	0.07074	- 7.4
13	50	50	0.03125	- 16.6	50	0.03547	- 7.8	50	0.03648	- 5.6
14	300	300	0.01563	- 11.9	300	0.01819	- 2.4	300	0.01882	- 0.0

remains idle. Since leasing would only gain a few hundred dollars, most companies would choose to avoid risk by selecting alternative (a), i.e., retain the existing machine.

References for Chapter 3

1. Abrams, H. J., *The Chemical Engineer*, No. 241 (1970)
2. Allen, D. H., *Chem. Eng.*, **74**, No. 14 (1967)
3. Canada, J. R., 'Intermediate Economic Analysis for Management and Engineering', p. 135, Englewood Cliffs, N.J., Prentice–Hall, Inc., 1971
4. Kroeger, H., *Chem. Eng.*, **67**, No. 10 (1960)
5. Rockley, L. E., 'Capital Investment Decisions', p. 102, London, Business Books Ltd., 1968
6. Sinclair, C. G., *Chem. and Proc. Eng.*, **47**, 137 (1966)
7. Street, H. H., *Chem. Eng.*, **70**, No. 10 (1963)

Problems for Chapter 3

(3.2-1) The net annual cash flows after tax A_{CF} for a project are as follows:

year 0 −\$10,000
year 1 −\$10,000
year 2 −\$10,000
year 3 +\$30,000

and for each subsequent year +\$4,000.

Calculate the following parameters:

(a) the equivalent maximum investment period (EMIP)
(b) the interest recovery point (IRP)
and
(c) the discounted breakeven point (DBEP) if the cost of capital is 10 per cent.

(3.2-2) The discounted cash flow rate of return (DCFRR) has been estimated to be 15 per cent for a future project. The estimate is based on predicted net annual cash flows after tax which in turn are based on an assumed inflation rate of 6 per cent per year. What is the true (DCFRR) of the project on the basis of current costs?

(3.3-1) Recalculate the net present value (NPV) given in Table (3.3-1a) based on the following approximate discount factors f_d:

year	0	1	2	3	4	5	6	7	8	9	10
f_d	1.0,	0.9,	0.8,	0.8,	0.7,	0.6,	0.6,	0.5,	0.5,	0.4,	0.4

Estimate the percentage error in the calculated (NPV) using this approximate method.

(3.3-2) A savings policy requires annual premiums of \$1,000, \$900, \$800, \$700, \$600, and \$500 in years 0, 1, 2, 3, 4, and 5 respectively after which no further premiums are necessary. The policy matures at the end of year 10. Calculate the amount of the lump sum payable at maturity to give a discounted cash flow rate of return (DCFRR) of 5 per cent.

(3.3-3) A savings policy requires fixed annual premiums of \$100 over a twenty-year period. The policy matures at the end of year 20. Calculate the amount of the lump sum payable at maturity to give a discounted cash flow rate of return (DCFRR) of 5 per cent.

(3.3-4) In what year of operation does the discounted cash flow rate of return (DCFRR) reach 10 per cent for a project described by the following data:

(i) an annual cash income $A_{CI} = \$200{,}000/\text{year}$ in year 1 and in each subsequent year
(ii) fixed capital investment $C_{FC} = \$200{,}000$ made in year 0
(iii) zero salvage value of plant items
(iv) working capital $C_{WC} = \$30{,}000$
(v) cost of land $C_L = \$20{,}000$
(vi) no tax allowances other than depreciation, i.e. $A_A = 0$
(vii) 100 per cent depreciation allowed in year 1
(viii) fractional tax rate $t = 0.50$

(3.4-1) Projects A and B have net present values (NPV) as follows:

cost of capital $i\%$	project A	project B
4	+\$100,000	+\$62,000
8	+\$41,000	+\$28,000
12	−\$2,000	+\$10,000
16	−\$32,000	−\$4,000

Use graphical interpolation to estimate the discounted cash flow rate of return (DCFRR) for each project. Discuss which project is the most profitable.

(3.4-2) Projects A, B, and C have net annual cash flows after tax in \$ as follows:

year	project A	project B	project C
0	−5,000	−5,000	−5,000
1	+3,000	+1,000	+2,000
2	+2,000	+2,000	+2,000
3	+1,000	+3,000	+2,000

Calculate the cumulative annual cash flows $\sum A_{CF}$ and the cumulative discounted annual cash flows $\sum A_{DCF}$ for projects A, B, and C and rank in order of merit. Make approximate estimates of the discounted cash flow rate of return (DCFRR) for projects A, B, and C and rank in order of merit. Take the cost of capital as 10 per cent.

(3.4-3) A company invests \$50,000 in a manufacturing process which gives positive net annual cash flows after tax A_{CF} of \$10,000 in each subsequent year. During the third year of operation an alternative process becomes available. The new process would require an investment of \$40,000 which would give positive net annual cash flows after tax A_{CF} of \$20,000 in each subsequent year. The cost of capital is 10 per cent. It is estimated that a market will exist for the product for at least a further six years. Should the company continue with the existing process (project A) or should it scrap project A and adopt the new process (project B)?

(3.4-4) A machine in a process generates a positive net annual cash flow A_{CF} of \$1,000. Two alternatives are available: machine A costing \$2,000 requires replacement every four years and machine B costing \$3,000 requires replacement every six years. Neither machine has any scrap value. The cost of capital is 10 per cent. Which machine is the most profitable to operate?

(3.4-5) A company can invest in either projects A or B. Projects A and B involve investing \$10,000 and \$7,000 respectively to give constant positive net annual cash flows A_{CF} over ten years. The discounted cash flow rate of return (DCFRR) is 16 per cent for project A and 18 per cent for project B.

Calculate

(a) the constant positive net annual cash flow for each project
(b) the net present value (NPV) at the end of year 10 for each project at a cost of capital of 10 per cent
(c) the (DCFRR) for the difference between projects A and B

Discuss the relative merits of investing in the two projects.

Chapter 4

Uncertainties in Profitability Estimates

The accuracy of a profitability estimate is no better than the accuracy of the data on which it is based. If for example the revenue from sales turns out to be less than forecast, the project will be less profitable than expected. It is useful to determine the change in profitability produced by a given change in input data for various factors such as revenue from sales, total expenses, fixed capital investment, etc. This procedure which determines the sensitivity of the profitability to changes in each of a number of factors is known as sensitivity analysis.

An extension of sensitivity analysis is to assign probabilities to particular values of the various factors being attained. For example, there may be a 50 per cent chance of the revenue from sales reaching its predicted value, a 20 per cent chance of it being 10 per cent higher and a 30 per cent chance of it being 10 per cent lower. These probabilities can be used to calculate an expected value for the factor. Expected values can be used to construct decision trees.

4.1 The Effect of Cash Flow Variations on Cash Income

The annual cash income A_{CI} is given by Equation (2.1-1)

$$A_{CI} = A_S - A_{TE} \tag{2.1-1}$$

and is the relatively small difference between two relatively large numbers, the revenue A_S from annual sales and the total annual cost or expense A_{TE} required to produce and sell the product excluding any allowance for plant depreciation. Thus a small error in estimating A_S or A_{TE} can make a significant difference to the cash income and hence the profit.

The net annual cash income A_{NCI} is related to the annual cash income A_{CI} by Equation (2.1-2)

$$A_{NCI} = A_{CI} - A_{IT} \tag{2.1-2}$$

where A_{IT} is the annual amount of tax.

An economic study should pinpoint the areas which are most susceptible to change. It is easier to predict expenses than either sales or profits. Fairly accurate capital and processing cost estimates can be made. However, for the most part errors in these estimates have a correspondingly smaller effect than changes in sales price, sales volume, and raw materials and distribution costs.

Sales and raw materials prices may be affected by any of the following factors: discounts and allowances, availability of substitutes, contract pricing Government regulations, quality and form of the materials, competition.

Sales volume may be affected by any of the following factors: new uses for the product, new markets, advertising, quality, over-capacity, replacement by another product, competition, timing of entry into the market.

Distribution costs depend on the following factors:

(1) plant location
(2) physical state of material (whether liquid, gas, or solid)
(3) nature of material (whether corrosive, explosive, flammable, perishable, or toxic)
(4) freight rates
(5) labor costs

Distribution costs may be affected by any of the following factors: new methods of materials handling, safety regulations, productivity agreements, wage rates, transportation systems, storage systems, quality, losses, seasonal effects.

It is very worth while to make tables or plot curves which show the effect of variations in costs and prices on profitability. This procedure is called sensitivity analysis[1, 4, 5]. The purpose of sensitivity analysis is to determine which factors the profitability of a project is most sensitive to. Sensitivity analysis should always be carried out to observe the effect of departures from predicted values.

For many years, companies and countries have lived with the problem of inflation or the falling value of money. Costs and, in particular, labor costs tend to rise each year. Failure to account for this in predicting future cash flows can lead to serious errors and misleading profitability estimates.

Another important factor is the tendency of product prices to fall as the total national or international volume of production increases. Sales prices may fall by 20 per cent for a doubling in volume of production[6, 7].

It should always be remembered that no profitability estimate is better than the inherent accuracy of the data.

4.2 The Effect on Profitability of a Decrease in Revenue from Sales

The revenue A_S from annual sales is related to the annual cash income A_{CI} and the total annual cost A_{TE} by Equation (2.1-1).

$$A_{CI} = A_S - A_{TE} \tag{2.1-1}$$

If the revenue from annual sales falls below the base case value A_S by an amount ΔA_S, the annual cash income is reduced by an amount ΔA_{CI} given by the equation

$$\Delta A_{CI} = \Delta A_S \tag{4.2-1}$$

The annual amount of tax A_{IT} is given by Equation (2.1-3)

$$A_{IT} = (A_{CI} - A_D - A_A)\,t \tag{2.1-3}$$

where t is the fractional tax rate.

The effect of a reduction in A_S by an amount ΔA_S is to reduce A_{IT} by an amount ΔA_{IT} given by the equation

$$\Delta A_{IT} = \Delta A_{CI}\,t \tag{4.2-2}$$

which can also be combined with Equation (4.2-1) and written as

$$\Delta A_{IT} = \Delta A_S\,t \tag{4.2-3}$$

The net annual cash flow A_{CF} after tax is given by Equation (3.1-1)

$$A_{CF} = A_{CI} - A_{IT} - A_{TC} \tag{3.1-1}$$

where A_{TC} is the annual expenditure of capital which is not necessarily zero after the plant has been built.

The effect of a reduction in A_S by an amount ΔA_S is to reduce A_{CF} by an amount ΔA_{CF} given by the equation

$$A_{CF} - \Delta A_{CF} = (A_{CI} - \Delta A_{CI}) - (A_{IT} - \Delta A_{IT}) - A_{TC} \tag{4.2-4}$$

which can be written in terms of Equation (3.1-1) as

$$\Delta A_{CF} = \Delta A_{CI} - \Delta A_{IT} \tag{4.2-5}$$

Substitute Equations (4.2-1) and (4.2-3) into Equation (4.2-5) and write

$$\Delta A_{CF} = \Delta A_S(1 - t) \tag{4.2-6}$$

The annual discounted cash flow A_{DCF} is related to A_{CF} by Equation (3.2-1)

$$A_{DCF} = A_{CF}\,f_d \tag{3.2-1}$$

where f_d is the discount factor.

The effect of a reduction in A_S by an amount ΔA_S is to reduce A_{DCF} by an amount ΔA_{DCF} given by the equation

$$\Delta A_{DCF} = \Delta A_{CF}\,f_d \tag{4.2-7}$$

which can be written in terms of Equation (4.2-6) as

$$\Delta A_{DCF} = \Delta A_S(1-t)f_d \tag{4.2-8}$$

The sum of the annual discounted cash flows over n years $\sum A_{DCF}$ is the net present value (NPV) given by Equation (3.2-2).

$$(\text{NPV}) = \sum A_{DCF} \tag{3.2-2}$$

The effect of a reduction in A_S by an amount ΔA_S is to reduce the (NPV) by an amount Δ(NPV) given by the equation

$$\Delta(\text{NPV}) = \sum \Delta A_{DCF} \tag{4.2-9}$$

which can be written in terms of Equation (4.2-8) as

$$\Delta(\text{NPV}) = \sum \Delta A_S(1-t)f_d \tag{4.2-10}$$

4.3 The Effect on Profitability of an Increase in Total Expense

The total annual cost or expense A_{TE} is related to the annual cash income A_{CI} and the revenue A_S from annual sales by Equation (2.1-1).

$$A_{CI} = A_S - A_{TE} \tag{2.1-1}$$

If the total annual expense is increased above the base value A_{TE} by an amount ΔA_{TE}, the annual cash income is reduced by an amount ΔA_{CI} given by the equation

$$\Delta A_{CI} = \Delta A_{TE} \tag{4.3-1}$$

The effect of a reduction in A_{CI} by an amount ΔA_{CI} is to reduce the annual amount of tax A_{IT} by an amount ΔA_{IT} given by Equation (4.2-2).

$$\Delta A_{IT} = \Delta A_{CI}\, t \tag{4.2-2}$$

Equation (4.2-2) can be combined with Equation (4.3-1) and written as

$$\Delta A_{IT} = \Delta A_{TE}\, t \tag{4.3-2}$$

The net annual cash flow A_{CF} after tax is given by Equation (3.1-1)

$$A_{CF} = A_{CI} - A_{IT} - A_{TC} \tag{3.1-1}$$

The effect of an increase in A_{TE} by an amount ΔA_{TE} is to reduce A_{CF} by an amount ΔA_{CF} given by Equation (4.2-5)

$$\Delta A_{CF} = \Delta A_{CI} - \Delta A_{IT} \tag{4.2-5}$$

Substitute Equations (4.3-1) and (4.3-2) into Equation (4.2-5) and write

$$\Delta A_{\mathrm{CF}} = \Delta A_{\mathrm{TE}}(1 - t) \tag{4.3-3}$$

The effect of an increase in A_{TE} by an amount ΔA_{TE} is to reduce the annual discounted cash flow A_{DCF} by an amount ΔA_{DCF} given by Equation (4.2-7).

$$\Delta A_{\mathrm{DCF}} = \Delta A_{\mathrm{CF}} f_{\mathrm{d}} \tag{4.2-7}$$

Equation (4.2-7) can be written in terms of Equation (4.3-3) as

$$\Delta A_{\mathrm{DCF}} = \Delta A_{\mathrm{TE}}(1 - t) f_{\mathrm{d}} \tag{4.3-4}$$

The effect of an increase in A_{TE} by an amount ΔA_{TE} is to reduce the net present value (NPV) by an amount Δ(NPV) given by Equation (4.2-9)

$$\Delta(\mathrm{NPV}) = \sum \Delta A_{\mathrm{DCF}} \tag{4.2-9}$$

Equation (4.2-9) can be written in terms of Equation (4.3-4) as

$$\Delta(\mathrm{NPV}) = \sum \Delta A_{\mathrm{TE}}(1 - t) f_{\mathrm{d}} \tag{4.3-5}$$

4.4 The Effect on Profitability of an Increase in Fixed Capital Investment

An increase in fixed capital investment C_{FC} will require an increase in the annual depreciation charge A_{D} by an amount ΔA_{D}.

The annual amount of tax A_{IT} is given by Equation (2.1-3)

$$A_{\mathrm{IT}} = (A_{\mathrm{CI}} - A_{\mathrm{D}} - A_{\mathrm{A}}) t \tag{2.1-3}$$

where t is the fractional tax rate.

The effect of an increase in A_{D} by an amount ΔA_{D} is to reduce A_{IT} by an amount ΔA_{IT} given by the equation

$$\Delta A_{\mathrm{IT}} = \Delta A_{\mathrm{D}} t \tag{4.4-1}$$

The net annual cash flow A_{CF} after tax is given by Equation (3.1-1)

$$A_{\mathrm{CF}} = A_{\mathrm{CI}} - A_{\mathrm{IT}} - A_{\mathrm{TC}} \tag{3.1-1}$$

where A_{TC} is the annual expenditure of capital which is not necessarily zero after the plant has been built.

If A_{TC} is increased by an amount ΔA_{TC} as a result of an increase in C_{FC}, the effect is to reduce A_{CF} by an amount ΔA_{CF} given by the equation

$$A_{\mathrm{CF}} - \Delta A_{\mathrm{CF}} = A_{\mathrm{CI}} - (A_{\mathrm{IT}} - \Delta A_{\mathrm{IT}}) - (A_{\mathrm{TC}} + \Delta A_{\mathrm{TC}}) \tag{4.4-2}$$

which can be written in terms of Equation (4.4-1) as

$$\Delta A_{\mathrm{CF}} = \Delta A_{\mathrm{TC}} - \Delta A_{\mathrm{D}} t \tag{4.4-3}$$

The effect of a reduction in A_{CF} by ΔA_{CF} is to reduce the annual discounted cash flow A_{DCF} by an amount ΔA_{DCF} given by Equation (4.2-7)

$$\Delta A_{\mathrm{DCF}} = \Delta A_{\mathrm{CF}} f_{\mathrm{d}} \tag{4.2-7}$$

Equation (4.2-7) can be written in terms of Equation (4.4-1) as

$$\Delta A_{\mathrm{DCF}} = (\Delta A_{\mathrm{TC}} - \Delta A_{\mathrm{D}} t) f_{\mathrm{d}} \tag{4.4-4}$$

The effect of a reduction in A_{DCF} by an amount ΔA_{DCF} is to reduce the net present value (NPV) by an amount Δ(NPV) given by Equation (4.2-9)

$$\Delta(\mathrm{NPV}) = \sum \Delta A_{\mathrm{DCF}} \tag{4.2-9}$$

Equation (4.2-9) can be written in terms of Equation (4.4-4) as

$$\Delta(\mathrm{NPV}) = \sum (\Delta A_{\mathrm{TC}} - \Delta A_{\mathrm{D}} t) f_{\mathrm{d}} \tag{4.4-5}$$

After the fixed capital investment has been made, the value of ΔA_{TC} may be zero in subsequent years. However, the increase in annual depreciation charge ΔA_{D} will continue in subsequent years.

Example (4.4-1)

Calculate

(a) net present value (NPV) with straight line depreciation and 10 per cent discount factor

(b) the discounted cash flow rate of return (DCFRR) with straight line depreciation

for the project described in Example (3.3-1) with the following modifications:

(i) revenue A_{S} reduced in each year by 10 per cent
(ii) revenue A_{S} reduced in each year by 20 per cent
(iii) total expense A_{TE} increased in each year by 10 per cent
(iv) fixed capital investment C_{FC} increased by 10 per cent
(v) A_{S} reduced in each year by 10 per cent,
A_{TE} increased in each year by 10 per cent,
and C_{FC} increased by 10 per cent

(a) (i) and (ii) (NPV) *with* A_S *reduced in each year by* 10 *per cent and by* 20 *per cent*

Required equations:

$$(\text{NPV}) = \sum A_{\text{DCF}} \tag{3.2-2}$$

$$\Delta A_{\text{DCF}} = \Delta A_S(1-t)f_d \tag{4.2-8}$$

$$\Delta(\text{NPV}) = \sum \Delta A_S(1-t)f_d \tag{4.2-10}$$

In year 1, the revenue A_S = \$400,000/year; 10 per cent of this is

$$\Delta A_S = \$40{,}000/\text{year}$$

The decrease in discounted net cash flow ΔA_{DCF} for year 1 when $t = 0.5$ and $f_d = 0.909\,09$ is given by Equation (4.2-8) to be

$$\begin{aligned}\Delta A_{\text{DCF}} &= \Delta A_S(1-t)f_d \\ &= (\$40{,}000/\text{year})(0.5)(0.909\,09) \\ &= \$18{,}180/\text{year}\end{aligned}$$

Values for subsequent years are calculated in the same way and listed in Table (4.4-1).

The decrease in net present value for year 10 is given by Equation (4.2-10) to be

$$\begin{aligned}\Delta(\text{NPV}) &= \sum \Delta A_S(1-t)f_d \\ &= +\$140{,}760\end{aligned}$$

for i = 10 per cent and ΔA_S = 10 per cent of A_S

and $\Delta(\text{NPV}) = +\$281{,}540$

for i = 10 per cent and ΔA_S = 20 per cent of A_S

Δ(NPV) for ΔA_S = 10 per cent of A_S is found by summing the values of ΔA_{DCF} in Table (4.4-1). A similar procedure is used for ΔA_S = 20 per cent of A_S.

The base net present value (NPV) for year 10 is

$$(\text{NPV}) = +\$276{,}210$$

for i = 10 per cent

Therefore the reduced net present value for year 10 is

$$\begin{aligned}(\text{NPV}) &= +\$276{,}210 - \$140{,}760 \\ &= +\$135{,}450\end{aligned}$$

for i = 10 per cent and ΔA_S = 10 per cent of A_S

TABLE (4.4-1)

Annual cash flows with straight line depreciation and 10 per cent discount factor

for revenue A_S reduced by 10 per cent

year	base revenue A_S	base net present value (NPV) $= \Sigma A_{DCF}$	decrease in revenue ΔA_S	discount factor at i=10% f_d	decrease in discounted net cash flow ΔA_{DCF} for t=0.5	decrease in net present value Δ(NPV) $= \Sigma \Delta A_{DCF}$	reduced net present value (NPV) $= \Sigma A_{DCF}$
0	0	-1,100,000	0	1.0000	0	0	-1,100,000
1	400,000	- 918,180	40,000	0.90909	18,180	18,180	- 936,360
2	500,000	- 711,570	50,000	0.82645	20,660	38,840	- 750,410
3	500,000	- 527,500	50,000	0.75131	18,780	57,620	- 585,120
4	500,000	- 363,580	50,000	0.68301	17,070	74,690	- 438,270
5	520,000	- 211,460	52,000	0.62092	16,140	90,830	- 302,290
6	520,000	- 73,160	52,000	0.56447	14,680	105,510	- 178,670
7	520,000	+ 50,000	52,000	0.51316	13,340	118,850	- 68,850
8	390,000	+ 131,640	39,000	0.46651	9,100	127,950	+ 3,690
9	350,000	+ 195,250	35,000	0.42410	7,420	135,370	+ 59,880
10	280,000	+ 276,210	28,000	0.38554	5,390	140,760	+ 135,450

and

$$(\text{NPV}) = +\$276{,}210 - \$281{,}540$$

$$= -\$5{,}330$$

for $i = 10$ per cent and $\Delta A_S = 20$ per cent of A_S

(b) (i) and (ii) (DCFRR) *with* A_S *reduced in each year by* 10 *per cent and by* 20 *per cent*

Net present value is given by Equation (3.2-2)

$$(\text{NPV}) = \sum A_{\text{DCF}} \tag{3.2-2}$$

The value of the interest rate i which makes (NPV) = 0 after 10 years in this case is the discounted cash flow rate of return (DCFRR).

The base

$$(\text{DCFRR}) = 16.4 \text{ per cent}$$

$$(\text{DCFRR}) = 12.9 \text{ per cent}$$

for $\Delta A_S = 10$ per cent of A_S

and

$$(\text{DCFRR}) = 9.8 \text{ per cent}$$

for $\Delta A_S = 20$ per cent of A_S

(a) (iii) (NPV) *with* A_{TE} *increased in each year by* 10 *per cent*

Required equations:

$$(\text{NPV}) = \sum A_{\text{DCF}} \tag{3.2-2}$$

$$\Delta A_{\text{DCF}} = \Delta A_{\text{TE}}(1 - t) f_d \tag{4.3-4}$$

$$\Delta(\text{NPV}) = \sum \Delta A_{\text{TE}}(1 - t) f_d \tag{4.3-5}$$

The calculations are similar to those in parts (i) and (ii).

The decrease in net present value for year 10 is given by Equation (4.3-5) to be

$$\Delta(\text{NPV}) = \sum \Delta A_{\text{TE}}(1 - t) f_d$$

$$= +\$37{,}780$$

for $i = 10$ per cent and $\Delta A_{\text{TE}} = 10$ per cent of A_{TE}

The reduced net present value for year 10 is

$$(\text{NPV}) = +\$276{,}210 - \$37{,}780$$
$$= +\$238{,}430$$

for $i = 10$ per cent and $\Delta A_{TE} = 10$ per cent of A_{TE}

(b) (iii) (DCFRR) *with* A_{TE} *increased in each year by* 10 *per cent*

By a procedure similar to that in parts (i) and (ii) it is found that

$$(\text{DCFRR}) = 15.0 \text{ per cent}$$

for $\Delta A_{TE} = 10$ per cent of A_{TE}

(a) (iv) (NPV) *with* C_{FC} *increased by* 10 *per cent*

Required equations:

$$A_D = \frac{(C_{FC} - S)}{s} \tag{2.4-1}$$

$$(\text{NPV}) = \sum A_{DCF} \tag{3.2-2}$$

$$\Delta A_{DCF} = (\Delta A_{TC} - \Delta A_D t) f_d \tag{4.4-4}$$

$$\Delta(\text{NPV}) = \sum (\Delta A_{TC} - \Delta A_D t) f_d \tag{4.4-5}$$

For the base case, the annual rate of straight line depreciation of the fixed capital investment from \$1,000,000, at start up, to zero value at the end of ten years of productive life is given by Equation (2.4-1) to be

$$A_D = \frac{(C_{FC} - S)}{s}$$

$$= \frac{\$1{,}000{,}000 - \$0}{10 \text{ years}}$$

$$= \$100{,}000/\text{year}$$

The effect of an increase in fixed capital cost $C_{FC} = \$1{,}000{,}000$ by 10 per cent, i.e. $\Delta C_{FC} = \$100{,}000$, is an increase in A_D, by an amount $\Delta A_D = \$10{,}000$/year.

In year 0

$$\Delta A_{TC} = \Delta C_{FC} = \$100{,}000/\text{year}$$

The decrease in discounted net cash flow A_{DCF} for year 0 when $f_d = 1.0000$

is given by Equation (4.4-4) to be

$$\begin{aligned}\Delta A_{\mathrm{DCF}} &= (\Delta A_{\mathrm{TC}} - \Delta A_{\mathrm{D}}\, t) f_{\mathrm{d}} \\ &= [\$100{,}000/\text{year} - (\$10{,}000/\text{year})(0.5)](1.0000) \\ &= \$95{,}000/\text{year}\end{aligned}$$

For subsequent years $\Delta A_{\mathrm{TC}} = 0$ and $\Delta A_{\mathrm{D}} = \$10{,}000/\text{year}$.

The decrease in net present value for year 10 is given by Equation (4.4-5) to be

$$\begin{aligned}\Delta(\mathrm{NPV}) &= \sum (\Delta A_{\mathrm{TC}} - \Delta A_{\mathrm{D}}\, t) f_{\mathrm{d}} \\ &= +\$69{,}320\end{aligned}$$

The reduced net present value for year 10 is

$$\begin{aligned}(\mathrm{NPV}) &= +\$276{,}210 - \$69{,}320 \\ &= \$206{,}890\end{aligned}$$

$$\text{for } i = 10 \text{ per cent and } \Delta C_{\mathrm{FC}} = 10 \text{ per cent of } C_{\mathrm{FC}}$$

(b) (iv) (DCFRR) *with* C_{FC} *increased by* 10 *per cent*

By a procedure similar to that in parts (i) and (ii) it is found that

$$(\mathrm{DCFRR}) = 14.0 \text{ per cent}$$

$$\text{for } \Delta C_{\mathrm{FC}} = 10 \text{ per cent of } C_{\mathrm{FC}}$$

(a) and (b) (v) (NPV) *and* (DCFRR) *with* A_{S} *reduced in each year by* 10 *per cent*, A_{TE} *increased in each year by* 10 *per cent, and* C_{FC} *increased by* 10 *per cent*

The results are listed in Table (4.4-2).

TABLE (4.4-2)

(NPV) and (DCFRR) values for various circumstances

circumstance	(NPV) for i = 10%	(DCFRR)
base case	\$276,210	15.76% ≅ 16%
A_S reduced by 10%	\$135,450	12.89% ≅ 13%
A_S' reduced by 20%	\$- 5,330	9.88% ≅ 10%
A_{TE} increased by 10%	\$238,430	15.02% ≅ 15%
C_{FC} increased by 10%	\$206,890	14.01% ≅ 14%
A_S, A_{TE}, and C_{FC} all varied by 10%	\$ 28,420	10.57% ≅ 11%

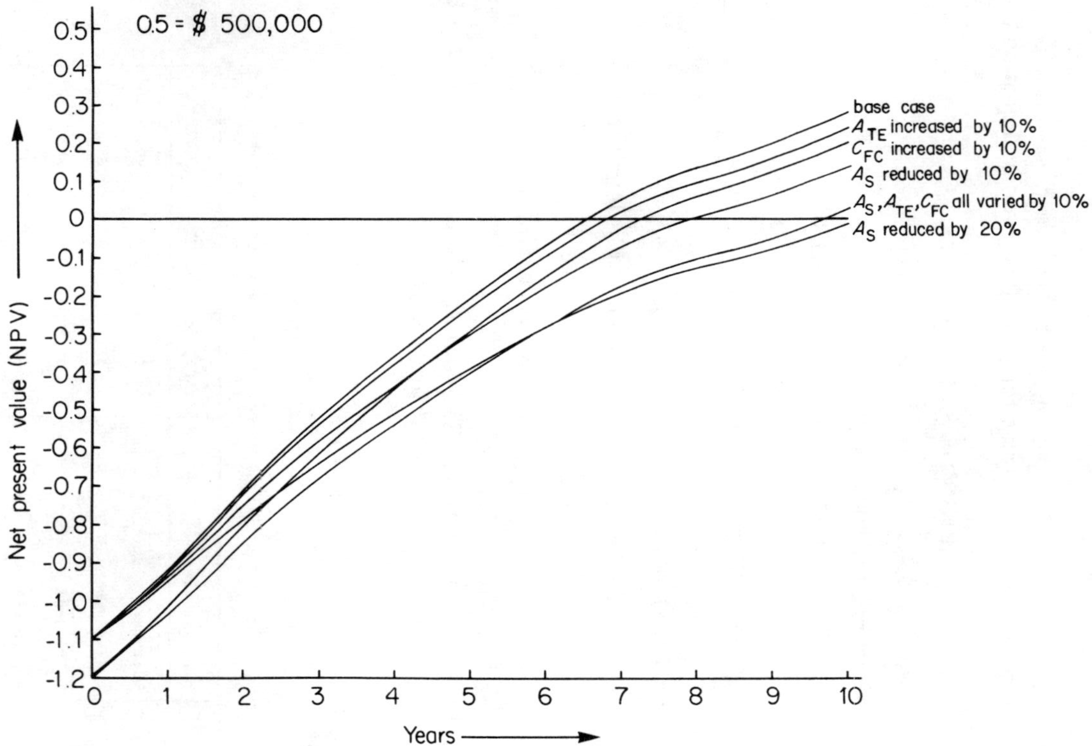

Figure (4.4-1) Variation of net present value (NPV) for Example (4.4-1)

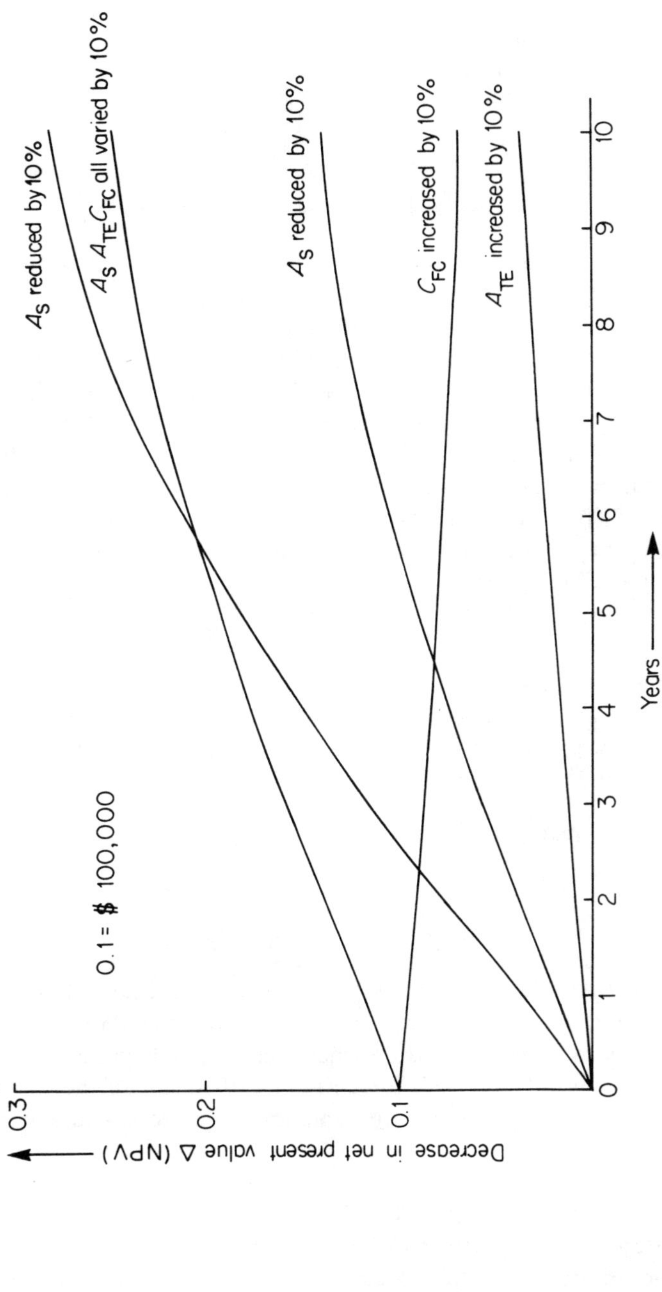

Figure (4.4-2) Decrease in net present value Δ(NPV) for Example (4.4-1)

The results of the sensitivity analysis carried out in this example are presented graphically in Figures (4.4-1) and (4.4-2). These are not the only factors that could have been used. A sensitivity analysis can be carried out on the basis of any relevant factors such as delay time in start up, change in taxation rate, etc. Factors can also be divided. For example, revenue from sales is the product of the sales volume and the selling price per unit and these can be treated as separate factors.

4.5 Comparative Profitability in the Presence of Uncertainty

Table (4.4-2) shows the effect on profitability of reduced revenues and increased costs for the project described in Example (4.4-1).

So far nothing has been said about the probability of any of these events occurring. For example, what is the probability of the revenue A_S from annual sales falling 10 per cent below the estimated value or the probability of the total annual cost A_{TE} rising 10 per cent above the estimated value?

An event or outcome which will definitely occur can be assigned a probability $p = 1$. An event or outcome which will definitely not occur can be assigned a probability $p = 0$. When a coin is tossed there is an equal chance of the outcome being a head or a tail. In this case the probability of a head is $p_1 = 0.5$ and the probability of a tail is $p_2 = 0.5$ where

$$p_1 + p_2 = 1.0 \tag{4.5-1}$$

The net present values (NPV) resulting from the various economic circumstances listed in Table (4.4-2) can each, including the base case, be assigned a probability p. A weighted average $(\text{NPV})_W$ known as the expected value can be calculated from the equation

$$(\text{NPV})_W = p_1(\text{NPV})_1 + p_2(\text{NPV})_2 + \ldots \tag{4.5-2}$$

where

$$p_1 + p_2 + \ldots = 1.0 \tag{4.5-3}$$

If the base case is certain to occur then $p_1 = 1.0$ and p_2 etc. all equal zero.

Equation (4.5-2) gives the expected net present value $(\text{NPV})_W$. Analogous equations may be written in terms of other quantities which measure profitability such as net profit. Methods for estimating the value of the probability p for the occurrence of a particular outcome are discussed in Chapter 7.

Example (4.5-1)

The project described in Example (3.3-1) is for the manufacture of a product at a maximum production rate of 5,200,000 lb/year and with a sales price of

10¢/lb. Although the process is protected by patents up to the end of year 10, it is likely that competition will enter the field in year 8 with an improved product. It is assumed that this will result in a reduction in both selling price and sales volume.

The following three courses of action are being considered in an attempt to combat competition.

(a) The base case which is to reduce the selling price in year 8 by 2¢/lb with further reductions of 1¢/lb in each subsequent year in order to maintain the revenues A_S from annual sales at the estimated values.

(b) Make the initial selling price 12¢/lb. This should reduce sales by 10 per cent in the first five years and bring in competition in year 5. Reduce the selling price by 2¢/lb in year 5 with further reductions of 1¢/lb in each subsequent year to maintain the annual sales volumes at the estimated values from year 5 onwards.

(c) Make the initial selling price 8¢/lb. This should keep competition out during the 10-year proposed life of the plant. The estimated sales volumes should not be affected up to year 7. However in subsequent years the sales volume should continue at the maximum output of 5,200,000 lb/year.

The sales data for the three options are listed in Table (4.5-1).

Determine the best pricing strategy on the basis of the following information and assumptions:

(1) The sales forecasts made by the sales division for the last ten projects were correct to ±5 per cent in seven cases, from 5 to 15 per cent high in two cases, and 20 per cent high in one case.

(2) In all cases the total annual expense A_{TE} is the same as listed in Table (3.3-1a).

(3) The following data are as in Example (3.3-1):

- (i) straight line depreciation and 10 per cent discount factor
- (ii) fixed capital investment $C_{FC} = \$1,000,000$
- (iii) zero salvage value of plant items
- (iv) working capital $C_{WC} = \$90,000$
- (v) cost of land $C_L = \$10,000$
- (vi) no tax allowances other than depreciation, i.e., $A_A = 0$
- (vii) fractional tax rate $t = 0.50$

Required equation:

$$(\text{NPV})_W = p_1(\text{NPV})_1 + p_2(\text{NPV})_2 + \dots \qquad (4.5\text{-}2)$$

(a) *Option* (a)

The net present value for the base case has already been calculated in Example (3.3-1) to be

$$(\text{NPV}) = +\$276,210$$

TABLE (4.5-1)

Sales data for options (a), (b), and (c)

year	option (a)			option (b)			option (c)		
	sales volume lb/year	sales price ¢/lb	revenue A_S $/year	sales volume lb/year	sales price ¢/lb	revenue A_S $/year	sales volume lb/year	sales price ¢/lb	revenue A_S $/year
1	4,000,000	10	400,000	3,600,000	12	432,000	4,000,000	8	320,000
2	5,000,000	10	500,000	4,500,000	12	540,000	5,000,000	8	400,000
3	5,000,000	10	500,000	4,500,000	12	540,000	5,000,000	8	400,000
4	5,000,000	10	500,000	4,500,000	12	540,000	5,000,000	8	400,000
5	5,200,000	10	520,000	4,680,000	10	468,000	5,200,000	8	416,000
6	5,200,000	10	520,000	5,200,000	9	468,000	5,200,000	8	416,000
7	5,200,000	10	520,000	5,200,000	8	416,000	5,200,000	8	416,000
8	4,875,000	8	390,000	4,875,000	7	341,250	5,200,000	8	416,000
9	5,000,000	7	350,000	5,000,000	6	300,000	5,200,000	8	416,000
10	4,667,000	6	280,000	4,667,000	5	233,330	5,200,000	8	416,000

The net present values have already been calculated in Example (4.4-1) to be

$$(\text{NPV}) = +\$135{,}450$$

for the revenue A_S reduced in each year by 10 per cent and

$$(\text{NPV}) = -\$5{,}330$$

for the revenue A_S reduced in each year by 20 per cent.

Since seven out of ten previous sales forecasts were correct to ±5 per cent the probability for the base case

$$p_1 = 0.7$$

Since two out of ten previous sales forecasts were from 5 to 15 per cent (mean 10 per cent) too high the probability of the revenue A_S being reduced in each year by 10 per cent is

$$p_2 = 0.2$$

Since only one out of ten previous sales forecasts was 20 per cent too high the probability of the revenue A_S being reduced in each year by 20 per cent is

$$p_3 = 0.1$$

The expected value of the net present value $(\text{NPV})_W$ is given by Equation (4.5-2) to be

$$\begin{aligned}(\text{NPV})_W &= p_1(\text{NPV})_1 + p_2(\text{NPV})_2 + p_3(\text{NPV})_3 \\ &= (0.7)(\$276{,}210) + (0.2)(\$135{,}450) - (0.1)(\$5{,}330) \\ &= \$219{,}900\end{aligned}$$

TABLE (4.5-2)

(NPV) values for various circumstances

revenue from sales	(NPV) in \$ for option (a)	(NPV) in \$ for option (b)	(NPV) in \$ for option (c)
as estimated	+276,210	+247,500	+ 84,760
10% down	+135,450	+109,600	- 36,870
20% down	- 5,330	- 28,310	-158,500
$(\text{NPV})_W$	+219,900	+192,340	+ 36,110

(b) and (c) *Options* (b) *and* (c)

The net present values (NPV) are calculated by the methods used in Examples (3.3-1) and (4.4-1) and the results are listed in Table (4.5-2).

The expected values $(NPV)_W$ are calculated as for option (a) and the results are listed in Table (4.5-2).

Table (4.5-2) shows that the apparently attractive option of eliminating the competition altogether is the least profitable alternative.

4.6 Decision Trees[2,3]

Consider two investment options A and B. Let option B be a safe investment which gives a base net present value $(NPV)_B$ which is independent of any competition. Let option A yield a net present value $(NPV)_{A1}$ if no competition exists and $(NPV)_{A2}$ if competition exists. Let the probabilities of no competition and competition be p_1 and $p_2 = 1 - p_1$ respectively.

The expected value of the net present value for option A can be written in terms of Equations (4.5-1) and (4.5-2) as

$$(NPV)_{WA} = p_1(NPV)_{A1} + (1 - p_1)(NPV)_{A2} \tag{4.6-1}$$

The expected value of the net present value for option B can be written in terms of Equations (4.5-1) and (4.5-2) as

$$(NPV)_{WB} = p_1(NPV)_B + (1 - p_1)(NPV)_B$$

which simplifies to

$$(NPV)_{WB} = (NPV)_B \tag{4.6-2}$$

The gain in the expected value of option A over option B is

$$\Delta(NPV)_W = (NPV)_{WA} - (NPV)_{WB} \tag{4.6-3}$$

which can be written in terms of Equations (4.6-1) and (4.6-2) as

$$\Delta(NPV)_W = [p_1(NPV)_{A1} + (1 - p_1)(NPV)_{A2}] - (NPV)_B \tag{4.6-4}$$

The options are diagrammatically represented in Figure (4.6-1) which is called a decision tree.

If $(NPV)_{A1} = 2(NPV)_B$ and $(NPV)_{A2} = 0.5(NPV)_B$ Equation (4.6-4) can be written as

$$\Delta(NPV)_W = [2p_1 + 0.5(1 - p_1) - 1](NPV)_B$$

If in this case the probability of no competition is $p_1 = 0.5$

$$\Delta(NPV)_W = +0.25(NPV)_B$$

and option A should be taken.

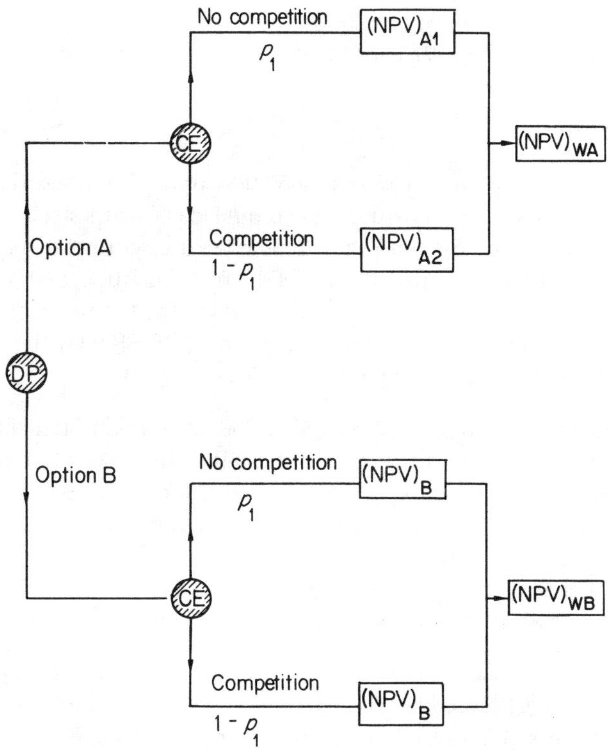

Figure (4.6-1) Decision tree for options

If the probability of no competition is $p_1 = 0.3$

$$\Delta(\mathrm{NPV})_{\mathrm{W}} = -0.05(\mathrm{NPV})_{\mathrm{B}}$$

and option B should be taken.

Options A and B are equally desirable when

$$\Delta(\mathrm{NPV})_{\mathrm{W}} = 0$$

i.e., when $p_1 = 0.33$.

References for Chapter 4

1. Foord, A., *Chem. and Proc. Eng.*, **49**, No. 2 (1968)
2. Leibson, I., and Trischman, C. A., *Chem. Eng.*, **79**, No. 2 (1972)
3. Riggs, J. L., 'Economic Decision Models for Engineers and Managers', p. 21, New York, McGraw–Hill Book Co. Inc., 1968
4. Ibid., p. 344
5. Rudd, D. F., and Watson, C. C., 'Strategy of Process Engineering', p. 334, New York, John Wiley and Sons, Inc., 1968

6. Seglin, L., *Chem. Eng.*, **70**, No. 19 (1963)
7. Stobaugh, R., *Chem. Eng.*, **72**, No. 24 (1965)

Problems for Chapter 4

(4.1-1) A company plans to invest \$450,000 in a manufacturing process which is estimated to give positive net annual cash flows after tax A_{CF} of \$100,000 in each of the next ten years. This gives a discounted cash flow rate of return (DCFRR) on the investment of 18 per cent. It is assumed that at the end of year 10, there will be no further market for the product. Calculate the required increase in A_{CF} to maintain the same (DCFRR) if the investment in the project is delayed for one year.

(4.1-2) A company plans to invest \$335,000 in a manufacturing process which is estimated to give positive net annual cash flows after tax A_{CF} of \$100,000 in each of the next five years. This gives a discounted cash flow rate of return (DCFRR) on the investment of 15 per cent. It is assumed that at the end of year 5, there will be no further market for the product. Calculate the required increase in A_{CF} to maintain the same (DCFRR) if the project is delayed for one year after the investment has been made.

(4.1-3) A company plans to invest \$500,000 in a manufacturing process for a product with an estimated market life of five years. The positive net annual cash flows after tax A_{CF} in each of the next five years have been estimated to lie in the range \$140,000 to \$160,000. Calculate the discounted cash flow rates of return (DCFRR) on the investment for the lower and upper estimates of A_{CF} respectively.

(4.2-1) Tables (3.3-1a) and (3.3-1b) give the data for the calculation of net present value (NPV) with straight line depreciation and discount factors of 10 and 20 per cent respectively for the project described in Example (3.3-1). Recalculate the (NPV)s for these tables on the basis of a reduction in revenue from annual sales of \$50,000 for each of the ten years. Also calculate the reduction in discounted cash flow rate of return (DCFRR) from the base case value of 16.4 per cent.

Chapter 5

Capital Cost

Capital cost estimation is an important part of investment appraisal. Various types of estimate can be made[5]. These range from order of magnitude estimates which can be done fairly rapidly to detailed estimates which require considerable time, effort, and data. Detailed estimates should only be done when absolutely necessary.

Of all the required costs in a profitability estimate, the capital cost can usually be obtained with the best accuracy. However, there is little point in spending more time on a capital cost estimate than is justified by the accuracy of the other factors in a profitability forecast such as manufacturing cost and revenue from annual sales. Most engineers involved in investment appraisal are not concerned with capital cost estimates better than those which can be obtained using factors.

The total capital cost C_{TC} of a project consists of the fixed capital cost C_{FC} plus the working capital cost C_{WC} plus the cost of land and other non-depreciable costs C_L.

$$C_{TC} = C_{FC} + C_{WC} + C_L \tag{2.5-1}$$

Methods for estimating the working capital cost C_{WC} are discussed in Chapter 2. This chapter is largely concerned with methods for estimating the fixed capital cost C_{FC}. The estimation of the cost of land is best done by a professional valuer.

Capital cost estimations are made for a variety of reasons. Some of these are to:

(1) enable feasibility studies to be carried out
(2) enable a manufacturing company to select from alternative investments
(3) assist in selection from alternative designs
(4) provide information for planning the appropriation of capital
(5) enable a contractor to tender for a new project

The purpose of the estimate influences the amount of time and money to be spent on it. This in turn determines the method of estimation and its probable accuracy.

Capital may be expended for a wide variety of projects which may include any of the following:

(1) purchase of land
(2) construction of a production plant on a 'green field' site
(3) construction of a production plant on a site equipped with services, drainage, etc.
(4) extensions to an existing production plant to provide additional capacity
(5) replacement or modification of part of an existing production plant to increase efficiency
(6) construction of non-productive facilities such as effluent treatment units, safety and welfare facilities, etc.

Limits known as 'battery limits' are frequently defined for a project and the cost of service pipework, etc. outside these boundary limits is not included in the estimate.

5.1 General Considerations in Fixed Capital Cost Estimation

Many capital cost estimation methods are in general use and these range from rapid order of magnitude estimates to those which require a detailed design. The American Association of Cost Engineers lists the following five categories of capital cost estimation:

(1) order of magnitude (ratio estimate);
probable accuracy ± 30 per cent
(2) study (factored estimate);
probable accuracy ± 30 per cent
(3) preliminary (budget authorization estimate);
probable accuracy ± 20 per cent
(4) definitive (project control estimate);
probable accuracy ± 10 per cent
(5) detailed (firm estimate);
probable accuracy ± 5 per cent

The capital cost and design philosophy of a plant are interrelated. The design and hence the cost of a plant is a function of the particular points of view of the design engineers engaged on the project. Many design engineers are reluctant to practise intelligent risk taking. Overdesign covers up errors of judgment. Almost any plant can be made to work if enough money is spent even though the basic design may be a rather poor one.

Factors which tend to increase the capital cost of a plant include the following:

(1) overprovision for safety

(2) overprovision of standby equipment
(3) unnecessarily robust supporting structures
(4) building enclosures
(5) inclusion of non-standard size equipment resulting from too rigid an adherence to theory
(6) expensive materials of construction

It may well be more economic to use cheaper materials of construction even though this may lead to more frequent breakdowns and higher maintenance

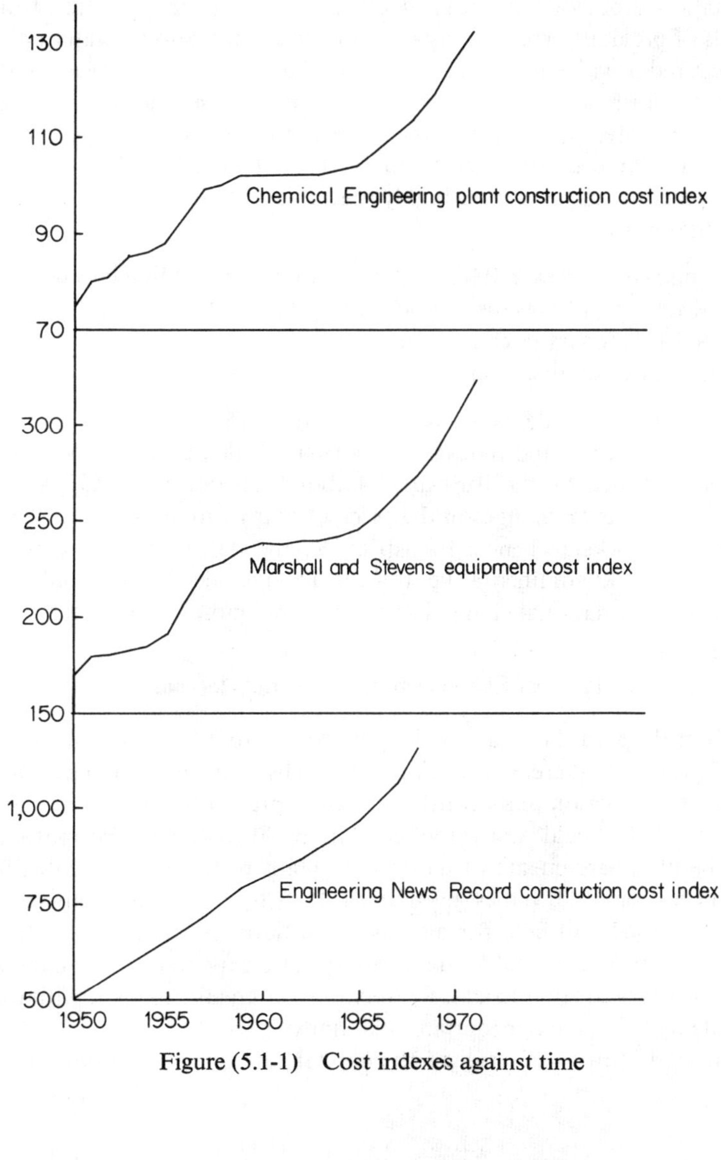

Figure (5.1-1) Cost indexes against time

costs. The design engineer may feel that management will give him more credit for lower maintenance costs than for correspondingly greater savings on capital expenditure.

Management when presented with a plant design and capital cost estimation should ask for a further design with a significantly lower capital cost. The risks involved with this second design should of course be clearly stated. It is quite wrong for design engineers to take implicit policy decisions in their plant design without making management aware of all the factors involved.

Money continuously falls in value owing to inflation. Hence all published cost data are out of date even at the time of publication. Data from cost records of previous projects may be converted to present-day values by means of a cost index which expresses the relative cost of an item in terms of the cost at a particular base time. There are many types of cost index intended to cover almost every area of interest. Some are based on national averages, others on local costs. Some are designed to cover broad areas of building, construction or equipment costs, others are highly specialized. A few of the more frequently used indexes are:

(1) Engineering News–Record construction and building indexes
(2) Marshall and Stevens installed equipment index
(3) Nelson refinery construction index
(4) Chemical Engineering plant construction index

Some of the above indexes are plotted in Figure (5.1-1).

The above compound indexes are normally calculated from various price indexes published by the Bureau of Labor Statistics of the Department of Labor, which cover changes in the price of many products and in the hourly earnings of workers in most industries. Salary trends for engineers, draftsmen, clerical and administrative staff are also included[7]. A cost index usually reflects average national changes and therefore ignores local factors.

5.2 Rapid Capital Cost Estimations using Ratio Methods

Haselbarth[12] published data giving the total capital investment per unit of annual production rate, C_{TC}/R. Table (5.2-1) lists the ratios for many processes involving production units constructed on a previously developed site. Units built on a 'green field' site would cost about 30 to 40 per cent more. On the other hand, enlargements of an existing plant would cost roughly 20 to 30 per cent less than the values given in Table (5.2-1). All costs apply to the first quarter of 1967 and hold for average conditions. For plant capacities other than those given in the table, the capacity ratio exponents listed may be used within a twofold ratio of sizes. Corrections for change of costs with time can be made by using the appropriate cost indexes.

Lynn and Howland[17] studied the capital ratios for 17 process industries.

The capital ratio (CR) for a 'green field' site process plant is defined as the ratio of the fixed capital investment C_{FC} to the annual sales revenue A_S.

$$(CR) = \frac{C_{FC}}{A_S} \tag{5.2-1}$$

TABLE (5.2-1)

1967 data for process plants[12]

product	plant capacity tons/year	total capital cost $	capital cost per annual ton $	source or method
acetaldehyde	50,000	3,500,000	70	ethylene
acetylene	75,000	9,500,000	127	natural gas
ammonia	500,000	16,000,000	32	
ammonium phosphate	250,000	2,500,000	10	
ammonium sulfate	140,000	1,200,000	9	
butadiene	100,000	50,000,000	500	butane
butadiene	200,000	70,000,000	350	butylene
cyclohexane	100,000	800,000	8	
ethyl alcohol	75,000	3,750,000	50	ethylene
ethylene	300,000	15,000,000	50	refinery gases
ethylene dichloride	25,000	3,200,000	127	
ethylene oxide	100,000	9,000,000	90	ethylene
glycerol	35,000	5,500,000	157	
hydrogen	60,000	6,500,000	108	
methanol	210,000	9,000,000	43	natural gas
methyl chloride	10,000	500,000	50	methanol
oxygen	150,000	2,250,000	15	
phosphoric acid (as P_2O_5)	100,000	2,400,000	24	
polyisoprene	30,000	5,000,000	320	
sulfuric acid	280,000	2,100,000	8	contact process

Fixed capital was taken to include money invested in land, production facilities, warehousing, etc., research and development costs, and any auxiliary facilities necessary to support the process. In any given year they considered C_{FC} in Equation (5.2-1) to represent the estimated replacement value of the depreciable facilities. Some typical values of capital ratios for the year 1958 are listed in Table (5.2-2).

Both the previous methods are very useful for rough screening. They have the advantage that they do not require design work or the establishment of heat and mass balances for the process. However, both methods must be used with common sense and discretion. They are obviously most valid where a substantial amount of up to date company data exists.

Factors which tend to make the capital ratio (CR) high are:

(1) large scale operations
(2) low sales price per unit of production
(3) technologically sophisticated operations
(4) products remote from the consumer

TABLE (5.2-2)[17]

industry	capital ratio for 1958
fibers, synthetic	3.44
petroleum	3.08
inorganics, heavy	2.24
chemicals, general	2.02
resins and plastics	1.90
glass	1.46
rubber	1.04
pharmaceuticals	0.92
soap and detergents	0.69
foodstuffs, processed	0.66

Factors which tend to make the capital ratio (CR) low are:

(1) small scale operations (even though the companies may be large)
(2) diverse product lines
(3) high sales price per unit of production
(4) fairly simple processing equipment
(5) products close to the consumer

There is a general tendency for capital ratios to increase with time because of the following factors:

(1) rising costs, particularly of labour

(2) increasing expenditure on non-productive facilities for landscaping, welfare, effluent treatment, etc.

(3) increasing technological sophistication

(4) increasing national and international competition

5.3 Rapid Capital Cost Estimations using Capacity Ratio Exponents

This method, which is based on existing cost data, also has the advantage of not requiring any design work or the establishment of heat and mass balances.

Let the cost of a piece of equipment or plant of size or capacity Q_1 be C_1. The cost C_2 of a similar piece of equipment or plant of size or capacity Q_2 can be calculated from the equation

$$C_2 = C_1\left(\frac{Q_2}{Q_1}\right)^{\psi} \qquad (2.8\text{-}1)$$

TABLE (5.3-1)[5]

equipment	ψ
compressors, reciprocating	0.7
turbo blowers	0.5
electric motors	0.8
evaporators	0.5
heat exchangers	0.65 to 0.95
instruments and controls	0.0
piping	0.7 to 0.9
pumps	0.7
tanks, rectangular	0.5
spherical	0.7
towers, constant diameter	0.7
constant height	1.0

where the value of the exponent ψ depends on the type of equipment or plant. Cost indexes should be used to bring the cost data to a common year. Some typical values of ψ for various items of equipment are given in Table (5.3-1) but it is preferable to calculate them from data in the company cost files. From Equation (2.8-1) it is possible to derive a unit cost equation for equipment

$$\frac{C_2}{Q_2} = \frac{C_1}{Q_1}\left(\frac{Q_2}{Q_1}\right)^{\psi-1} \qquad (5.3\text{-}1)$$

For complete process plants the exponent ψ is usually taken to be 0.7. However, where the capacity increase is achieved by duplicating a number of pieces of

TABLE (5.3-2)

process plant	ψ
acetylene	0.75
ammonia	0.74
ammonium nitrate	0.54
benzene	0.61
butadiene	0.59
caustic soda	0.35
chlorine	0.35
ethanol	0.60
ethylene	0.58
ethylene oxide	0.79
formaldehyde	0.55
hydrogen cyanide	0.71
isopropyl alcohol	0.60
methanol	0.83
nitric acid	0.56
oxygen	0.64
phosphoric acid	0.58
polyethylene (low pressure)	0.67
polyethylene (high pressure)	0.90
styrene	0.68
sulfuric acid (contact)	0.62
urea	0.59

equipment, the exponent will be higher and may even approach a value of 1.0. Continuous and highly instrumented processes will have a value of ψ lower than 0.7. Some typical values of ψ for various types of complete process units are given in Table (5.3-2)[8, 14]. This method is most accurate where a substantial amount of company data exists for the calculation of base factors and ψ.

5.4 Capital Cost Estimation Methods based on Design

Process designs range from preliminary designs based on approximate technical data, calculations, and cost data to final designs based on accurate technical data, calculations, and firm quotations. Final designs require a considerable technical effort and are not justified until required sales and profitability can be fairly firmly forecast. During the development of a process from the laboratory to the construction stage, the proposed plant is almost continuously being redesigned and cost estimated.

Design and economics should be interrelated and good design is not possible without corresponding cost estimates. Management should be kept supplied with this information so that they can take the necessary decisions to avoid uneconomic commitments. In this way many processes will not proceed beyond the preliminary design stage. Some projects may be taken much further than they should be if the transmission of information is inadequate.

A number of texts are available which deal with process design in considerable detail[2, 13, 19, 24]. The main steps in preparing a capital cost estimation based on design are as follows:

(1) initial idea for the process and specification of the size and type of operation

(2) collection of physical and chemical data either from the literature or from laboratory experiments

(3) preparation of a preliminary equipment flow sheet incorporating the required unit operations and showing the main items of equipment

(4) preparation of heat and mass balances

(5) specification of temperatures and pressures at various points on the equipment flow sheet

(6) design calculations to size the main items of equipment such as pumps, heat exchangers, reactors, columns, tanks, etc.

(7) preparation of a coded list of items of major process equipment such as storage tanks, reactors, columns, circulating pumps, heat exchangers, etc., together with details such as size, capacity, materials of construction, pressures, temperatures, etc.

(8) collection of cost data from the literature, company records and quotations

(9) estimation of the total delivered cost of all the items of major process equipment $\sum C_{EQ}$ such as storage tanks, reactors, columns, circulating pumps, heat exchangers, etc.

In many cases the purchased cost of equipment, free on board (FOB), is quoted by a supplier and this may be multiplied by a factor of 1.03 to give the approximate delivered cost.

The simplest method for estimating the fixed capital cost C_{FC} of a plant based on design is the Lang factor method[15, 16] given by the equation

$$C_{FC} = f_L \sum C_{EQ} \tag{5.4-1}$$

where $f_L = 3.10$ for solids processing

$f_L = 3.63$ for mixed solids–fluid processing

$f_L = 4.74$ for fluid processing

and $\sum C_{EQ}$ is the sum of the costs of the major pieces of equipment. The method is most effective in companies which use their own Lang factors based on their own company data.

A refinement of the Lang factor method used by Hand[11] is given by the equation

$$C_{FC} = \sum f_L C_{EQ} \tag{5.4-2}$$

where different Lang factors are used for different types of equipment,

e.g., $f_L = 4.0$ for pumps, pressure vessels, and fractionating columns
$f_L = 3.5$ for heat exchangers
$f_L = 2.5$ for compressors

Again Hand's modified Lang factor method is most effective when the factors are based on comprehensive company data. A comprehensive list of such factors was given by Wroth[26].

A number of attempts have been made to break the Lang factor down into a series of other factors[3,4,21] which more accurately represent the type of plant and process.

The equation

$$C_{FC} = \phi_1 \phi_2 \phi_3 \sum C_{EQ} \tag{5.4-3}$$

incorporates factors listed by Rudd and Watson[23] which are based on the work of Chilton[6].

Equations (5.4-1), (5.4-2), and (5.4-3) all relate the fixed capital cost C_{FC} of a plant to the delivered cost of all the items of major process equipment $\sum C_{EQ}$. However, Chilton[6] used installed equipment costs. A factor ϕ_1 is used in Equation (5.4-3) to convert delivered equipment costs to installed equipment costs.

In Equation (5.4-3)

$\phi_1 = 1.45$ for solids processing
$\phi_1 = 1.39$ for mixed solids–fluid processing
$\phi_1 = 1.47$ for fluid processing[23]
$\phi_2 = 1 + f_1 + f_2 + f_3 + f_4 + f_5$
$\phi_3 = 1 + f_6 + f_7 + f_8$

the process piping factor ranges are

$f_1 = 0.07$ to 0.10 for solids processing
$f_1 = 0.10$ to 0.30 for mixed solids–fluid processing
$f_1 = 0.30$ to 0.60 for fluid processing

the instrumentation factor ranges are

$f_2 = 0.02$ to 0.05 for little automatic control
$f_2 = 0.05$ to 0.10 for some automatic control
$f_2 = 0.10$ to 0.15 for complex automatic control

the buildings factor ranges are

$f_3 = 0.05$ to 0.20 for outdoor units
$f_3 = 0.20$ to 0.60 for mixed indoor and outdoor units
$f_3 = 0.60$ to 1.00 for indoor units

the facilities factor ranges are

$f_4 = 0$ to 0.05 for minor additions
$f_4 = 0.05$ to 0.25 for major additions
$f_4 = 0.25$ to 1.00 for a new site

the outside lines factor ranges are

$f_5 = 0$ to 0.05 for existing plant
$f_5 = 0.05$ to 0.15 for separated units
$f_5 = 0.15$ to 0.25 for scattered units

the engineering and construction factor ranges are

$f_6 = 0.20$ to 0.35 for straightforward plants
$f_6 = 0.35$ to 0.50 for complex plants

the size factor ranges are

$f_7 = 0$ to 0.05 for large plants
$f_7 = 0.05$ to 0.15 for small plants
$f_7 = 0.15$ to 0.35 for experimental plants

the contingency factor ranges are

$f_8 = 0.10$ to 0.20 for a firm process
$f_8 = 0.20$ to 0.30 for a process subject to change
$f_8 = 0.30$ to 0.50 for a tentative process

These factor ranges are only approximate and are no substitute for comprehensive company data.

The capital cost estimation methods so far considered are all preliminary methods which can be done in a few days or at most in a week or so.

The capital cost estimation of a plant based on detailed design may take up to several months to complete. In addition to equipment flow sheets, piping and instrument diagrams, design specifications, equipment drawings, electrical diagrams, etc., are also required. All material is priced in detail. Labor is priced on the basis of unit cost records. This method has been described in detail by a number of authors[1, 3, 4, 9, 10, 20, 22, 25].

Sometimes the capital cost of only part of a plant is estimated in detail. The rest of the plant is estimated on the basis of factors. It may be possible to divide the equipment flowsheet into a number of standard systems for which a great deal of cost information is available. It is then only necessary to estimate the non-standard systems in detail.

The accuracy and reliability of a capital cost estimate is a function of the following factors:

(1) the accuracy and completeness of the physical and chemical data
(2) the accuracy and completeness of the process design
(3) the particular method used for capital cost estimation
(4) the accuracy and extent of the cost data
(5) the experience and capability of the estimators

Accuracies may range from ±30 per cent for preliminary estimates based on Lang factors to ±5 per cent for detailed design estimates. Nevertheless it is possible to receive tenders from contractors based on the detailed design of a particular plant which differ from each other by a great deal more than 5 per cent. Conversely some preliminary estimates on factors may have accuracies which are a great deal better than ±30 per cent.

In many cases management will be satisfied with an estimating system of about ±15 per cent. Factor estimates are usually within this range and their other advantages are:

(1) speed in preparation
(2) low cost compared with definitive estimates
(3) when the scope is vague their accuracy may be better than a detailed estimate
(4) usually the accuracy is similar to that of a budget authorization estimate

In practice, factor estimates are often as good or better than estimates obtained by the more tedious procedures based on detailed design.

Example (5.4-1)

A company installed a process plant to produce 3,000,000 lb/year of a liquid product in 1964. Estimate the fixed capital cost of a plant to produce 6,000,000 lb/year of the same product in 1971 on the basis of the following information:

(i) the same process is used in both cases
(ii) delivered costs of major items of process equipment for the smaller plant listed in Table (5.4-1) at 1964 prices
(iii) a Marshall and Stevens equipment cost index of 242 in 1964 and 321 in 1971 based on an index of 100 in 1926
(iv) $\psi = 0.7$ in Equation (2.6-1) for the scale up of the fixed capital cost of the complete plant
(v) the fixed capital cost of the plant is related to the cost of the major items of process equipment by Equation (5.4-3)
(vi) factors for Equation (5.4-3) listed in Table (5.4-2)

TABLE (5.4-1)

Cost of major items of equipment for smaller plant at 1964 prices

equipment item	quantity	delivered cost, C_{EQ} (1964$)
storage tanks	3	26,250
centrifugal pumps	4	2,500
reactor	1	6,200
reboiler	1	6,500
distillation column	1	15,000
reflux divider	1	630
condenser	1	5,320
		ΣC_{EQ} = 62,400

TABLE (5.4-2)

Cost factors for use in Equation (5.4-3)

description	approximate factor
process piping, f_1	0.50
automatic control, f_2	0.10
buildings, f_3	0.20
facilities, f_4	0.10
outside lines, f_5	0.10
	ϕ_2 = 1+ 1.00 = 2.00
engineering and construction, f_6	0.25
size factor, f_7	0.10
contingency, f_8	0.25
	ϕ_3 = 1+ 0.60 = 1.60

Required equations:

$$C_2 = C_1\left(\frac{Q_2}{Q_1}\right)^{\psi} \tag{2.8-1}$$

$$C_{FC} = \phi_1\phi_2\phi_3 \sum C_{EQ} \tag{5.4-3}$$

where $\phi_1 = 1.45$ for solids processing

$\phi_1 = 1.39$ for mixed solids–fluids processing

$\phi_1 = 1.47$ for fluid processing

$\phi_2 = 1 + f_1 + f_2 + f_3 + f_4 + f_5$

$\phi_3 = 1 + f_6 + f_7 + f_8$

$\phi_1 = 1.47$ for a fluid processing plant and values for ϕ_2 and ϕ_3 are calculated in Table (5.4-2) to be

$\phi_2 = 2.00$

$\phi_3 = 1.60$

The total delivered cost of the major items of process equipment for the smaller plant at 1964 prices is given in Table (5.4-1) as

$$\sum C_{EQ} = \$62{,}400$$

The total delivered cost of the major items of process equipment for the smaller plant at 1971 prices adjusted for the increase in the Marshall and Stevens equipment cost index is

$$\sum C_{EQ} = (\$62{,}400)\left(\frac{321}{242}\right)$$
$$= \$82{,}770$$

The total delivered cost of the major items of process equipment for the larger plant at 1971 prices is given by Equation (2.8-1) to be

$$C_2 = C_1\left(\frac{Q_2}{Q_1}\right)^{\psi}$$
$$= (\$82{,}770)\left(\frac{6{,}000{,}000 \text{ lb/year}}{3{,}000{,}000 \text{ lb/year}}\right)^{0.7}$$
$$= \$134{,}500$$

The fixed capital cost of the larger plant at 1971 prices is given by Equation (5.4-3) to be

$$C_{FC} = \phi_1 \phi_2 \phi_3 \sum C_{EQ}$$
$$= (1.47)(2.00)(1.60)(\$134{,}500)$$
$$= \$632{,}700$$

In this case the overall Lang factor

$$f_L = \phi_1 \phi_2 \phi_3$$
$$= 4.704$$

5.5 Capital Cost Estimations using Computer Methods

At the present time there is an increasing interest in the use of digital computers for cost estimations. It is necessary to feed in the following information:

(1) process design data, perhaps generated by another computer program
(2) cost data for delivered equipment
(3) cost indexes to update the cost data
(4) process design equations
(5) various factors similar to those in Equations (5.4-1), (5.4-2), and (5.4-3)

The output from the computer will be a process design and the capital cost estimate for a particular process design specification, which can be used as a basis for cost optimization by the computer or otherwise. The process specification should make use of standard sizes of equipment wherever feasible as these will be available and lower in cost than any non-standard special item.

A capital cost estimation based on detailed design of a plant may take up to several months to complete. In addition to equipment flow sheets, piping and instrument diagrams, design specifications, equipment drawings, electrical diagrams, etc., are also required. All material is priced in detail. Labor is priced on the basis of unit cost records. The method is described in detail in the literature[22].

Sometimes the capital cost of only part of a plant is estimated in detail. The remainder of the plant is estimated on the basis of factors. It is often possible to divide the equipment flowsheet into a number of standard systems for which a great deal of cost information is available. It is then only necessary to estimate non-standard systems in detail.

Miller[18] developed a method of estimation which is adaptable for computer use and usually has an accuracy of ± 15 per cent. He pointed out that in addition to the nature of the process, e.g. liquids, solids, and mixed, three other factors affect estimates. These are (i) the size of the equipment, (ii) the materials of construction, and (iii) the operating pressures. In the main, these three factors can be taken into account using the 'average unit cost' of the process equipment.

$$\text{average unit cost} = \frac{\text{total cost of main plant items}}{\text{total number of main plant items}}$$

From the actual cost records for many plants Miller examined the data and developed factors for all the components within the battery limit. A complete set of factors is given in Miller's paper for estimating the cost of battery limit plants. The method applies strictly only to battery limit plants but there are four areas involved in a plant estimate:

(1) battery limit
(2) storage and handling
(3) utilities
(4) services

The last three areas are often grouped together as auxiliaries. Their estimation has been well covered in the literature[22] and Miller also gives factors for their estimation.

The accuracy of this method depends on the accuracy of the cost data for the main plant items. If a good estimate has been made for the process equipment and the scope is fairly well defined, then the total estimate should be sufficiently accurate for the authorization of expenditure stage.

References for Chapter 5

1. Aries, R. S., and Newton, R. D., 'Chemical Engineering Cost Estimation', p. 3, New York, McGraw–Hill Book Co. Inc., 1955
2. Backhurst, J. R., and Harker, J. H., 'Process Plant Design', p. 31, London, Heinemann Educational Books Ltd., 1973
3. Bauman, H. C., 'Fundamentals of Cost Engineering in the Chemical Industry', p. 38, New York, Reinhold Publishing Corporation, 1964
4. Ibid., p. 155
5. 'Capital Cost Estimation', London, The Institution of Chemical Engineers, 1969
6. Chilton, C. H., *Chem. Eng.*, **56**, No. 6 (1949)
7. *Eng. News–Record*, **180**, 77, March 21 (1968)
8. Gallagher, J. T., *Chem. Eng.*, **74**, No. 13 (1967)
9. Hackney, J. W., *Chem. Eng.*, **67**, No. 5 (1960)
10. Hackney, J. W., *Chem. Eng.*, **67**, No. 7 (1960)
11. Hand, W. E., *Petrol. Refiner*, **37**, No. 9 (1958)
12. Haselbarth, J. E., *Chem. Eng.*, **74**, No. 25 (1967)
13. Jeffreys, G. V., 'The Manufacture of Acetic Anhydride', London, The Institution of Chemical Engineers, 1964
14. Jelen, F. C., 'Cost and Optimization Engineering', p. 312, New York, McGraw–Hill Book Co. Inc., 1970
15. Lang, H. J., *Chem. Eng.*, **54**, No. 10 (1947)

16. Lang, H. J., *Chem. Eng.*, **55**, No. 6 (1948)
17. Lynn, L., and Howland, R. F., *Chem. Eng.*, **67**, No. 3 (1960)
18. Miller, C. A., *Chem. Eng.*, **72**, No. 19 (1965)
19. Peters, M. S., and Timmerhaus, K. D., 'Plant Design and Economics for Chemical Engineers', 2nd ed., p. 57, New York, McGraw–Hill Book Co. Inc., 1968
20. Ibid., p. 116
21. Ibid., p. 117
22. Popper, H. (Ed.), 'Modern Cost Engineering Techniques', New York, McGraw–Hill Book Co. Inc., 1970
23. Rudd, D. F., and Watson, C. C., 'Strategy of Process Engineering', p. 125, New York, John Wiley and Sons, Inc., 1968
24. Vilbrandt, F. C., and Dryden, C. E., 'Chemical Engineering Plant Design', p. 40, New York, McGraw–Hill Book Co. Inc., 1959
25. White, D. A. F., *The Cost Engineer*, **508**, Sept (1965)
26. Wroth, W. F., *Chem. Eng.*, **67**, No. 21 (1960)

Problems for Chapter 5

(5.2-1) The capital ratio (CR) is given by the equation

$$(\mathrm{CR}) = \frac{C_{\mathrm{FC}}}{A_{\mathrm{S}}} \qquad (5.2\text{-}1)$$

where A_{S} is the annual sales revenue and C_{FC} is the fixed capital investment.

Estimate the expected revenue from annual sales from a fixed capital investment of $1,000,000 in a detergent plant using the data given in Table (5.2-2).

(5.3-1) In 1967 the fixed capital cost of a plant to produce $140,000 ton/year of urea was $4,300,000. Estimate the fixed capital cost of a new plant completed in 1971 to produce 200,000 ton/year of urea. Use the exponential scaling method of estimation together with the following information:

(i) the same process is used in both cases

(ii) a Marshall and Stevens equipment cost index of 263 in 1967 and 321 in 1971

(iii) exponential scaling factor for urea plants to be taken as 0.59 from Table (5.3-2)

(5.3-2) A process plant with a capacity of 30,000,000 pounds of product per year has a current fixed capital cost of $1,000,000. Estimate the fixed capital cost of a similar plant with a capacity of 60,000,000 pounds of product per year using an assumed capacity ratio scale-up exponent of 0.7. Calculate the percentage error introduced if the correct capacity ratio exponent is 0.8.

(5.3-3) In 1971 it was decided that growing demand for ethylene from refinery gases warranted expansion of an existing plant from 200,000 ton/year to 260,000 ton/year. It was suggested that if production were increased to

300,000 ton/year then the excess ethylene could be transformed into about 65,000 ton/year of ethanol. Use ratio techniques to obtain a rapid estimate of the economic feasibility of the alcohol process. In particular, obtain estimates of

(a) the cost of the ethanol plant

(b) the cost of the necessary extension to the ethylene plant

(c) the cost of the excess extension attributable to the cost of the ethanol plant

(d) the minimum price differential between ethylene and ethanol to justify more detailed consideration of the project if a 15 per cent rate of return on fixed capital investment is required

(5.5-1) A company wishes to estimate the installed cost of a distillation section. The process flowsheet indicates that the main plant items will consist of a header tank, the fractionating tower, a reboiler, condenser, reflux drum, two reflux pumps, two bottoms pumps, and a steam ejector. From the cost data and factors given below, estimate the total installed cost of the distillation section.

equipment	no. off	del. cost min/max	erection	piping	instr.	elect.	civil	str/bldg.	lagging
header tank	1	3,100 3,540	0.14	1.57	1.20	0.16	0.14	0.61	0.21
fractionating tower	1	13,900 18,800	0.30	0.89	1.30	0.08	0.08	0.39	0.10
reboiler	1	3,710 5,000	0.12	1.57	1.10	0.10	0.14	0.11	0.17
condenser	1	2,730 3,530	0.14	1.94	1.90	0.15	0.14	0.72	0.21
reflux drum	1	930 1,060	0.30	2.84	2.50	0.40	0.14	0.69	0.30
reflux pump	2	720 940	0.38	2.84	0.52	0.80	0.28	0.69	0.45
bottoms pump	2	620 830	0.38	2.84	0.52	0.80	0.28	0.69	0.45
steam ejector	1	390 460	0.38	2.84	1.10	0.40	0.68	0.59	0.45

Chapter 6
Manufacturing Cost

Manufacturing cost estimation is an integral part of the investment appraisal of manufacturing processes. Most estimates are based on an analysis of historical costs. These in turn are used as the basis for projections into the future. Obviously estimates are most valid when company data exist for the manufacture of the same or similar products. However, there are dangers in placing too much reliance on past costs. These may be the product of a deficient costing system. Moreover the costs may be for a process which has been operated very inefficiently. Models and simulation techniques are being used increasingly to forecast costs. This is particularly the case with entirely new products. However, there is a danger in this case of omitting a component cost. One should not only be aware of quantity breaks in materials prices but also of the possibility of sudden changes in prices.

A special case of investment appraisal is the make or buy decision. Even though it may be cheaper to manufacture a product, it may be more expedient to buy. Government policy may limit the degree of vertical integration. In addition a company may wish to retain its flexibility and to avoid tying up large amounts of capital in a product with an uncertain future.

Sometimes manufacturing cost estimates are made to establish a product price. For a new product the ratio of manufacturing expense to sales price c_{ME}/c_S should be compared with the ratio of total manufacturing cost or expense to sales revenue for the company as a whole. If the ratio c_{ME}/c_S is less than or equal to the ratio for the company, then the proposed sales price c_S appears to be reasonable and the product is probably commercially viable. This comparison is of course only used as an approximate guide in preliminary assessments.

The annual manufacturing cost or expense A_{ME} can be written as the sum of the direct manufacturing or prime cost A_{DME} and the indirect manufacturing or overhead cost A_{IME}.

$$A_{ME} = A_{DME} + A_{IME} \tag{2.2-1}$$

The determination of direct or prime costs is more straightforward than the determination of indirect or overhead costs. When more than one product is involved the question arises as to the correct distribution of overhead costs between the various products.

The division of costs into fixed and variable elements is popular with accountants. Variable costs vary directly with the volume of production. For a particular plant fixed costs do not vary with the volume of production. Fixed costs are also known as period costs since they are a function of time. In addition to fixed and variable costs there are mixed or semivariable costs. These have a fixed and a variable element. The variable element can vary with production linearly, stepwise, or in a curvilinear manner. However, it is a convenient simplification to divide all manufacturing costs into fixed and linearly variable costs. This is the basis of the methods considered in this chapter.

6.1 General Considerations in Estimating Manufacturing Costs

Manufacturing costs are best considered in the context of the manufacturing, trading, and profit and loss accounts. Typical examples of these are shown in Tables (6.1-1), (6.1-2), and (6.1-3) respectively. These tables are based on the conventional accountancy period of one year.

The gross annual profit A_{GP} in Table (6.1-2) is dependent on the balance sheet annual depreciation charge A_{BD} which is not necessarily the same as the depreciation allowance used for tax purposes. Since A_{BD} is arbitrarily chosen, it can be used to make the gross annual profit A_{GP} high or low according to company policy.

The gross annual profit A_{GP} is also dependent on the method of valuing the inventory. For example, raw materials may have been purchased at the beginning of the accounting year at say 9¢/lb. The purchase price may have risen to say 12¢/lb at the end of the accounting year. If valuation of the inventory is made at the higher purchase price, the production cost is lower and the gross profit higher than if the valuation is made at the lower purchase price. Although in this case the profit looks better, a higher tax is payable.

The profit is also dependent on the method of valuing the work in progress. Consider the manufacture of 100,000 lb of product with a prime or direct manufacturing cost of 10¢/lb and an additional indirect manufacturing expense of 5¢/lb. Assume that 90,000 lb of the product are sold and 10,000 lb are stored in inventory. The value of the inventory is $1,000 on the basis of prime or direct cost and $1,500 when the indirect manufacturing expense is included. It is still a controversial question as to whether inventory should be valued at direct cost or whether manufacturing overheads should be absorbed in the cost. The latter is known as absorption costing and is the traditional accounting method. Direct costing is being increasingly used and is particularly favoured by engineers.

Equation (2.3-1) gives the annual cash income A_{CI} before tax in terms of

TABLE (6.1-1)

Manufacturing account for the year ended 31 December 1973

	$			$
inventory of raw materials 1 Jan 1973	70,000		production cost of products	2,644,000
add purchases	1,740,000			
add carriage inwards	50,000			
	1,860,000			
less inventory of raw materials 31 Dec 1973	102,000			
cost of raw materials consumed	1,758,000			
direct wages	244,000			
direct utilities	44,000			
other direct expenses	208,000			
prime cost or direct manufacturing expense A_{DME}	2,254,000	2,254,000		
payroll overhead	56,000			
general plant overhead	104,000			
other indirect expenses	104,000			
indirect manufacturing expense A_{IME}	264,000			
depreciation A_{BD}	136,000			
	400,000	400,000		
		2,654,000		
add work in progress 1 Jan 1973		60,000		
		2,714,000		
less work in progress 31 Dec 1973		70,000		
production cost of products		2,644,000		2,644,000

TABLE (6.1-2)

Trading account for the year ended 31 December 1973

	$		$
inventory of finished products 1 Jan 1973	400,000	sales	4,000,000
add production cost of products	2,644,000		
	3,044,000		
less inventory of finished products 31 Dec 1973	380,000		
	2,664,000		
gross profit	1,336,000		
	4,000,000		4,000,000

TABLE (6.1-3)

Profit and loss account for the year ended 31 December 1973

		$		$
administration	148,000		gross profit	1,336,000
sales and shipping	248,000			
advertising and marketing	80,000			
technical service	20,000			
research and development	120,000			
	616,000	616,000		
net profit before taxes		720,000		
		1,336,000		1,336,000

the revenue A_S from the annual sales of a product and the components of the total annual cost or expense required to produce and sell the product excluding any allowance for plant depreciation.

$$A_{CI} = [A_S - (A_{VGE} + A_{VME})] - (A_{FGE} + A_{FME}) \qquad (2.3\text{-}1)$$

In Equation (2.3-1) A_{VGE} and A_{VME} are the annual variable general and variable manufacturing expenses respectively; A_{FGE} and A_{FME} are the annual fixed general and fixed manufacturing expenses respectively.

The revenue A_S from annual sales is the product of the annual production rate R and the sales price c_S per unit of production for a constant inventory level.

$$A_S = Rc_S \qquad (2.3\text{-}3)$$

Similarly the annual variable general expense A_{VGE} and the annual variable manufacturing expense A_{VME} can be taken as proportional to the annual production rate R and the variable general expense c_{VGE} and the variable manufacturing expense c_{VME} per unit of production respectively.

$$A_{VGE} = Rc_{VGE} \tag{6.1-1}$$

$$A_{VME} = Rc_{VME} \tag{6.1-2}$$

In practice annual direct variable costs such as raw materials, utilities, etc., are not necessarily always directly proportional to the production rate[10].

Substitute Equations (6.1-1) and (6.1-2) into the first term on the right of Equation (2.1-9) to give

$$A_S - (A_{VGE} + A_{VME}) = R[c_S - (c_{VGE} + c_{VME})] \tag{6.1-3}$$

In Equation (6.1-3) the term $[c_S - (c_{VGE} + c_{VME})]$ is called the contribution to cash income.

In the case of the simultaneous production of more than one product, Equation (6.1-3) can be written in the form

$$\begin{aligned} A_S - (A_{VGE} + A_{VME}) = {} & R_1\{(c_S)_1 - [(c_{VGE})_1 + (c_{VME})_1]\} \\ & + R_2\{(c_S)_2 - [(c_{VGE})_2 + (c_{VME})_2]\} + \dots \end{aligned} \tag{6.1-4}$$

where 1, 2, etc., refer to the various coproducts.

The contribution to cash income made by a particular product depends on the method of accounting. Widely different values for the contribution can be calculated using different methods of assigning manufacturing expenses[9].

The cost of each item in a cost estimate should be presented in such a way that the estimate can be modified and updated at any time in the future when revised data become available.

Published data and short cut estimating methods can be used to calculate the approximate manufacturing costs of a new product. However, most companies have extensive data on various items of cost such as overheads, property taxes, etc. These data should be used wherever possible to give the estimate which is most valid for a particular company.

The cost of additional production can be estimated on the basis either of allocated or incremental costs. The incremental or marginal cost is defined as the cost of making one additional unit of product without an additional investment in facilities[6]. The alternative is for the additional unit of product to be allocated a proportional share of the general expense together with a proportional share of the direct, indirect, and fixed manufacturing expenses.

Consider a raw material which is already purchased by a company. An additional amount of material is purchased for use in a new facility. Assume that the larger volume permits a reduction in the purchase price per unit of material. On an allocated cost basis, the raw material for the new facility would be charged at the new average cost. On an incremental cost basis the raw material would be charged at the lower purchase price for the additional material[13, 15].

6.2 One Main Product plus Byproducts

Let one unit of raw material yield x_1, x_2, etc., weights of products 1, 2, etc., respectively. Let the variable general expense per unit of raw material be c_{VGE} and the variable manufacturing expense per unit of raw material be c_{VME}. It should be noted that the unit of raw material may either be a single material or a mixture of several components. Leibson and Trischman[11] showed the effects on manufacturing expenses of alternate feedstocks with different compositions and costs for producing the same products.

If product 1 is the main product then this carries all the variable expenses so that

$$(c_{VGE})_1 = \frac{c_{VGE}}{x_1} \tag{6.2-1}$$

and

$$(c_{VME})_1 = \frac{c_{VME}}{x_1} \tag{6.2-2}$$

where $(c_{VGE})_1$ and $(c_{VME})_1$ are the variable general and variable manufacturing expenses per unit of product 1 respectively.

For the byproduct 2, etc., $(c_{VGE})_2 = 0$ and $(c_{VME})_2 = 0$, etc., so that for this case Equation (6.1-4) becomes

$$A_S - (A_{VGE} + A_{VME}) = R_1\left[(c_S)_1 - \frac{(c_{VGE} + c_{VME})}{x_1}\right] + R_2(c_S)_2 + \ldots \tag{6.2-3}$$

If R is the annual rate at which the raw material is consumed, then

$$R_1 = x_1 R \tag{6.2-4}$$

and

$$R_2 = x_2 R \tag{6.2-5}$$

In terms of one unit of raw material Equation (6.2-3) can be combined with Equations (6.2-4) and (6.2-5) and written as

$$\frac{A_S - (A_{VGE} + A_{VME})}{R} = x_1(c_S)_1 - (c_{VGE} + c_{VME}) + x_2(c_S)_2 + \ldots \tag{6.2-6}$$

Equation (6.2-6) gives the contribution of products 1, 2, etc., per unit of raw material.

In this particular case the contribution of the main product is

$$x_1(c_S)_1 - (c_{VGE} + c_{VME})$$

per unit weight of raw material.

The contribution of product 2 is $x_2(c_S)_2$, i.e., its selling price per unit weight of raw material.

6.3 Two Main Products Accounted for by Weight

Let one unit of raw material yield x_1 and x_2 weights of products 1 and 2 respectively. Let the variable general expense per unit of raw material be c_{VGE} and the variable manufacturing expense per unit of raw material be c_{VME}.

If the variable expenses are shared by weight then

$$(c_{VGE})_1 = \frac{x_1 \, c_{VGE}}{(x_1 + x_2)\, x_1} \tag{6.3-1}$$

and

$$(c_{VME})_1 = \frac{x_1 \, c_{VME}}{(x_1 + x_2)\, x_1} \tag{6.3-2}$$

where $(c_{VGE})_1$ and $(c_{VME})_1$ are the variable general and variable manufacturing expenses per unit of product 1 respectively.

$$(c_{VGE})_2 = \frac{x_2 \, c_{VGE}}{(x_1 + x_2)\, x_2} \tag{6.3-3}$$

and

$$(c_{VME})_2 = \frac{x_2 \, c_{VME}}{(x_1 + x_2)\, x_2} \tag{6.3-4}$$

where $(c_{VGE})_2$ and $(c_{VME})_2$ are the variable general and variable manufacturing expenses per unit of product 2 respectively.

For this case Equation (6.1-4) becomes

$$A_S - (A_{VGE} + A_{VME}) = R_1\left[(c_S)_1 - \frac{(c_{VGE} + c_{VME})}{(x_1 + x_2)}\right] + R_2\left[(c_S)_2 - \frac{(c_{VGE} + c_{VME})}{(x_1 + x_2)}\right] \tag{6.3-5}$$

In Equations (6.3-1) to (6.3-5) the sum $(x_1 + x_2)$ may be equal to or less than 1. The above analysis can be extended for any number of coproducts.

In terms of one unit of raw material, Equation (6.3-5) can be combined with Equations (6.2-4) and (6.2-5) and written as

$$\frac{A_S - (A_{VGE} + A_{VME})}{R} = x_1\left[(c_S)_1 - \frac{(c_{VGE} + c_{VME})}{(x_1 + x_2)}\right] + x_2\left[(c_S)_2 - \frac{(c_{VGE} + c_{VME})}{(x_1 + x_2)}\right] \tag{6.3-6}$$

Equation (6.3-6) gives the contribution of products 1 and 2 per unit weight of raw material.

6.4 Two Main Products Accounted for by Value

Let one unit of raw material yield x_1 and x_2 weights of products 1 and 2 respectively with values of $x_1(c_S)_1$ and $x_2(c_S)_2$ respectively; $(c_S)_1$ and $(c_S)_2$ are the sales prices of products 1 and 2 per unit of production respectively.

Let the variable general expense per unit of raw material be c_{VGE} and the variable manufacturing expense per unit of raw material be c_{VME}.

If the variable expenses are shared by value then

$$(c_{VGE})_1 = \frac{x_1(c_S)_1\, c_{VGE}}{[x_1(c_S)_1 + x_2(c_S)_2]\, x_1} \tag{6.4-1}$$

and

$$(c_{VME})_1 = \frac{x_1(c_S)_1\, c_{VME}}{[x_1(c_S)_1 + x_2(c_S)_2]\, x_1} \tag{6.4-2}$$

where $(c_{VGE})_1$ and $(c_{VME})_1$ are the variable general and variable manufacturing expenses per unit of product 1 respectively.

$$(c_{VGE})_2 = \frac{x_2(c_S)_2\, c_{VGE}}{[x_1(c_S)_1 + x_2(c_S)_2]\, x_2} \tag{6.4-3}$$

and

$$(c_{VME})_2 = \frac{x_2(c_S)_2\, c_{VME}}{[x_1(c_S)_1 + x_2(c_S)_2]\, x_2} \tag{6.4-4}$$

where $(c_{VGE})_2$ and $(c_{VME})_2$ are the variable general and variable manufacturing expenses of product 2 respectively.

For this case Equation (6.1-4) becomes

$$A_S - (A_{VGE} + A_{VME}) = R_1\left\{(c_S)_1 - \frac{(c_S)_1(c_{VGE} + c_{VME})}{[x_1(c_S)_1 + x_2(c_S)_2]}\right\}$$

$$+ R_2\left\{(c_S)_2 - \frac{(c_S)_2(c_{VGE} + c_{VME})}{[x_1(c_S)_1 + x_2(c_S)_2]}\right\} \qquad (6.4\text{-}5)$$

The above analysis can be extended for any number of coproducts.

In terms of one unit of raw material Equation (6.4-5) can be combined with Equations (6.2-4) and (6.2-5) and written as

$$\frac{A_S - (A_{VGE} + A_{VME})}{R} = x_1\left\{(c_S)_1 - \frac{(c_S)_1(c_{VGE} + c_{VME})}{[x_1(c_S)_1 + x_2(c_S)_2]}\right\}$$

$$+ x_2\left\{(c_S)_2 - \frac{(c_S)_2(c_{VGE} + c_{VME})}{[x_1(c_S)_1 + x_2(c_S)_2]}\right\} \qquad (6.4\text{-}6)$$

Equation (6.4-6) gives the contribution of products 1 and 2 per unit weight of raw material.

Example (6.4-1)

1 lb of raw material is used to manufacture 0.32 lb of product 1 and 0.64 lb of product 2. The balance of the raw material goes to waste. Product 1 sells at 20¢/lb and product 2 sells at 6¢/lb. The variable general and variable manufacturing expenses including raw materials total 5¢/lb of raw material.

Calculate:

(a) the total contribution to cash income per pound of raw material
(b) the indidual contributions of each product to cash income per pound of raw material

for the following cases:

(i) product 1 as the main product charged for all the variable expenses
(ii) product 2 as the main product charged for all the variable expenses
(iii) products 1 and 2 sharing the variable expenses on the basis of weight
(iv) products 1 and 2 sharing the variable expenses on the basis of value

(i) *Product* 1 *as the main product charged for all the variable expenses*

Required equation:

$$\frac{A_S - (A_{VGE} + A_{VME})}{R} = x_1(c_S)_1 - (c_{VGE} + c_{VME}) + x_2(c_S)_2 \qquad (6.2\text{-}6)$$

TABLE (6.4-1)

Contribution to cash income using different methods of assigning manufacturing expenses

	$A_S - (A_{VGE} + A_{VME})$	$\dfrac{A_S - (A_{VGE} + A_{VME})}{R}$
one main product plus byproducts	$R_1\left[(c_S)_1 - \dfrac{(c_{VGE}+c_{VME})}{x_1}\right] + R_2(c_S)_2 + \ldots.$	$x_1(c_S)_1 - (c_{VGE}+c_{VME}) + x_2(c_S)_2 + \ldots.$
two main products accounted for by weight	$R_1\left[(c_S)_1 - \dfrac{(c_{VGE}+c_{VME})}{(x_1+x_2)}\right] + R_2\left[(c_S)_2 - \dfrac{(c_{VGE}+c_{VME})}{(x_1+x_2)}\right]$	$x_1\left[(c_S)_1 - \dfrac{(c_{VGE}+c_{VME})}{(x_1+x_2)}\right] + x_2\left[(c_S)_2 - \dfrac{(c_{VGE}+c_{VME})}{(x_1+x_2)}\right]$ $= x_1(c_S)_1 - (c_{VGE}+c_{VME}) + x_2(c_S)_2$
two main products accounted for by value	$R_1\left\{(c_S)_1 - \dfrac{(c_S)_1(c_{VGE}+c_{VME})}{\left[x_1(c_S)_1+x_2(c_S)_2\right]}\right\} + R_2\left\{(c_S)_2 - \dfrac{(e_S)_2(c_{VGE}+c_{VME})}{\left[x_1(c_S)_1+x_2(c_S)_2\right]}\right\}$	$x_1\left\{(c_S)_1 - \dfrac{(c_S)_1(c_{VGE}+c_{VME})}{\left[x_1(c_S)_1+x_2(c_S)_2\right]}\right\} + x_2\left\{(c_S)_2 - \dfrac{(c_S)_2(c_{VGE}+c_{VME})}{\left[x_1(c_S)_1+x_2(c_S)_2\right]}\right\}$ $= x_1(c_S)_1 - (c_{VGE}+c_{VME}) + x_2(c_S)_2$

In the present case

$$\begin{aligned} c_{\text{VGE}} + c_{\text{VME}} &= 5¢/\text{lb} \\ (c_{\text{S}})_1 &= 20¢/\text{lb} \\ (c_{\text{S}})_2 &= 6¢/\text{lb} \\ x_1 &= 0.32 \text{ lb} \\ x_2 &= 0.64 \text{ lb} \end{aligned}$$

(i) (a) From Equation (6.2-6) the total contribution per pound of raw material

$$\begin{aligned} &= x_1(c_{\text{S}})_1 + x_2(c_{\text{S}})_2 - (c_{\text{VGE}} + c_{\text{VME}}) \\ &= (0.32)(20¢/\text{lb}) + (0.64)(6¢/\text{lb}) - 5¢/\text{lb} \\ &= 6.4¢/\text{lb} + 3.84¢/\text{lb} - 5¢/\text{lb} \\ &= 5.24¢/\text{lb} \end{aligned}$$

(i) (b) The individual contribution of product 1 as the main product

$$\begin{aligned} &= 6.4¢/\text{lb} - 5¢/\text{lb} \\ &= 1.4¢/\text{lb of raw material} \end{aligned}$$

The individual contribution of product 2 as the byproduct

$$= 3.84¢/\text{lb of raw material}$$

(ii) *Product 2 as the main product charged for all the variable expenses*

Required equation:

as in part (i)

(ii) (a) From Equation (6.2-6) the total contribution per pound of raw material

$$\begin{aligned} &= x_1(c_{\text{S}})_1 + x_2(c_{\text{S}})_2 - (c_{\text{VGE}} + c_{\text{VME}}) \\ &= 6.4¢/\text{lb} + 3.84¢/\text{lb} - 5¢/\text{lb} \\ &= 5.24¢/\text{lb} \end{aligned}$$

(ii) (b) The individual contribution of product 2 as the main product

$$\begin{aligned} &= 3.84¢/\text{lb} - 5¢/\text{lb} \\ &= -1.16¢/\text{lb of raw material} \end{aligned}$$

The individual contribution of product 1 as the byproduct

$$= 6.4¢/\text{lb of raw material}$$

(iii) *Products* 1 *and* 2 *sharing the variable expenses on the basis of weight*

Required equation:

$$\frac{A_S - (A_{VGE} + A_{VME})}{R} = x_1\left[(c_S)_1 - \frac{(c_{VGE} + c_{VME})}{(x_1 + x_2)}\right] + x_2\left[(c_S)_2 - \frac{(c_{VGE} + c_{VME})}{(x_1 + x_2)}\right] \tag{6.3-6}$$

(iii) (a) From Equation (6.3-6) the total contribution per pound of raw material

$$= x_1(c_S)_1 + x_2(c_S)_2 - \frac{x_1(c_{VGE} + c_{VME})}{(x_1 + x_2)} - \frac{x_2(c_{VGE} + c_{VME})}{(x_1 + x_2)}$$

This is equal to the term $x_1(c_S)_1 + x_2(c_S)_2 - (c_{VGE} + c_{VME})$ in Equation (6.2-6)

$$x_1(c_S)_1 = 6.4¢/\text{lb}$$
$$x_2(c_S)_2 = 3.84¢/\text{lb}$$
$$\frac{x_1}{(x_1 + x_2)}(c_{VGE} + c_{VME}) = \frac{(0.32)}{0.96}(5¢/\text{lb}) = 1.67¢/\text{lb}$$
$$\frac{x_2}{(x_1 + x_2)}(c_{VGE} + c_{VME}) = \frac{(0.64)}{0.96}(5¢/\text{lb}) = 3.33¢/\text{lb}$$

Total contribution

$$= 6.4¢/\text{lb} + 3.84¢/\text{lb} - 1.67¢/\text{lb} - 3.33¢/\text{lb}$$
$$= 5.24¢/\text{lb of raw material}$$

(iii) (b) The individual contribution of product 1

$$= 6.4¢/\text{lb} - 1.67¢/\text{lb}$$
$$= 4.73¢/\text{lb of raw material}$$

The individual contribution of product 2

$$= 3.84¢/\text{lb} - 3.33¢/\text{lb}$$
$$= 0.51¢/\text{lb of raw material}$$

(iv) *Products* 1 *and* 2 *sharing the variable expenses on the basis of value*

Required equation:

$$\frac{A_S - (A_{VGE} + A_{VME})}{R} = x_1\left\{(c_S)_1 - \frac{(c_S)_1(c_{VGE} + c_{VME})}{[x_1(c_S)_1 + x_2(c_S)_2]}\right\} + x_2\left\{(c_S)_2 - \frac{(c_S)_2(c_{VGE} + c_{VME})}{[x_1(c_S)_1 + x_2(c_S)_2]}\right\} \quad (6.4\text{-}6)$$

(iv) (a) From Equation (6.4-6) the total contribution per pound of raw material

$$= x_1(c_S)_1 + x_2(c_S)_2 - \frac{x_1(c_S)_1(c_{VGE} + c_{VME})}{x_1(c_S)_1 + x_2(c_S)_2} - \frac{x_2(c_S)_2(c_{VGE} + c_{VME})}{x_1(c_S)_1 + x_2(c_S)_2}$$

This is equal to the term $x_1(c_S)_1 + x_2(c_S)_2 - (c_{VGE} + c_{VME})$ in Equation (6.2-6)

$$\frac{x_1(c_S)_1(c_{VGE} + c_{VME})}{x_1(c_S)_1 + x_2(c_S)_2} = \frac{(6.4¢/\text{lb})(5¢/\text{lb})}{(6.4¢/\text{lb} + 3.84¢/\text{lb})} = 3.12¢/\text{lb}$$

$$\frac{x_2(c_S)_2(c_{VGE} + c_{VME})}{x_1(c_S)_1 + x_2(c_S)_2} = \frac{(3.84¢/\text{lb})(5¢/\text{lb})}{(6.4¢/\text{lb} + 3.84¢/\text{lb})} = 1.88¢/\text{lb}$$

Total contribution

$$= 6.4¢/\text{lb} + 3.84¢/\text{lb} - 3.12¢/\text{lb} - 1.88¢/\text{lb}$$
$$= 5.24¢/\text{lb}$$

(iv) (b) The individual contribution of product 1

$$= 6.4¢/\text{lb} - 3.12¢/\text{lb}$$
$$= 3.28¢/\text{lb of raw material}$$

The individual contribution of product 2

$$= 3.84¢/\text{lb} - 1.88¢/\text{lb}$$
$$= 1.96¢/\text{lb of raw material}$$

6.5 Direct Manufacturing Costs[1,12]

Raw materials: The cost of raw materials is normally the largest item of expense in the manufacturing cost of a chemical product. However, this is not always the case. For example in the case of the manufacture of liquid oxygen, the raw material cost is essentially zero. The quantities of raw materials consumed can be calculated from material balances.

Material costs are conveniently presented in tables which give the following information: name of material, form and grade, method of delivery, unit of measure, cost per unit, source of cost, annual consumption, annual cost, fractional consumption per unit of production, cost per unit of production. Net consumption of materials should be used in the case of catalysts, solvents, filter aids, etc., which may have a recovery value. Current prices of chemicals are published in various journals, such as *Chemical and Engineering News* and *European Chemical News*. However, quotations from suppliers should be used wherever possible.

It may be possible for a company to negotiate the purchase of a material at a cost per unit which is significantly lower than the current published price. This is particularly true if large quantities are involved. Thus estimates should be presented for both minimum and maximum costs. Price trends, availability, and quality are other factors which should be considered[14]. A knowledge of price trends is particularly important in the case of a product which a company may not manufacture for several years.

The yield in a chemical reaction determines the quantities of materials in the material balance. Assumed yields are used to obtain approximate exploratory estimates. In this case possible range should be given. Firmer estimates require yields based on laboratory or preferably pilot plant work.

Operating labor: The cost of operating labor is frequently the second largest item of expense in the manufacturing cost of a product. Labor requirements for a process can be estimated from an intelligent study of the equipment flow sheet paying careful attention to the various primary process steps such as fractionation, filtration, etc. The hourly wage rate c_L should be that currently paid in the company. Once N, the number of men required per shift, has been estimated for a particular production rate, the annual labor cost and the labor cost per unit of production can be estimated.

Wessel[16] made a study of the operating labor requirements in the U.S. chemical industry and presented the data as a plot of man hours per ton per processing step against plant capacity in tons per day. The processing step may be a single item of plant but is more usually a group of associated plant under the control of the same operators. Wessel's data can be represented by the following equation:

$$\log_{10} Y = -0.783 \log_{10} X + 1.252 + B \qquad (6.5\text{-}1)$$

where $Y =$ operating labor man hours/ton/processing step

$X =$ plant capacity tons/day

$B =$ a constant

$B = 0.132$ where multiple units are used to increase capacity or where the process is completely batch operation

$B = 0$ for average chemical processing plant

$B = -0.167$ for large highly automated plants or those concerned only with fluid processing

Wessel's data are for the U.S. chemical industry and refer to the short ton equal to 2,000 lb. Labor requirements are higher in countries with lower productivities.

The approximate cost of supervision for operating labor is equivalent to 10 per cent of the labor cost for simple operations and 25 per cent of the labor cost for complex operations[2].

Utilities: These include steam, cooling water, process water, electricity, fuel, compressed air, and refrigeration. The consumption of utilities can be estimated from the material and energy balances for the process together with the equipment flow sheet. Consider a cooler in the equipment flow sheet. The required rate of heat removal is known from the balances. The rate of cooling water can be readily calculated once the inlet and outlet temperatures of the water have been specified. The calculation of the consumption of the other utilities is also straightforward. Allowances should be made for wastage.

The current cost per unit for each utility is usually well known in a company. Thus the annual utilities cost and the utilities cost per unit of production can be estimated. The latter is normally much smaller than the raw materials and labor costs. However a great deal more work is involved in calculating the utilities cost than for any other item in the manufacturing cost.

Unfortunately there are no satisfactory short cut methods for estimating the utilities cost item in the manufacturing cost. However, where this item is relatively small, it may be possible to make an intelligent guess on the basis of known costs for similar processes in the company. Alternatively published data for the consumption of utilities per unit of production for various processes may be used[3].

Miscellaneous direct costs: Estimates for the cost of maintenance and repairs, operating supplies, royalties, and patents are best based on company records for similar processes. A rough average figure for the annual cost of maintenance is 6 per cent of the capital cost of the plant C_{FC}. However this percentage can vary from 2 to 10 depending on the severity of plant operation. Approximately half the maintenance costs are for materials and half for labor.

Royalty and patents costs are of the order of 1 to 5 per cent of the sales price of the product[3].

6.6 Indirect Manufacturing Costs

Estimates for the cost of payroll overhead, control laboratory, general plant overhead, packaging, and storage facilities are best based on company records for similar processes.

Payroll overhead includes the cost of pensions, holidays, sick pay, etc. It is normally equivalent to between 15 and 20 per cent of the operating labor cost[4].

Laboratory work is required for product quality control. The cost is approximately equivalent to 10 to 20 per cent of the operating labor cost[5].

Plant overhead includes the cost of medical, safety, recreational, effluent disposal, and warehousing facilities, etc. In general the larger the plant the lower the overhead per unit of production. The plant overhead cost can vary between the equivalent of 50 and 150 per cent of the operating labor cost.

Packaging costs depend on the physical and chemical nature of the product as well as its use and value. The cost of packaging is as high as one-third the selling price for soaps and pharmaceuticals.

Fixed manufacturing costs are a function of the fixed capital investment and are independent of the production rate of the plant.

Property taxes or rates depend on location. They may be taken as 2 per cent of the fixed capital cost of the plant C_{FC} in the absence of specific data.

The cost of insurance depends on both location and the hazardous nature of the materials handled. This cost is normally of the order of 1 per cent of the fixed capital cost of the plant C_{FC}.

6.7 Rapid Manufacturing Cost Estimations

The manufacturing cost of a product is the sum of the processing or conversion cost and the cost of the raw materials[7,8]. The processing cost can be roughly broken down into the following three parts: investment related costs, labor related costs, and utility costs.

Companies usually include in the charge for overheads the following items: operating supplies, supervision, indirect payroll expenses, plant protection, plant office, general plant overhead and control laboratory[7]. This charge is frequently taken as an equivalent percentage of the direct labor cost. The percentage is best obtained from company records. Although it can vary over a wide range, 125 per cent is a reasonable value. In this case the labor related costs would be 2.25 times the direct labor cost. For a 6,000 hour year and N men per shift earning c_L per hour, the annual labor related costs would be $13{,}500 c_L N$.

Consider a plant of fixed capital cost C_{FC}. If the annual property rates or taxes are taken as $0.02C_{FC}$, the insurance as $0.01C_{FC}$ and the maintenance as $0.06C_{FC}$, the annual investment related costs would be $0.09C_{FC}$ excluding depreciation. The annual utilities cost is A_U.

The annual processing cost A_P can be represented by an equation of the form

$$A_P = \eta_1 C_{FC} + \eta_2 c_L N + A_U \tag{6.7-1}$$

where the factors η_1 and η_2 can be obtained from the data available in a particular company. Substitute the information given above into Equation (6.7-1) to obtain

$$A_P = 0.09C_{FC} + 13{,}500 c_L N + A_U \tag{6.7-2}$$

Equation (6.7-2) represented very closely the processing costs of a particular company excluding depreciation and is typical of the coefficients to be expected.

The total annual expense A_{TE} required to produce and sell a product can be written as the sum of the annual general expense A_{GE} and the annual manufacturing cost or expense A_{ME}.

$$A_{TE} = A_{GE} + A_{ME} \tag{2.1-5}$$

The annual manufacturing cost can be written as

$$A_{ME} = A_P + Rc_{RM} \tag{6.7-3}$$

where c_{RM} is the cost of raw materials per unit of production.

Substitute Equation (6.8-1) into Equation (2.1-5) to give the annual total expense in terms of the annual production rate R.

$$A_{TE} = A_{GE} + A_P + Rc_{RM} \tag{6.7-4}$$

6.8 Approximate Scale Up of Processing Costs

For a plant with a fixed capital cost C_{FC1}, an annual production rate R_1 and an annual processing cost A_{P1}, Equation (6.7-1) can be written as

$$A_{P1} = \eta_1 C_{FC1} + \eta_2 c_L N_1 + A_{U1} \tag{6.8-1}$$

Equations (2.8-1) and (6.8-1) can be combined to give the annual processing cost A_{P2} for a plant with an annual production rate R_2 as follows

$$A_{P2} = \eta_1 C_{FC1}\left(\frac{R_2}{R_1}\right)^{0.7} + \eta_2 c_L N_1\left(\frac{R_2}{R_1}\right)^{0.25} + A_{U1}\left(\frac{R_2}{R_1}\right) \tag{6.8-2}$$

The processing cost per unit of production for a plant with an annual production rate R_2 is given by the equation

$$\frac{A_{P2}}{R_2} = \frac{100}{R_2}\left[\eta_1 C_{FC}\left(\frac{R_2}{R_1}\right)^{0.7} + \eta_2 c_L N_1\left(\frac{R_2}{R_1}\right)^{0.5} + A_{U1}\left(\frac{R_2}{R_1}\right)\right] \tag{6.8-3}$$

where A_{P2}/R_2 is in ¢/lb.

Equation (6.8-3) has been used to compute the data for Figure (6.8-1) which shows the decrease in processing cost per unit of production A_{P2}/R_2 with increasing size of plant.

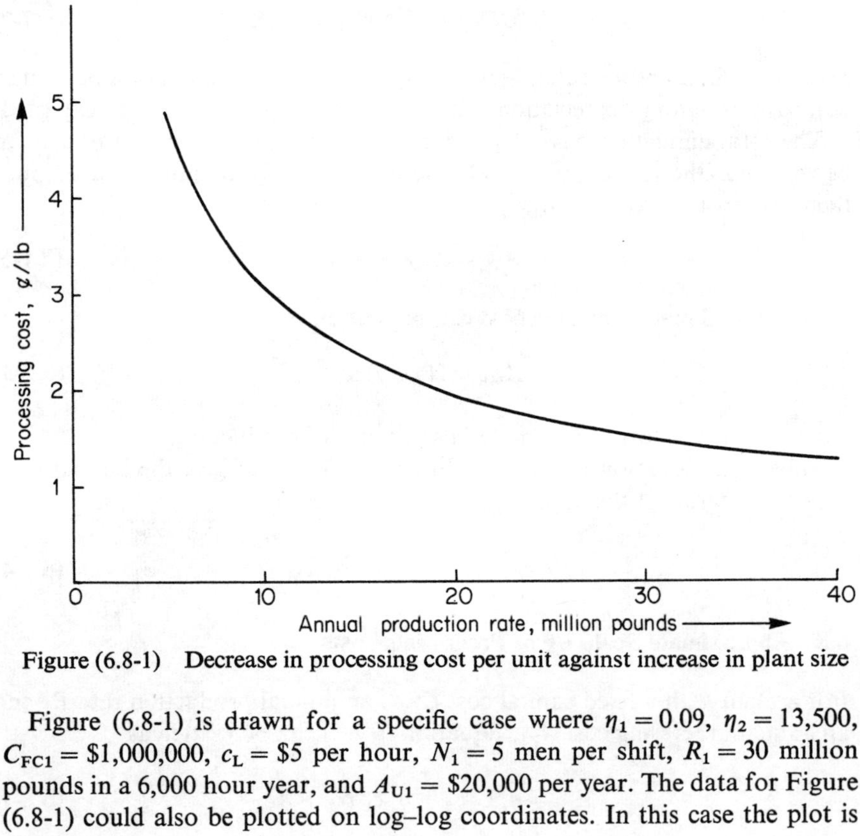

Figure (6.8-1) Decrease in processing cost per unit against increase in plant size

Figure (6.8-1) is drawn for a specific case where $\eta_1 = 0.09$, $\eta_2 = 13{,}500$, $C_{FC1} = \$1{,}000{,}000$, $c_L = \$5$ per hour, $N_1 = 5$ men per shift, $R_1 = 30$ million pounds in a 6,000 hour year, and $A_{U1} = \$20{,}000$ per year. The data for Figure (6.8-1) could also be plotted on log–log coordinates. In this case the plot is a straight line.

6.9 Manufacturing Cost as a basis for Product Pricing

Pricing on the basis of cost plus a fair profit has the disadvantage of ignoring demand. The modern approach is to price on the basis of market research.

However the classic cost plus fair profit approach can still give useful complementary information. This can be done by any of the following three methods:

(1) absorption pricing
(2) rate of return pricing
(3) marginal pricing

The gross annual profit A_{GP} for a product is given by Equation (2.1-6)

$$A_{GP} = A_S - A_{ME} - A_{BD} \tag{2.1-6}$$

where A_S is the revenue from annual sales, A_{ME} is the annual manufacturing cost, and A_{BD} is the balance sheet annual depreciation charge.

Equation (2.1-6) can also be combined with Equation (2.2-3) and rewritten in the form

$$A_S = A_{GP} + A_{VME} + A_{FME} + A_{BD} \tag{6.9-1}$$

where A_{VME} and A_{FME} are the annual variable and fixed manufacturing costs or expenses respectively.

Rewrite Equation (6.9-1) in terms of Equations (2.3-3) and (6.1-2) to give

$$c_S = c_{VME} + \frac{A_{GP}}{R} + \frac{A_{FME} + A_{BD}}{R} \tag{6.9-2}$$

where R is the annual sales volume taken as equal to the annual production rate, c_S is the sales price per unit of production, and c_{VME} is the variable manufacturing expense per unit of production.

Absorption pricing is based on a normal annual production rate R. The gross profit per unit A_{GP}/R is taken as a fixed percentage x of the fixed plus variable manufacturing costs given by the equation

$$\frac{A_{GP}}{R} = \left(\frac{x}{100}\right)\left[c_{VME} + \left(\frac{A_{FME} + A_{BD}}{R}\right)\right] \tag{6.9-3}$$

Combine Equations (6.9-2) and (6.9-3) to give

$$c_S = \left(\frac{100 + x}{100}\right)\left[c_{VME} + \left(\frac{A_{FME} + A_{BD}}{R}\right)\right] \tag{6.9-4}$$

Equations (6.9-2), (6.9-3), and (6.9-4) are based on a fixed normal annual production rate R.

Consider a change in annual production rate to $R + \Delta R$. In order to maintain the gross profit per unit as A_{GP}/R, the sales price per unit of production would need to be $c_S - \Delta c_S$. For this case Equation (6.9-2) can be written in the modified form

$$c_S - \Delta c_S = c_{VME} + \frac{A_{GP}}{R} + \frac{A_{FME} + A_{BD}}{R + \Delta R} \tag{6.9-5}$$

Subtract Equation (6.9-5) from Equation (6.9-2) to give

$$\Delta c_S = \frac{\Delta R}{R}\left(\frac{A_{FME} + A_{BD}}{R + \Delta R}\right) \tag{6.9-6}$$

Equation (6.9-6) gives the overpricing Δc_S per unit of production for an increase in annual production rate ΔR. Equation (6.9-6) also gives the underpricing Δc_S per unit of production for a decrease in annual production rate ΔR. In the first case the fixed costs or overheads are said to be overabsorbed and in the second case underabsorbed.

Absorption pricing is rigid and arbitrary and may result in business being turned away if the fixed sales price c_S cannot be obtained even though the business may give a useful contribution to fixed costs.

Rate of return pricing is a modified form of absorption pricing. It is based on the equation

$$\frac{A_{GP}}{A_{ME}} = \left(\frac{C_{TC}}{A_{ME}}\right)\left(\frac{A_{GP}}{C_{TC}}\right) \tag{6.9-7}$$

where C_{TC} is the total capital employed. Equation (6.9-7) can also be written as

$$\begin{matrix}\text{percentage}\\ \text{mark up on cost}\end{matrix} = \left(\begin{matrix}\text{capital turnover}\\ \text{ratio}\end{matrix}\right)\left(\begin{matrix}\text{projected rate}\\ \text{of return on capital}\end{matrix}\right)$$

The percentage mark up on cost is calculated for a known capital turnover ratio and a desired rate of return on capital. As with absorption pricing, the percentage mark up on manufacturing cost per unit of production is calculated for a normal annual production rate. If this production rate is exceeded, the rate of return on capital will be higher than projected because of the decrease in unit cost. Conversely, if the production rate is lower than normal, the rate of return on capital will be lower than projected because of the increase in unit cost. For production rates both higher and lower than the normal production rate, the percentage mark up is based on the normal unit cost. Thus the method is only strictly valid for the normal production rate.

With marginal pricing a company chooses its selling prices so as to maximize the total contribution $\sum R(c_S - c_{VME})$ from its various products. The method is particularly useful for large multiproduct companies with extensive existing facilities since it is the marginal cost that must be considered as the base case when entering into competition with another company. The lowest acceptable price for a product is that which gives the lowest worthwhile contribution to fixed costs. Marginal pricing enables a company to develop a more aggressive pricing policy than when using absorption or rate of return pricing.

In this section, absorption, rate of return, and marginal pricing have been considered on the basis of manufacturing cost. Total cost which is the sum of the manufacturing and general costs can also be considered as the basis. In this case the appropriate profit to consider is the net annual profit rather than the gross annual profit.

References for Chapter 6

1. Aries, R. S., and Newton, R. D., 'Chemical Engineering Cost Estimation', p. 118, New York, McGraw–Hill Book Co. Inc., 1955
2. Ibid., p. 163
3. Ibid., p. 168
4. Ibid., p. 173
5. Ibid., p. 174
6. Bauman, H. C., 'Fundamentals of Cost Engineering in the Chemical Industry', p. 314, New York, Reinhold Publishing Corporation, 1964
7. Holland, F. A., and Brinkerhoff, R., *Brit. Chem. Eng.*, **9**, 384 (1964)
8. Holland, F. A., and Brinkerhoff, R., *Chem. Eng.*, **70**, No. 3 (1963)
9. Keim, C. R., *Chem. Eng.*, **78**, No. 26 (1971)
10. Leibson, I., and Trischman, C. A., *Chem. Eng.*, **78**, No. 12 (1971)
11. Leibson, I., and Trischman, C. A., *Chem. Eng.*, **78**, No. 13 (1971)
12. Peters, M. S., and Timmerhaus, K. D., 'Plant Design and Economics for Chemical Engineers', 2nd ed., p. 127, New York, McGraw–Hill Book Co. Inc., 1968
13. Ross, J., Marsik, F. V., Douglas, F. R., and Wagner, R. L., *Chem. Eng.*, **70**, No. 16 (1963)
14. Teplitsky, G., *Chem. Eng.*, **73**, No. 4 (1966)
15. Weinberger, A. J., *Chem. Eng.*, **70**, No. 26 (1963)
16. Wessel, H. E., *Chem. Eng.*, **59**, No. 7 (1952)

Problems for Chapter 6

(6.1-1) The total capital cost for a chemical plant is \$10,000,000 and the plant produces 20 million lb of product per year selling at an average price of \$0.40/lb. Annual fixed charges for the plant amount to \$1,600,000 and distribution costs may be taken as 4 per cent of the total cost of manufacture. Raw material costs per lb of product are \$0.12/lb, labour \$0.05/lb, utilities \$0.03/lb and packing \$0.005/lb. Estimate the following values:

(a) total cost of manufacture per year and per pound of product
(b) profit per pound of product before taxes
(c) annual rate of return based on the original total investment

(6.1-2) A plant is designed to produce 7,500 ton/year of a product selling at \$610/ton. The total capital investment is \$1,250,000 and the plant operates for 8,400 hours per year.

Each ton of product requires:

3,100 lb of raw materials at \$0.13/lb
280 kWh of electricity at 1.5¢/kWh
10,000 lb of steam at \$0.65/1,000 lb
8,000 gal of water at \$0.40/1,000 gal
800 ft^3 of natural gas at \$0.60/1,000 ft^3

Labor requirements are 6 men per eight hour shift at \$5 per hour. Plant overheads amount to 50 per cent of the labor payroll. Supervision costs are \$20,000 per year. Repairs and maintenance cost 10 per cent per annum of total capital investment and depreciation is charged at 10 per cent per annum on the same basis. Selling and distribution expenses total \$20/ton of product and general overheads are allocated at 10 per cent of sales revenue.

Calculate the gross profit when the plant is operating at 100, 80, and 50 per cent of design capacity. Assume that labor and supervision costs do not vary with change of capacity.

(6.5-1) Sulfuric acid produced from sulfur by the contact process requires the following major plant items:

(i) a sulfur melting tank
(ii) a sulfur burner to produce the sulfur dioxide–air mixture
(iii) a gas cooler which supplies hot air to a waste heat boiler
(iv) two stages of catalytic conversion to sulfur trioxide
(v) three intercoolers to control the inlet temperatures to the converters and to the gas scrubbers
(vi) two scrubbers to remove the sulfur trioxide produced by washing first with 105 per cent sulfuric acid (oleum) and then with 98 per cent sulfuric acid
(vii) four circulation and blending tanks to produce the various strengths of acid required
(viii) a drying tower to remove water from the air supply to the sulfur burner by contact with recycled concentrated acid

Estimate the number of operators required for such a plant producing 50 short tons of acids per day using the equation

$$\log_{10} Y = -0.783 \log_{10} X + 1.252 + B \tag{6.5-1}$$

(6.7-1) The annual processing cost of product X including depreciation is given by the equation

$$A_P = 0.19C_{FC} + 13{,}500c_L N + A_U$$

where C_{FC} is the fixed capital cost, N is the number of men per shift, c_L is their rate of pay per hour which is currently \$5 per hour, and A_U is the annual utilities cost.

Which of the following two alternatives is preferable assuming a wage inflation rate of 5 per cent per year?

(1) a capital intensive plant

$$\text{where } C_{FC} = \$2{,}000{,}000$$
$$N = 4$$
$$A_U = \$20{,}000 \text{ per year}$$

(2) a labor intensive plant

$$\text{where } C_{FC} = \$1{,}000{,}000$$
$$N = 6$$
$$A_U = \$70{,}000 \text{ per year}$$

(6.9-1) A chemical plant has a normal production rate of 10,000,000 lb/year of product. The variable manufacturing expense is 9¢/lb and the annual fixed manufacturing expense including depreciation is $600,000/year. The company has fixed the selling price of the product to give a gross profit per lb of product equal to 20 per cent of the fixed plus variable manufacturing costs at the normal production rate.

Calculate the following:

(a) the gross profit per lb of product
(b) the selling price of the product
(c) the overpricing per lb if the production rate is raised to 15,000,000 lb/year
(d) the increase in annual gross profit for the increased production rate.

PART TWO

Elements of Decision Making

Chapter 7

Numerate Methods for Decision Makers

The use of discounted cash flow rate of return (DCFRR) and net present value (NPV) as measures of profitability for specific cash flow data are illustrated in Part 1 of this text. The effect of variations in cash flow data on the values of (DCFRR) and (NPV) are also illustrated in Part 1. Since cash flow data for future projects are necessarily subject to uncertainty, values of (DCFRR) and (NPV) for future projects can never be predicted with absolute certainty. It is therefore desirable when stating predicted values of (DCFRR) and (NPV) for future projects also to give a measure of confidence in the predictions. Discerning decision makers will wish to know the probability that the (DCFRR) or (NPV) will attain a particular value. For example for a particular future project it may have been estimated that there is a 90 per cent chance of the (DCFRR) being greater than 10 per cent, 50 per cent chance of the (DCFRR) being greater than 16 per cent, and only 10 per cent chance of the (DCFRR) being greater than 20 per cent. Management still has the power of decision but the probability data provide a desirable background of information. The estimation of probabilities requires the use of statistics. Thus statistical methods are playing an increasing role in decision making.

7.1 Statistical Measures and Methods

Predictions of future sales price, sales volume, etc., are normally based on a very limited amount of data about past events. Furthermore, it would not be convenient to use the entire population of past events even if it were available. A statistic is a measure, based on limited information from a sample, which allows the corresponding parameter of the population to be estimated. For example, the mean $\bar{x}$ of a property x is a statistic based on a sample of n items. It is defined by Equation (7.1-1).

$$\bar{x} = \frac{x_1 + x_2 + x_3 + \dots x_n}{n} \tag{7.1-1}$$

The mean $\bar{x}$ is the statistic corresponding to the parameter μ which is the arithmetic average of all the items in the population. The population may for example consist of one thousand items whilst the sample may only consist of ten items.

In many cases the x values will not all be different. In this case, Equation (7.1-1) can be rewritten in the form

$$\bar{x} = \frac{\sum x_i f(x_i)}{\sum f(x_i)} \tag{7.1-2}$$

where $f(x_i)$ is the frequency with which a particular value x_i occurs. If $f(x_i)$ is obtained by counting the number of occurrences of the value x_i, then $f(x_i)$ will have an integer value which may also be zero; $\sum f(x_i)$ will be the total number of items n in the sample. It is often convenient to divide the frequency of occurrence by n. In this case $f(x_i)$ becomes the relative frequency of occurrence of the value x_i and $\sum f(x_i) = 1$.

The values of x may either be discrete or continuous. The number of sales of, say, cars in any one day must be an integer. If a business sells 4 cars, this represents all possible values of x in the range 3.5 to 4.5. It is normal practice to diagrammatically represent the frequency of various values of x as a bar chart or a histogram with the frequency constant over the range of the x interval as shown in Figure (7.2-1e). Where x is continuous, the mid value of x over a range may be taken. In this case the ordinate should be the frequency per unit width of x. This makes the area under any bar proportional to the probability that the value of x will lie in the given range. If the relative frequency is plotted as ordinate, the sum of the areas under all the bars is unity. If x is continuous and the intervals are made smaller and smaller, eventually a smooth curve will result. The area under the curve between x_1 and x_2 represents the probability that a randomly selected item will have a value of x lying in the range x_1 to x_2. This is the information which is desired.

When data are available from past experience, they can be used to generate frequency distribution curves. However, in business situations it is often necessary to generate frequency distributions on the basis of the opinions of one or more experts.

Various mathematical models have been developed to fit the various types of distribution curves. It is most unlikely that any frequency distribution curve obtained in practice will fit exactly a curve plotted from any of these mathematical models. Nevertheless the approximations are extremely useful particularly in view of the inherent inaccuracies involved in practical data. The most commonly used distributions are the Binomial[3,5,17], Poisson[1,6,18], and Normal or Gaussian[2,7,19] distributions.

A Normal distribution curve has a bell type shape as shown in Figure (A2-1). The curve obeys the equation

$$f(x) = \frac{\exp[-(x-\mu)^2/2\sigma^2]}{\sigma(2\pi)^{0.5}} \tag{7.1-3}$$

where σ is known as the true standard deviation. The standard deviation s^* from a sample is given by the equation

$$s^* = \left[\frac{\sum (x_i - \bar{x})^2 f(x_i)}{\sum f(x_i) - 1}\right]^{0.5} \tag{7.1-4}$$

The standard deviation s^* for the sample corresponds to the true standard deviation σ for the whole population in the same way that the mean $\bar{x}$ of the sample corresponds to the arithmetic average μ for the whole population.

Equation (7.1-3) can be rewritten more compactly in the form

$$f(z) = \frac{\exp(-z^2/2)}{(2\pi)^{0.5}} \tag{7.1-5}$$

where the standard score

$$z = \frac{(x - \mu)}{\sigma} \tag{7.1-6}$$

The area under the curve of $f(z)$ is unity if the abscissa extends from $-\infty$ to $+\infty$. The area under the curve between z_1 and z_2 is the probability that a randomly selected value of z will lie in the range z_1 to z_2.

An event or outcome which will definitely occur has a probability $p = 1$. An event or outcome which will definitely not occur has a probability $p = 0$. When a coin is tossed the probability of a head $p_1 = 0.5$ and the probability of a tail $p_2 = 0.5$.

Equation (7.1-5) can be integrated between limits to determine the probability that a random value lies between the selected limits. Extensive tables of $f(z)$ and the associated integral are available[4]. An abbreviated version is given in Table (A2-1) in Appendix 2.

A frequency distribution curve can be used to plot a cumulative frequency curve which is the curve of most importance in business decision making. Figure (A2-2) shows a cumulative frequency curve plotted from a normal frequency distribution curve. The curve represents the probability of a random value z of having a value say z_1 or less.

If a property or variable c is a function of several other variables x_1, x_2, etc., then it can be written in the form

$$c = \phi(x_1, x_2, \ldots x_n) \tag{7.1-7}$$

It can be shown[15] that if each x is a normally distributed independent variable then

$$\sigma_c^2 = \left(\frac{\partial c}{\partial x_1}\right)^2 \sigma_1^2 + \left(\frac{\partial c}{\partial x_2}\right)^2 \sigma_2^2 + \ldots \left(\frac{\partial c}{\partial x_n}\right)^2 \sigma_n^2 \tag{7.1-8}$$

where σ_c is the standard deviation of the variable c and σ_1, σ_2 etc., are the standard deviations of the variables x_1, x_2, etc.

If c is related to x_1, x_2, etc., by a linear function of the form

$$c = k_1 x_1 + k_2 x_2 + \ldots k_n x_n \tag{7.1-9}$$

then Equation (7.1-8) can be written in the form

$$\sigma_c^2 = k_1^2 \sigma_1^2 + k_2^2 \sigma_2^2 + \ldots k_n^2 \sigma_n^2 \tag{7.1-10}$$

For the case of a product function

$$c = x_1 x_2 \tag{7.1-11}$$

Equation (7.1-8) can be written in the form

$$\frac{\sigma_c^2}{c^2} = \frac{\sigma_1^2}{x_1^2} + \frac{\sigma_2^2}{x_2^2} \tag{7.1-12}$$

It was shown in Part 1 of this text that discounted cash flow rate of return (DCFRR) and net present value (NPV) are both functions of the cumulative revenue $\sum A_S$ from annual sales, the cumulative total annual cost or expense $\sum A_{TE}$ and the fixed capital cost C_{FC} of the plant amongst other factors.

Equation (7.1-8) can be written for (DCFRR) in the form

$$\sigma^2_{(\text{DCFRR})} = \left[\frac{\partial(\text{DCFRR})}{\partial \sum A_S}\right]^2 \sigma^2_{\Sigma A_S} + \left[\frac{\partial(\text{DCFRR})}{\partial \sum A_{TE}}\right]^2 \sigma^2_{\Sigma A_{TE}} + \left[\frac{\partial(\text{DCFRR})}{\partial C_{FC}}\right]^2 \sigma^2_{C_{FC}} \tag{7.1-13}$$

and for (NPV) in the form

$$\sigma^2_{(\text{NPV})} = \left[\frac{\partial(\text{NPV})}{\partial \sum A_S}\right]^2 \sigma^2_{\Sigma A_S} + \left[\frac{\partial(\text{NPV})}{\partial \sum A_{TE}}\right]^2 \sigma^2_{\Sigma A_{TE}} + \left[\frac{\partial(\text{NPV})}{\partial C_{FC}}\right]^2 \sigma^2_{C_{FC}} \tag{7.1-14}$$

The differentials in Equations (7.1-13) and (7.1-14) are approximately equal to the sensitivity relationships determined in Chapter 4. In the case of (NPV)

$$\frac{\partial(\text{NPV})}{\partial \sum A_S} \simeq \frac{\Delta(\text{NPV})}{\Delta \sum A_S} \tag{7.1-15}$$

$$\frac{\partial(\text{NPV})}{\partial \sum A_{TE}} \simeq \frac{\Delta(\text{NPV})}{\Delta \sum A_{TE}} \tag{7.1-16}$$

and

$$\frac{\partial(\text{NPV})}{\partial C_{\text{FC}}} \simeq \frac{\Delta(\text{NPV})}{\Delta C_{\text{FC}}} \tag{7.1-17}$$

Similar approximations can be written in the case of (DCFRR).

The revenue A_S from annual sales is the product of the annual production rate R and the sales price c_S per unit of production.

$$A_S = Rc_S \tag{2.3-3}$$

For this case Equation (7.1-8) can be written in the form

$$\sigma_{A_S}^2 = \left(\frac{A_S}{R}\right)^2 \sigma_R^2 + \left(\frac{A_S}{c_S}\right)^2 \sigma_{c_S}^2 \tag{7.1-18}$$

Many distributions occurring in business situations are not symmetrical but are skewed. In such cases the Normal distribution curve is not a good fit. However, when data are based on estimates of future trends, the accuracy of the Normal approximation is usually acceptable. This is particularly the case as the number of component variables x_1, x_2, etc., in Equation (7.1-8) increases. Although the distributions of the individual variables x_1, x_2 may be skewed the property or variable c tends to approach the Normal distribution. For example, future revenues from sales tend to be less rather than greater than predicted values. To some extent this is balanced by the fact that future costs tend to be greater rather than less than predicted values.

The third column in Table (A2-1) gives the area under the right hand side of the Normal frequency distribution curve for a particular value of z. This area is also the corresponding ordinate in a cumulative Normal frequency distribution curve such as the one in Figure (A2-2). Although this curve is S-shaped it can be plotted as a straight line by rescaling the ordinate axis to give what is known as Normal probability graph paper. Such paper may be constructed from the data of Table (A2-1) and is illustrated by Figure (A2-3).

Very skew frequency distributions can sometimes be straightened by plotting on log normal graph paper[21].

Example (7.1-1)

Determine the cumulative probability of attaining various levels of net present value (NPV), and discounted cash flow rate of return (DCFRR) for a proposed project based on the following facts, opinions, and assumptions:

(i) uncertainties in all factors normally distributed about their means
(ii) sales volume in the range 13,000 ton/year to 17,000 ton/year
(iii) sales price in the range \$295/ton to \$305/ton

(iv) cost of raw materials \$135/ton of product

(v) a relatively simple plant which could be designed, financed, and completed during the current year

(vi) five independent estimates of fixed capital cost given as \$4,200,000, \$3,850,000, \$4,500,000, \$3,700,000, and \$4,250,000 respectively

(vii) 2 men on each of 3 shifts

(viii) labor rate $c_L = \$5.20$/hour

(ix) neglect annual utilities cost

(x) annual processing cost given by Equation (6.7-2)

(xi) working capital $C_{WC} = 0.12C_{FC}$

(xii) neglect cost of land

(xiii) annual general expense allocated to the product $A_{GE} = \$450{,}000$/year

(xiv) straight line depreciation over 5 years

(xv) zero salvage value of plant items

(xvi) cost of capital 10 per cent/year

(xvii) no tax allowance other than depreciation, i.e., $A_A = 0$

(xviii) fractional tax rate $t = 0.45$

Required equations:

$$A_{CI} = A_S - A_{TE} \tag{2.1-1}$$

$$A_{NCI} = A_{CI} - A_{IT} \tag{2.1-2}$$

$$A_{CF} = A_{NCI} - A_{TC} \tag{2.1-4}$$

$$A_{IT} = (A_{CI} - A_D - A_A)\,t \tag{2.1-3}$$

$$A_{TE} = A_{GE} + A_{ME} \tag{2.1-5}$$

$$C_{TC} = C_{FC} + C_{WC} + C_L \tag{2.5-1}$$

$$A_D = \frac{(C_{FC} - S)}{s} \tag{2.6-1}$$

$$A_{ME} = A_P + Rc_{RM} \tag{6.7-3}$$

$$A_{TE} = A_{GE} + A_P + Rc_{RM} \tag{6.7-4}$$

$$A_P = 0.09C_{CF} + 13{,}500c_L N + A_U \tag{6.7-2}$$

$$A_S = Rc_S \tag{2.3-3}$$

$$A_{DCF} = A_{CF} f_d \tag{3.2-1}$$

$$(\text{NPV}) = \sum A_{DCF} \tag{3.2-2}$$

$$(\text{NPV}) = \sum A_{DCF} = 0 \tag{3.2-3}$$

when $i = (\text{DCFRR})$

$$\bar{x} = \frac{x_1 + x_2 + x_3 + \ldots x_n}{n} \tag{7.1-1}$$

$$s^* = \left[\frac{\sum (x_i - \bar{x})^2 f(x_i)}{\sum f(x_i) - 1}\right]^{0.5} \tag{7.1-4}$$

$$z = \frac{(x - \mu)}{\sigma} \tag{7.1-6}$$

$$\sigma_c^2 = \left(\frac{\partial c}{\partial x_1}\right)^2 \sigma_1^2 + \left(\frac{\partial c}{\partial x_2}\right)^2 \sigma_2^2 + \ldots \left(\frac{\partial c}{\partial x_n}\right)^2 \sigma_n^2 \tag{7.1-8}$$

$$c = k_1 x_1 + k_2 x_2 + \ldots k_n x_n \tag{7.1-9}$$

$$\sigma_c^2 = k_1^2 \sigma_1^2 + k_2^2 \sigma_2^2 + \ldots k_n^2 \sigma_n^2 \tag{7.1-10}$$

$$\sigma_{A_\text{S}}^2 = \left(\frac{A_\text{S}}{R}\right)^2 \sigma_\text{R}^2 + \left(\frac{A_\text{S}}{c_\text{S}}\right)^2 \sigma_{c_\text{S}}^2 \tag{7.1-18}$$

Equation (6.7-2) gives the annual processing cost excluding depreciation. In the present case

$$A_\text{U} = 0$$

$$c_\text{L} = \$5.20/\text{hour}$$

$$N = 2$$

hence

$$\begin{aligned} A_\text{P} &= 0.09C_\text{FC} + 13{,}500c_\text{L} N + A_\text{U} \\ &= 0.09C_\text{FC} + 140{,}400 \quad \text{in \$/year} \end{aligned}$$

Equation (6.7-4) gives the annual total expense required to produce and sell the product. In the present case

$$A_\text{GE} = \$450{,}000/\text{year}$$

and

$$c_\text{RM} = \$135/\text{ton}$$

hence

$$\begin{aligned} A_\text{TE} &= A_\text{GE} + A_\text{P} + Rc_\text{RM} \\ &= 590{,}400 + 0.09C_\text{FC} + 135R \quad \text{in \$/year} \end{aligned}$$

where R is the sales volume of product in ton/year.

Equation (2.5-1) gives the total capital cost C_{TC}. In the present case

$$C_{WC} = 0.12C_{FC}$$

$$C_L = 0$$

hence

$$C_{TC} = C_{FC} + C_{WC} + C_L$$

$$= \$1.12C_{FC}$$

The annual rate of straight line depreciation of the fixed capital investment from C_{FC}, at start up, to zero value at the end of five years of productive life is given by Equation (2.6-1) to be

$$A_D = \frac{(C_{FC} - S)}{s}$$

$$= \frac{\$C_{FC} - \$0}{5 \text{ years}}$$

$$= \$0.2C_{FC}/\text{year}$$

The revenue A_S from the annual sales of the product is given by Equation (2.3-3)

$$A_S = Rc_S \tag{2.3-3}$$

The annual cash income A_{CI} when $A_S = Rc_S$ and $A_{TE} = 590{,}400 + 0.09C_{FC} + 135R$ is given by Equation (2.1-1) to be

$$A_{CI} = A_S - A_{TE}$$

$$= R(c_S - 135) - 590{,}400 - 0.09C_{FC} \quad \text{in \$/year}$$

The annual amount of tax A_{IT} when $A_{CI} = R(c_S - 135) - 590{,}400 - 0.09C_{FC}$, $A_A = 0$, and $t = 0.45$, is given by Equation (2.1-3) to be

$$A_{IT} = (A_{CI} - A_D - A_A)t$$

$$= [R(c_S - 135) - 590{,}400 - 0.09C_{FC}](0.45) - 0.45A_D \quad \text{in \$/year}$$

In this case the net annual cash flow A_{CF} after tax for years 1 to 5 is given by a combination of Equations (2.1-2) and (2.1-4) to be

$$A_{CF} = A_{CI} - A_{IT} - A_{TC}$$

$$= [R(c_S - 135) - 590{,}400 - 0.09C_{FC}]$$

$$- [R(c_S - 135) - 590{,}400 - 0.09C_{FC}](0.45) + 0.45A_D - A_{TC}$$

$$= 0.55R(c_S - 135) - 324{,}720 - 0.0495C_{FC} + 0.45A_D - A_{TC} \quad \text{in \$/year}$$

The net annual cash flow A_{CF} after tax for year 0 when $A_{CI} = \$0/\text{year}$, $A_{IT} = \$0/\text{year}$, and $A_{TC} = C_{TC} = \$1.12C_{FC}/\text{year}$ is given by a combination of Equations (2.1-2) and (2.1-4) to be

$$\begin{aligned} A_{CF} &= A_{CI} - A_{IT} - A_{TC} \\ &= \$0/\text{year} - \$0/\text{year} - \$1.12C_{FC}/\text{year} \\ &= -\$1.12C_{FC}/\text{year} \end{aligned}$$

The net annual cash flow A_{CF} after tax for years 1, 2, 3, and 4 when $A_D = \$0.2C_{FC}/\text{year}$ and $A_{TC} = \$0/\text{year}$ is

$$A_{CF} = 0.55R(c_S - 135) - 324{,}720 + 0.0405C_{FC} \quad \text{in \$/year}$$

The net annual cash flow A_{CF} after tax for year 5 when $A_D = \$0.2C_{FC}/\text{year}$ and $A_{TC} = -\$0.12C_{FC}/\text{year}$ (from the return of the working capital) is

$$A_{CF} = 0.55R(c_S - 135) - 324{,}720 + 0.1605C_{FC} \quad \text{in \$/year}$$

The equations

$$A_{CF} = -1.12C_{FC} \quad \text{for year 0}$$

$$A_{CF} = 0.55R(c_S - 135) - 324{,}720 + 0.0405C_{FC} \quad \text{for years 1, 2, 3, and 4}$$

and

$$A_{CF} = 0.55R(c_S - 135) - 324{,}720 + 0.1605C_{FC} \quad \text{for year 5}$$

can be used to obtain the net annual cash flows after tax in \$/year for various values of the variables R, c_S, and C_{FC}.

The net annual discounted cash flow A_{DCF} is given by Equation (3.2-1) to be

$$A_{DCF} = A_{CF} f_d$$

where the discount factor

$$f_d = \frac{1}{(1+i)^n}$$

The net present value (NPV) is given by Equation (3.2-2) to be

$$(\text{NPV}) = \sum A_{DCF}$$

In this case the sum of the values of A_{DCF} for the 5 year period is

$$\begin{aligned} (\text{NPV}) = {} & (-1.12C_{FC})(1.000\,00) + [0.55R(c_S - 135) - 324{,}720 + 0.0405C_{FC}] \\ & \times \left[\frac{1}{(1+i)} + \frac{1}{(1+i)^2} + \frac{1}{(1+i)^3} + \frac{1}{(1+i)^4}\right] \\ & + [0.55R(c_S - 135) - 324{,}720 + 0.1605C_{FC}]\left[\frac{1}{(1+i)^5}\right] \end{aligned}$$

which can also be written in the form

$$(\text{NPV}) = [0.55R(c_S - 135) - 324{,}720]\left\{\left[\frac{(1+i)^{n+1} - 1}{i(1+i)^n}\right] - 1\right\} + C_{FC}\sum_{k=0}^{n}\frac{K}{(1+i)^k}$$

where $n = 5$

$K = -1.12$ for year 0

$K = 0.0405$ for years 1 to 4

$K = 0.1605$ for year 5

and R and c_S do not vary from year to year.

Since for $i = 10$ per cent

$f_d = 0.909\ 09$ for year 1

$f_d = 0.826\ 45$ for year 2

$f_d = 0.751\ 31$ for year 3

$f_d = 0.683\ 01$ for year 4

$f_d = 0.620\ 92$ for year 5

and $\sum f_d = 3.790\ 78$

$$\begin{aligned}(\text{NPV}) &= -1.12C_{FC} + [0.55R(c_S - 135) - 324{,}720 + 0.0405C_{FC}]\,(3.790\ 78) \\ &\quad + (0.12C_{FC})(0.620\ 92) \\ &= 2.0849R(c_S - 135) - 0.891\ 96C_{FC} - 1{,}230{,}942 \\ &\quad \text{in \$ for } i = 10 \text{ per cent}\end{aligned}$$

The mean value of the net present value $(\overline{\text{NPV}})$ for year 5 can be obtained by using the mean values of the sales volume $\bar{R}$, the sales price $\bar{c}_S$, and the fixed capital cost $\bar{C}_{FC}$ to give

$$\overline{(\text{NPV})} = 2.0849\bar{R}(\bar{c}_S - 135) - 0.891\ 96\bar{C}_{FC} - 1{,}230{,}942 \quad \text{in \$ for } i = 10 \text{ per cent}$$

The mean value of a quantity is given by Equation (7.1-1) to be

$$\bar{x} = \frac{x_1 + x_2 + x_3 + \ldots x_n}{n}$$

The mean value of the sales volume is given by Equation (7.1-1) to be

$$\begin{aligned}\bar{R} &= \frac{13{,}000 \text{ ton/year} + 17{,}000 \text{ ton/year}}{2} \\ &= 15{,}000 \text{ ton/year}\end{aligned}$$

The mean value of the sales price is given by Equation (7.1-1) to be

$$\bar{c}_S = \frac{\$295/\text{ton} + \$305/\text{ton}}{2} = \$300/\text{ton}$$

The mean value of the fixed capital cost is given by Equation (7.1-1) to be

$$\bar{C}_{FC} = \frac{\$4{,}200{,}000 + \$3{,}850{,}000 + \$4{,}500{,}000 + \$3{,}700{,}000 + \$4{,}250{,}000}{5} = \$4{,}100{,}000$$

Substitute the mean values of $\bar{R}$, $\bar{c}_S$, and $\bar{C}_{FC}$ into the equation for the mean value of the net present value $(\overline{\text{NPV}})$ for year 5 to give

$$(\overline{\text{NPV}}) = (2.0849)(15{,}000)(300 - 135) - (0.891\,96)(4{,}100{,}000) - 1{,}230{,}942 = \$272{,}150 \quad \text{for } i = 10 \text{ per cent}$$

The standard deviation of a quantity is given by Equation (7.1-4) to be

$$s^* = \left[\frac{\sum (x_i - \bar{x})^2 f(x_i)}{\sum f(x_i) - 1}\right]^{0.5}$$

The standard deviation of the fixed capital cost is given by Equation (7.1-4) to be

$$\sigma_{C_{FC}} \cong s^*_{C_{FC}} = \left\{\frac{[(4.2 - 4.1)^2 + (3.85 - 4.1)^2 + (4.5 - 4.1)^2 + (3.7 - 4.1)^2 + (4.25 - 4.1)^2]}{5 - 1}\right\}^{0.5} \times (\$1{,}000{,}000) = \$322{,}100$$

Equation (7.1-4) cannot be used to estimate the standard deviations of the sales volume and sales price since there are insufficient values. An alternative estimation method is required.

Table (A2-1) shows that the cumulative probability of a normally distributed variable lying within four standard deviations of the mean is 0.499 97. It is therefore more than 99.99 per cent certain that a random value will lie within $\pm 4\sigma$ from the mean. Thus for practical purposes σ may be taken as one eighth of the range of certainty.

Therefore take the standard deviation of the sales volume to be

$$\sigma_R = \frac{(17{,}000 \text{ ton/year} - 13{,}000 \text{ ton/year})}{8} = 500 \text{ ton/year}$$

and the standard deviation of the sales price to be

$$\sigma_{c_S} = \frac{(\$305/\text{ton} - \$295/\text{ton})}{8}$$
$$= \$1.25/\text{ton}$$

The variance of the revenue A_S from annual sales is given by Equation (7.1-18) to be

$$\sigma_{A_S}^2 = \left(\frac{A_S}{R}\right)^2 \sigma_R^2 + \left(\frac{A_S}{c_S}\right)^2 \sigma_{c_S}^2$$

which can also be written as

$$\sigma_{A_S}^2 = \bar{c}_S^2 \sigma_R^2 + \bar{R}^2 \sigma_{c_S}^2$$

For this example, an analogous equation can be written in the form

$$\sigma_{R(c_S-135)}^2 = (\bar{c}_S - 135)^2 \sigma_R^2 + \bar{R}^2 \sigma^2{}_{(c_S-135)}$$

Since

$$\bar{c}_S - 135 = 300 - 135 = \$165/\text{ton}$$
$$\sigma_R = 500 \text{ ton/year}$$
$$\bar{R} = 15{,}000 \text{ ton/year}$$

and

$$\sigma_{c_S} = \$1.25/\text{ton}$$

$$\sigma_{R(c_S-135)}^2 = (\$165/\text{ton})^2 (500 \text{ ton/year})^2 + (15{,}000 \text{ ton/year})^2 (\$1.25/\text{ton})^2$$
$$= (\$84{,}604/\text{year})^2$$

If a variable c is a function of several other variables x_1, x_2, etc., where each is normally distributed, the variance of c is given by Equation (7.1-8) to be

$$\sigma_c^2 = \left(\frac{\partial c}{\partial x_1}\right)^2 \sigma_1^2 + \left(\frac{\partial c}{\partial x_2}\right)^2 \sigma_2^2 + \ldots \left(\frac{\partial c}{\partial x_n}\right)^2 \sigma_n^2$$

For this example, the mean value of the net present value for year 5

$$\overline{(\text{NPV})} = 2.0849\bar{R}(\bar{c}_S - 135) - 0.891\,96\bar{C}_{FC} - 1{,}230{,}942$$
$$\text{in \$ for } i = 10 \text{ per cent}$$

Since

$$\frac{\partial\overline{(\text{NPV})}}{\partial\bar{R}(\bar{c}_S - 135)} = 2.0849 \text{ year}$$

$$\frac{\partial\overline{(\text{NPV})}}{\partial \bar{C}_{\text{FC}}} = -0.891\ 96 C_{\text{FC}}$$

$$\sigma_{R(c_S - 135)} = \$84{,}604/\text{year}$$

and

$$\sigma_{\text{CFC}} = \$322{,}100$$

the variance of the (NPV) is given by Equation (7.1-8) to be

$$\begin{aligned}\sigma^2_{(\text{NPV})} &= (2.0849 \text{ year})^2 (\$84{,}604/\text{year})^2 + (-0.891\ 96)^2 (\$322{,}100)^2 \\ &= (\$337{,}128)^2\end{aligned}$$

Therefore the standard deviation of the net present value

$$\sigma_{(\text{NPV})} = \$337{,}128$$

Table (A2-1) can be used to estimate the cumulative probability of a given (NPV) for year 5 being attained on the basis of the (NPV) for year 5 being normally distributed about a mean value of \$272,150 with a standard deviation of \$337,128.

The standard score is given by Equation (7.1-6) to be

$$z = \frac{(x - \mu)}{\sigma}$$

For the (NPV) in this example, Equation (7.1-6) can be written as

$$\begin{aligned}z &= \frac{(\text{NPV}) - \overline{(\text{NPV})}}{\sigma_{(\text{NPV})}} \\ &= \frac{(\text{NPV}) - \$272{,}150}{\$337{,}128}\end{aligned}$$

which can also be written in the form

$$(\text{NPV}) = 337{,}128z + 272{,}150 \text{ in } \$$$

Read from Table (A2-1) that the area under the right hand side of the Normal distribution curve is 0.4000 when $z = 1.282$. Since the Normal distribution curve is symmetrical about the mean at $z = 0$, the area to the left of $z = -1.282$ is $0.5000 - 0.4000 = 0.1000$. There is therefore a cumulative probability of 10 per cent that a value of $z \leqslant -1.282$ will be attained. In this example this corresponds to a net present value given by the equation

$$(\text{NPV}) = 337{,}128z + 272{,}150$$

to be

$$\begin{aligned}(\text{NPV}) &= (337{,}128)(-1.282) + 272{,}150\\ &= -\$160{,}048\end{aligned}$$

There is also a cumulative probability of 90 per cent that a value of $z \leqslant 1.282$ will be attained. In this example this corresponds to a net present value given by the equation

$$(\text{NPV}) = 337{,}128z + 272{,}150$$

to be

$$\begin{aligned}(\text{NPV}) &= (337{,}128)(1.282) + 272{,}150\\ &= \$704{,}348\end{aligned}$$

Other values are calculated in the same way and listed in Table (7.1-1a). The probability of attaining a given (NPV) or less for year 5 is shown graphically in Figure (7.1-1a).

TABLE (7.1-1a)

Cumulative probability of attaining a given value of (NPV) or less

cumulative probability, per cent	z	(NPV) $	(DCFRR) per cent/year
0.00	- 4.000	- 1,076,362	0.88
2.00	- 2.054	- 420,311	6.38
10.00	- 1.282	- 160,048	8.56
20.00	- 0.842	- 11,712	9.81
30.00	- 0.524	+ 95,495	10.71
40.00	- 0.253	+ 186,857	11.47
50.00	0.000	+ 272,150	12.19
60.00	0.253	+ 357,443	12.91
70.00	0.524	+ 448,805	13.67
80.00	0.842	+ 556,012	14.57
90.00	1.282	+ 704,348	15.82
98.00	2.054	+ 964,611	18.00
100.00	4.000	+ 1,620,662	23.50

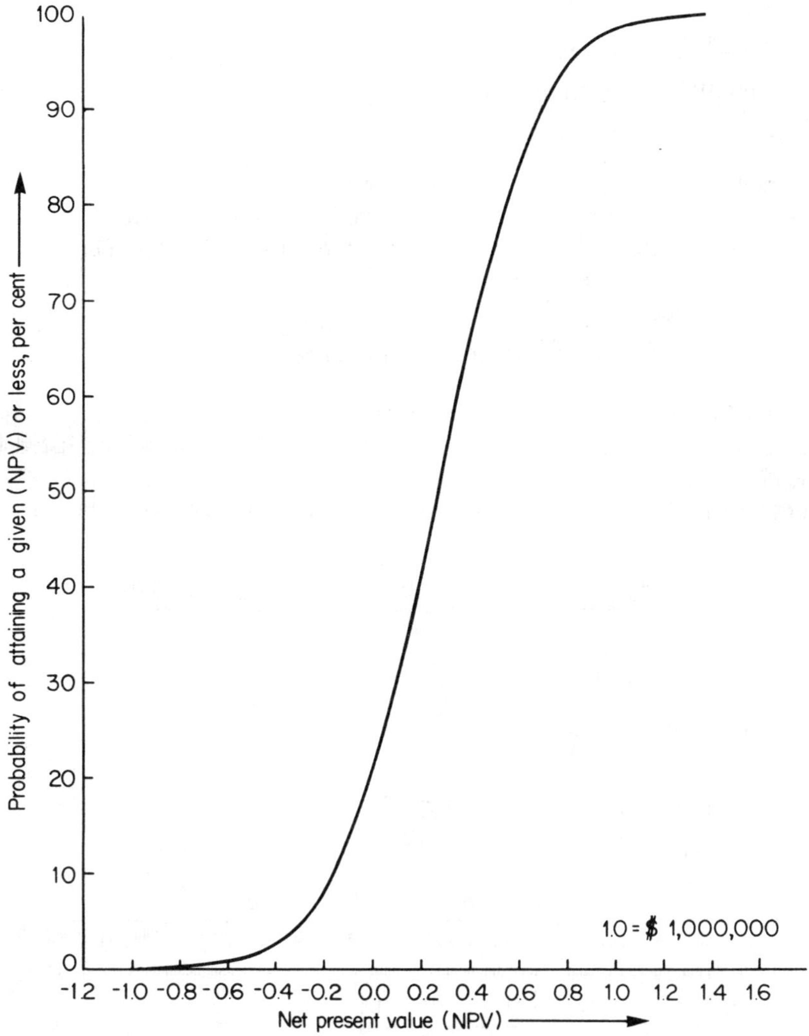

Figure (7.1-1a) Probability of attaining a given net present value (NPV) or less against (NPV)

The net present value (NPV) for year 5 for this example can be written in the form

$$(\text{NPV}) = [0.55R(c_S - 135) - 324{,}720]\left\{\left[\frac{(1+i)^{n+1} - 1}{i(1+i)^n}\right] - 1\right\}$$
$$+ C_{FC}\sum_{k=0}^{n}\frac{K}{(1+i)^k} \quad \text{in \$}$$

where $n = 5$

$K = -1.12$ for year 0

$K = 0.0405$ for years 1 to 4

$K = 0.1605$ for year 5

and R and c_S do not vary from year to year.

The value of the interest rate i which makes (NPV) = 0 after 5 years in this case is the discounted cash flow rate of return (DCFRR). This can be determined by an iterative procedure.

The mean value

$$\overline{(\text{DCFRR})} = 12.19 \text{ per cent}$$

is obtained on the basis of the mean values of the sales volume $\bar{R}$, the sales price $\bar{c}_S$, and the fixed capital cost $\bar{C}_{FC}$. The annual cash flows are listed in Table (7.1-1b).

Put (NPV) = 0 after 5 years and rewrite the derived equation in the form

$$\frac{\sum_{k=0}^{n} [K/(1+i)^k]}{\left\{\left[\dfrac{(1+i)^{n+1}-1}{i(1+i)^n}\right]-1\right\}} = \frac{0.55R(c_S - 135) - 324{,}720}{-C_{FC}}$$

Differentiate both sides to give

$$\left[\frac{\left\{\left[\dfrac{(1+i)^{n+1}-1}{i(1+i)^n}\right]-1\right\}\left[\displaystyle\sum_{k=0}^{n}\frac{-kK}{(1+i)^{k+1}}\right] - \left[\displaystyle\sum_{k=0}^{n}\frac{K}{(1+i)^k}\right]\left[-\dfrac{1}{i^2}+\dfrac{n}{i(1+i)^{n+1}}+\dfrac{1}{i^2(1+i)^n}\right]}{\left\{\left[\dfrac{(1+i)^{n+1}-1}{i(1+i)^n}\right]-1\right\}^2}\right] di$$

$$= \frac{(-C_{FC})\{0.55\, d[R(c_S - 135)]\} - [0.55R(c_S - 135) - 324{,}720]\, d(-C_{FC})}{(-C_{FC})^2}$$

and substitute

$$i = \overline{(\text{DCFRR})} = 12.19 \text{ per cent}$$

$$n = 5 \text{ years}$$

TABLE (7.1-1b)

Annual cash flows based on mean values of factors

year	before tax			depreciation charge plus other allowances	taxable income	when t=0.45 amount of tax A_{IT} =	net capital expenditure	after tax			
	revenue	total expenses	cash income					net cash flow A_{CF} =	discount factor at i= 12.19%	discounted net cash flow	net present value (NPV)
	A_S	A_{TE}	A_{CI}	$A_D + A_A$	$A_{CI}-A_D-A_A$	$(A_{CI}-A_D-A_A)t$	A_{TC}	$A_{CI}-A_{IT}-A_{TC}$	f_d	A_{DCF}	$= \Sigma A_{DCF}$
0	0	0	0	0	0	0	4,592,000	-4,592,000	1.00000	-4,592,000	-4,592,000
1	4,500,000	2,984,400	1,515,600	820,000	695,600	313,020	0	1,202,580	0.89138	1,071,952	-3,520,048
2	4,500,000	2,984,400	1,515,600	820,000	695,600	313,020	0	1,202,580	0.79455	955,514	-2,564,534
3	4,500,000	2,984,400	1,515,600	820,000	695,600	313,020	0	1,202,580	0.70825	851,723	-1,712,811
4	4,500,000	2,984,400	1,515,600	820,000	695,600	313,020	0	1,202,580	0.63131	759,206	- 953,605
5	4,500,000	2,984,400	1,515,600	820,000	695,600	313,020	-492,000	1,694,580	0.56274	953,607	+ 2

$$R = \bar{R} = 15{,}000 \text{ ton/year}$$
$$c_S = \bar{c}_S = \$300/\text{ton}$$
$$C_{FC} = \bar{C}_{FC} = \$4{,}100{,}000$$

to give the linear equation

$$di = \left(\frac{-0.680\,296}{4{,}100{,}000}\right) d[R(c_S - 135)] + \left(\frac{0.312\,703}{4{,}100{,}000}\right) dC_{FC}$$

where $i = (\text{DCFRR})$.

If a variable c is related to several other variables x_1, x_2, etc., by a linear function of the form

$$c = k_1 x_1 + k_2 x_2 + \ldots k_n x_n \tag{7.1-9}$$

then Equation (7.1-8) can be written in the form

$$\sigma_c^2 = k_1^2 \sigma_1^2 + k_2^2 \sigma_2^2 + \ldots k_n^2 \sigma_n^2 \tag{7.1-10}$$

For this example, the variance of (DCFRR) can be related to the variance of $R(c_S - 135)$ and the variance of C_{FC} by Equation (7.1-10) written in the form

$$\sigma_{(\text{DCFRR})}^2 = \left(\frac{-0.680\,296}{4{,}100{,}000}\right)^2 \sigma_{R(c_S-135)}^2 + \left(\frac{0.312\,703}{4{,}100{,}000}\right)^2 \sigma_{C_{FC}}^2$$

where

$$\sigma_{R(c_S-135)} = \$84{,}604/\text{year}$$

and

$$\sigma_{C_{FC}} = \$322{,}100$$

to give

$$\sigma_{(\text{DCFRR})} = 2.828 \text{ per cent}$$

The probability of attaining a given discounted cash flow rate of return (DCFRR) or less for year 5 is determined in a similar manner to that described for the net present value (NPV). The probabilities for various values of (DCFRR) are shown graphically in Figure (7.1-1b).

Decision makers often prefer to have graphs showing the probability of attaining a value greater than a given value. Such curves are easily obtained by subtracting each probability of achieving a given value or less from 100 per cent. Figure (7.1-1c) is obtained from the data in Figure (7.1-1b) in this way and shows the probability of attaining a (DCFRR) greater than a given (DCFRR).

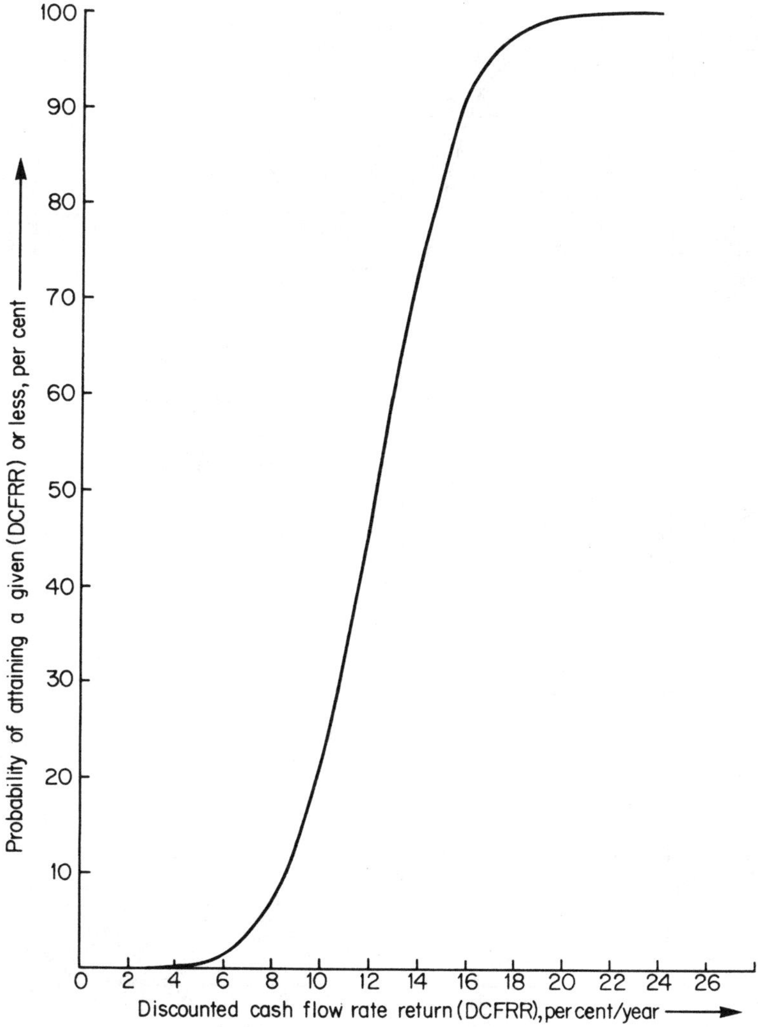

Figure (7.1-1b) Probability of attaining a given discounted cash flow rate of return (DCFRR) or less against (DCFRR)

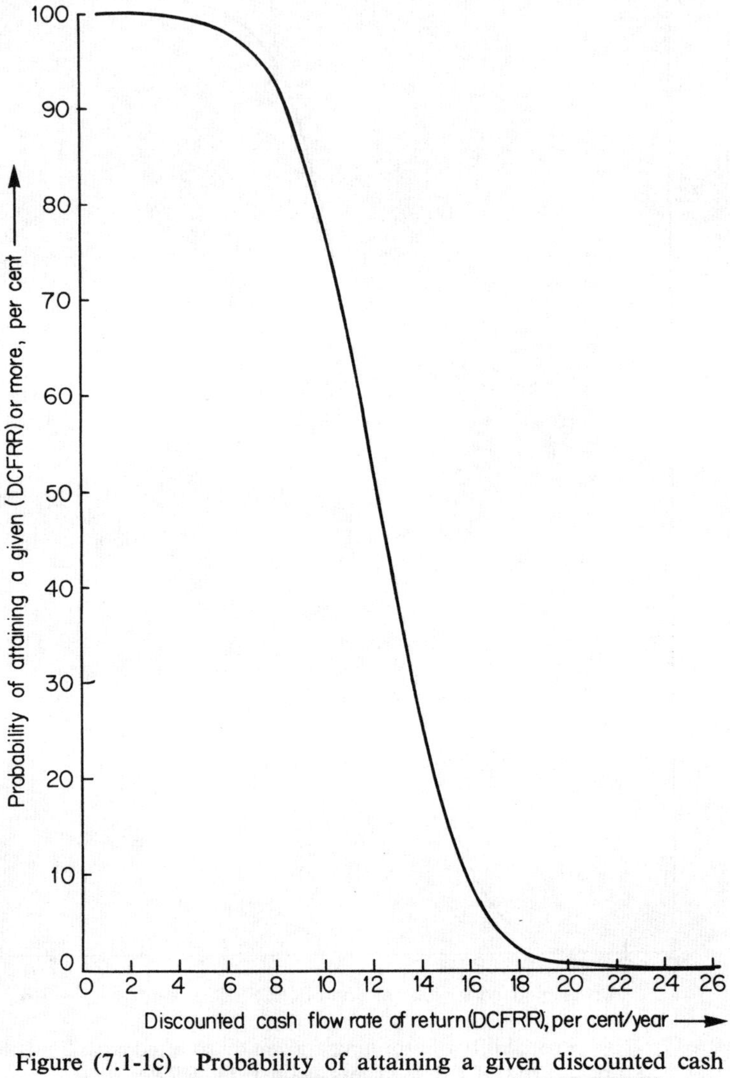

Figure (7.1-1c) Probability of attaining a given discounted cash flow rate of return (DCFRR) or more against (DCFRR)

7.2 Probability Techniques

The estimated discounted cash flow rate of return (DCFRR) and the net present value (NPV) for a proposed investment are only as accurate as the estimated cash flows on which they are based. The greatest uncertainty is in sales forecasting since the price of the product and the volume of sales are determined by the prevailing market conditions. Both sales price and volume are subject to change because of factors such as:

(1) competition entering or leaving the market in an unforeseen way
(2) technological change which may reduce the need for the product
(3) replacement by a better product
(4) Government legislation such as a change in import and export duties

Thus it is essential for a company to have an efficient commercial intelligence system to assess the market conditions. This can be done by taking an intelligent interest in technical meetings, technical and financial literature, patent applications, etc.

The accuracy of sales forecasting can also be increased by a careful study of past sales records, price trends, etc. However, the uncertainty of an estimate increases the further into the future that it is projected.

A great deal of sales and other types of forecasting is based on the opinions of experts. Quantitative estimates can be obtained by careful questioning. The panel of experts should not only include specialists in that particular field, e.g. sales, but also people who are directly affected by the forecasts made by others.

Experts should be able to estimate maximum, minimum, and most likely or modal values for a quantity. Of course the modal value is not necessarily midway between the minimum and maximum values since many distributions are skewed. An expert may be asked to estimate the probability of the occurrence of certain values on each side of the mode[14]. Where experts are questioned separately the method is known as the Delphi method. It is useful to make a comparison of the past predictions of each expert with the results obtained in practice. This information enables the opinions to be weighted. Where the experts work in close collaboration it is not possible to avoid some collusion. In this case it is better to arrive at a single consensus opinion by a free and open discussion. This is the Think Tank method. Its main disadvantage is that rank or aggressiveness might unduly weight one or more opinions.

The opinions of the experts provide a basis for plotting a frequency or probability distribution curve. If the relative frequency is plotted as ordinate, the total area under the curve is unity. The area under the curve between two values of the quantity is the probability that a randomly selected value will fall in the range between the two values of the quantity. It should be stressed that these probabilities are merely estimates and that their reliability depends mainly on the skill and experience of the forecasters.

The estimated discounted cash flow rate of return (DCFRR) and the estimated net present value (NPV) are both functions of the estimated cumulative revenue $\sum A_S$ from annual sales, the estimated cumulative total annual cost or expense $\sum A_{TE}$ and the estimated fixed capital cost C_{FC} of the plant. The revenue A_S from annual sales for each year is in turn the product of the sales price and the sales volume. Initially it is desirable to select those values from the distribution curves of $\sum A_S$, $\sum A_{TE}$, and C_{FC} which enable the maximum and minimum (DCFRR) and (NPV) values to be calculated. If the maximum values of (DCFRR) and (NPV) are not acceptable to the company, then the project should be promptly rejected. If the minimum values of (DCFRR) and (NPV) are acceptable then a detailed assessment should be put in hand. If the maximum values of (DCFRR) and (NPV) are acceptable but the minimum values are not, then the feasibility study should be continued.

If the frequency or probability distribution curves of all the factors such as $\sum A_S$ can be considered as Normal distribution curves, then the cumulative frequency or probability curves for attaining a definite level of (DCFRR) or (NPV) can readily be obtained by the method used in Example (7.1-1). If the frequency distribution curve of one or more of the factors cannot be taken as Normal the amount of calculation involved can be very large. For example, if there are say ten levels of sales volume, six levels of sales price, five levels of total annual expense, and three levels of fixed capital cost, the total number of different (DCFRR) or (NPV) calculations is $(10)(6)(5)(3) = 900$. This is a great deal of calculation for only a modest number of levels for each factor. Thus in most cases it is not practicable to obtain the cumulative probability curves for (DCFRR) and (NPV) by using all the possible combinations of factors. The problem can be greatly simplified by the use of Monte Carlo methods to sample the population consisting of all possible combinations of factors.

The Monte Carlo method makes use of random numbers. A digital computer can be used to generate pseudo-random numbers in the range 0 to 1. A short list of such numbers generated by a computer is given in Table (A2-2). Consider the frequency distribution curve of a particular factor, e.g. sales volume. Each value of the sales volume has a certain probability of occurrence. The cumulative probability of that value, or less, being realized is a number in the range 0 to 1. Thus a random number in the range 0 to 1 can be used to select a random value of the sales volume. In the same way random values of the other factors can be obtained. These can then be combined to give random values of (DCFRR) and (NPV). These, in turn, can be used to plot cumulative probability curves for (DCFRR) and (NPV). The computer may be required to perform some 10,000 to 50,000 calculations. The use of the Monte Carlo method is illustrated in Example (7.2-1).

It should be noted that the cumulative probability curves of (DCFRR) and (NPV) can never be more accurate than the opinions on which they are based.

Example (7.2-1)

A sales manager has given the following opinions about the sales potential of a proposed new speciality product:

(1) The sales volume will not be less than 1,000 ton/year nor more than 2,000 ton/year. All values in this range are equally likely.

(2) The sales price will lie in the range \$750/ton to \$900/ton with a most likely value of \$850/ton. The probability of intermediate values can be taken to vary linearly with sales price.

On the basis of these opinions, use the Monte Carlo technique to obtain a cumulative probability curve for attaining various levels of revenue A_S from annual sales.

Required equation:

$$A_S = Rc_S \tag{2.3-3}$$

Consider the probability curve of the sales volume. Let the total area under the curve equal unity. The area under the curve is

0 for $-\infty \leqslant R \leqslant 1{,}000$ ton/year

$1 = (p)(1{,}000$ ton/year) for $1{,}000$ ton/year $\leqslant R \leqslant 2{,}000$ ton/year

and 0 for $2{,}000$ ton/year $\leqslant R \leqslant \infty$

Thus $p = 1/1{,}000$. The probability plot for sales volume is shown in Figure (7.2-1a).

The cumulative probability of a sales volume less than, or equal to R occurring is $\int_{-\infty}^{R} f(R)\mathrm{d}R$. Since $\int_{-\infty}^{1{,}000} (0)\mathrm{d}R = 0$ and $\int_{2{,}000}^{\infty} (0)\mathrm{d}R = 0$, the

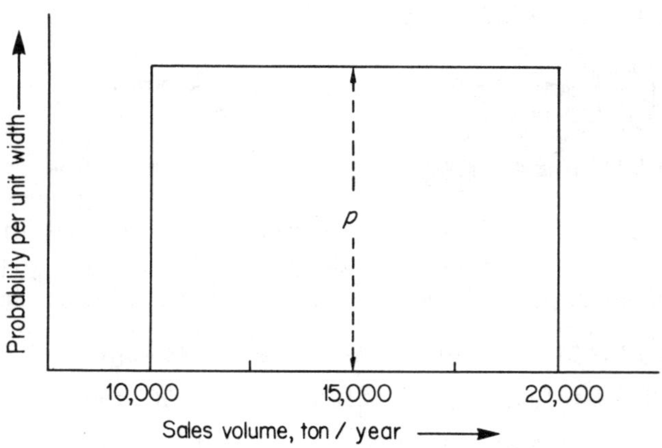

Figure (7.2-1a) Probability of attaining a particular sales volume

cumulative probability curve can be represented by the equation

$$\int_{1,000}^{R} (p)\,\mathrm{d}R = \left(\frac{1}{1,000}\right)(R - 1,000)$$

This curve is shown in Figure (7.2-1b).

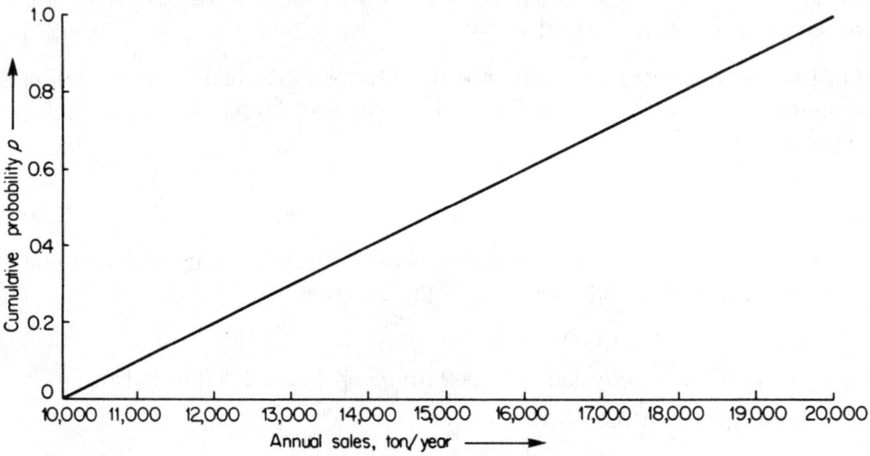

Figure (7.2-1b) Cumulative probability against annual sales of product

Consider the probability curve of the sales price. Let the total area under the curve equal unity. The area under the curve is

$$0 \text{ for } -\infty \leqslant c_S \leqslant \$750/\text{ton}$$

$$1 = \left(\frac{p_m}{2}\right)(900 - 750) \text{ for } \$750/\text{ton} < c_S \leqslant \$900/\text{ton}$$

and 0 for $\$900/\text{ton} < c_S \leqslant \infty$

Thus $p_m = 1/75 = 0.013\,33$ which is the probability at the most likely value of \$850/ton. The probability plot for sales price is shown in Figure (7.2-1c).

The ordinate of the probability curve can be represented by the expressions

$$(0.000\,133\,3)(c_S - 750) \text{ for } \$750/\text{ton} < c_S \leqslant \$850/\text{ton}$$

and $(0.000\,266\,6)(900 - c_S)$ for $\$850/\text{ton} < c_S \leqslant \$900/\text{ton}$

The cumulative probability of a sales price less than, or equal to c_S occurring is $\int_{-\infty}^{c_S} f(c_S)\mathrm{d}c_S$. Since $\int_{-\infty}^{750} (0)\mathrm{d}c_S = 0$ and $\int_{900}^{\infty} (0)\mathrm{d}c_S = 0$, the cumulative

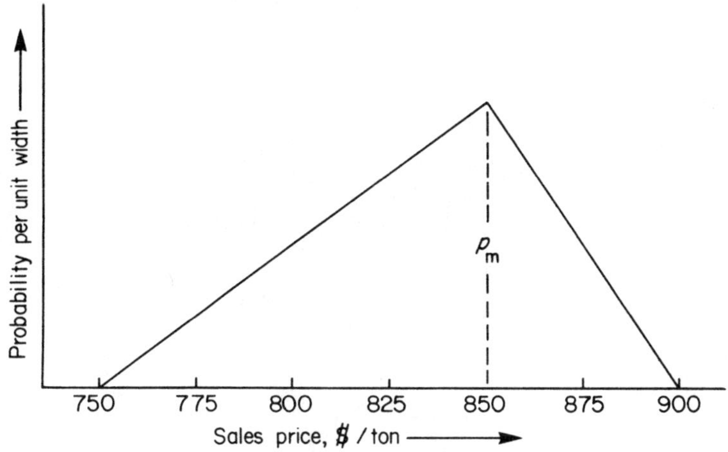

Figure (7.2-1c) Probability of attaining a particular sales price

probability curve can be represented by the equations

$$\int_{750}^{c_s} (0.000\,133\,3)(c_S - 750)\,dc_S = (0.000\,066\,66)(c_S - 750)^2$$

for \$750/ton $< c_S \leqslant$ \$850/ton

and

$$(0.000\,066\,66)(850 - 750)^2 + \int_{850}^{c_s} (0.000\,266\,6)(900 - c_S)\,dc_S$$

$$= (0.000\,066\,66)(850 - 750)^2 + (0.000\,133)(900 - 850)^2$$

$$- (0.000\,133)(900 - c_S)^2 = 1 - (0.000\,133\,3)(900 - c_S)^2$$

for \$850/ton $< c_S \leqslant$ \$900/ton

This curve is shown in Figure (7.2-1d).

Use the random numbers in Table (A2-2) to generate the required cumulative probability function by the Monte Carlo method. The random numbers can be used in any sequence provided that no number is re-used during a calculation.

Read the numbers in Table (A2-2) from left to right and top to bottom. Let each number of four digits represent two groups of two digits. Let the first of the two-digit figures represent a value of the sales volume R and the second of the two-digit figures represent a value of the sales price c_S. The use of

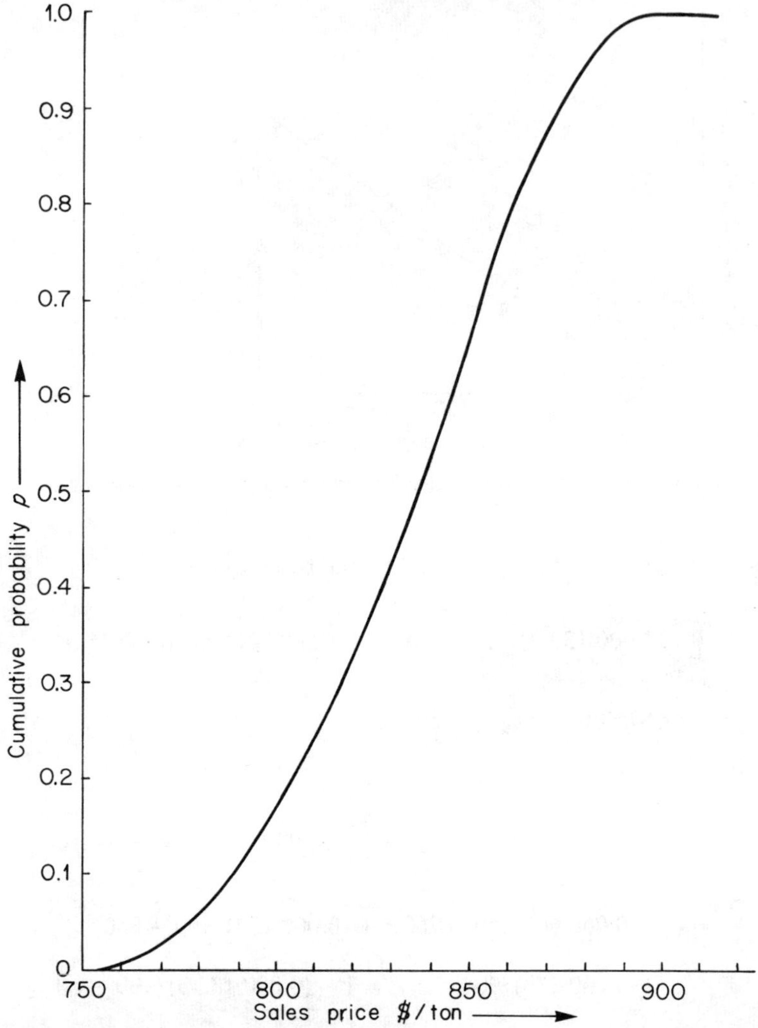

Figure (7.2-1d) Cumulative probability against sales price of product

two-digit figures limits the number of possible values of R and c_s to one hundred each.

The first number in Table (A2-2) is 3770. Let the first value of R be that which has a cumulative probability of 0.37. This is read from Figure (7.2-1c) to be 1,370 ton/year. Let the first value of c_s be that which has a cumulative probability of 0.70. This is read from Figure (7.2-1d) to be \$852.5/ton. Thus the value of the revenue A_s from annual sales generated from the first random

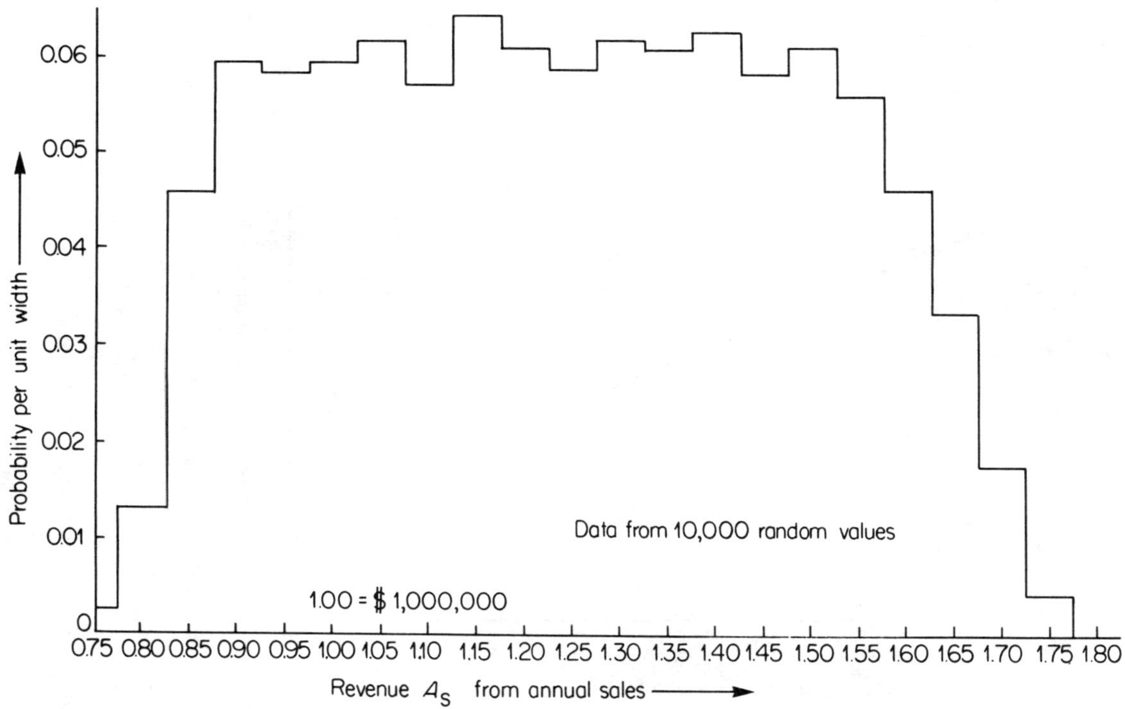

Figure (7.2-1e) Histogram of revenue from annual sales

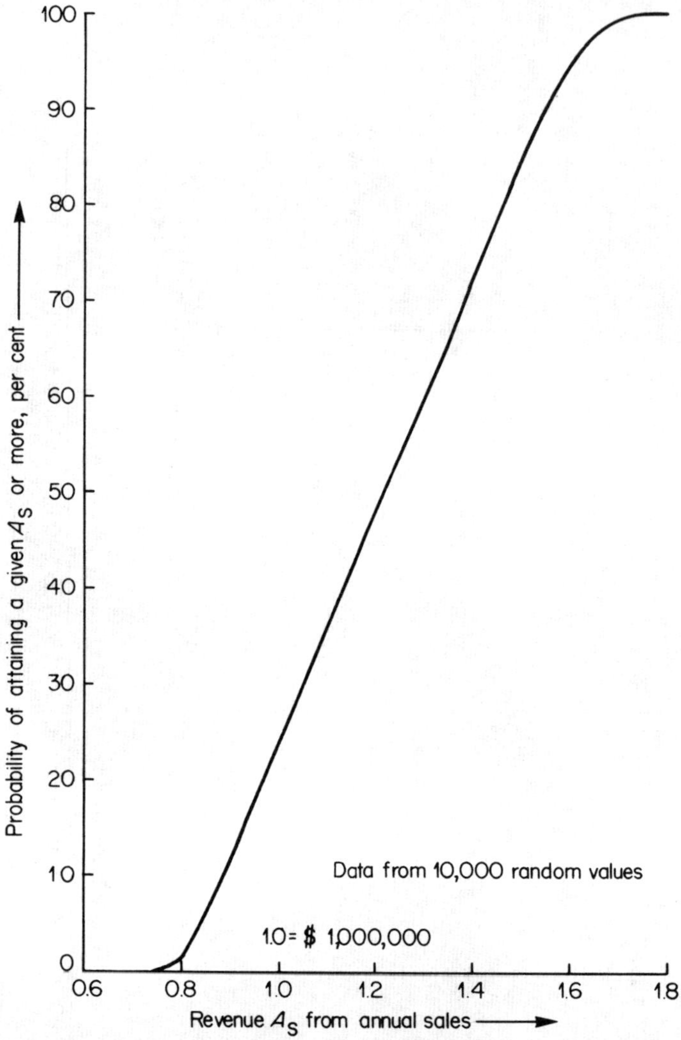

Figure (7.2-1f) Probability of attaining a given revenue A_s from annual sales or more against A_s

number is given by Equation (2.3-3) to be

$$A_s = Rc_s$$

$$= (1{,}370 \text{ ton/year})(\$852.5/\text{ton})$$

$$= \$1{,}167{,}900/\text{year}$$

TABLE (7.2-1)

Frequency distribution data for Example (7.2-1)

number in Monte Carlo sample	mid range value, $100,000/year																					
	7.5	8.0	8.5	9.0	9.5	10.0	10.5	11.0	11.5	12.0	12.5	13.0	13.5	14.0	14.5	15.0	15.5	16.0	16.5	17.0	17.5	18.0
1,000	0.10	1.70	5.00	6.00	6.30	5.80	7.30	5.10	7.40	5.70	4.80	7.90	5.50	5.60	4.90	6.20	6.00	3.40	3.80	1.30	0.20	0.00
2,000	0.05	1.45	4.95	6.55	5.60	5.80	6.70	5.40	6.95	5.75	5.45	6.65	6.15	5.85	5.45	6.05	5.85	4.15	3.30	1.65	0.25	0.00
3,000	0.07	1.50	4.60	6.63	5.83	5.47	6.93	5.70	6.77	5.73	5.97	6.20	6.17	6.27	5.30	5.90	5.53	4.50	3.20	1.43	0.30	0.00
4,000	0.08	1.43	4.37	6.35	6.05	5.82	6.20	5.90	6.78	5.70	5.97	6.20	6.00	6.13	5.75	5.93	5.42	4.68	3.37	1.50	0.37	0.00
5,000	0.06	1.30	4.40	5.98	5.96	6.08	6.18	5.70	6.76	5.92	6.04	6.10	6.12	5.98	6.02	5.98	5.40	4.52	3.42	1.72	0.36	0.00
6,000	0.08	1.28	4.40	5.98	5.80	6.12	6.28	5.73	6.45	5.97	6.03	6.13	6.15	5.95	5.88	6.05	5.53	4.57	3.42	1.70	0.50	0.00
7,000	0.11	1.23	4.43	5.96	5.80	5.90	6.34	5.79	6.30	6.06	6.01	6.27	6.07	6.14	5.83	5.90	5.77	4.64	3.29	1.67	0.49	0.00
8,000	0.11	1.25	4.45	5.96	5.89	5.84	6.20	5.93	6.40	5.94	5.94	6.29	6.04	6.19	5.81	5.91	5.65	4.75	3.31	1.71	0.43	0.00
9,000	0.11	1.30	4.50	5.91	5.81	5.92	6.10	5.78	6.49	5.96	5.82	6.37	6.09	6.22	5.76	6.07	5.60	4.67	3.42	1.69	0.41	0.00
10,000	0.12	1.30	4.58	5.94	5.82	5.93	6.16	5.70	6.43	6.07	5.86	6.17	6.07	6.25	5.82	6.09	5.59	4.61	3.33	1.76	0.40	0.00
total frequency based on 10,000 calculations	0.27	2.14	4.19	5.83	6.10	6.08	6.06	6.08	6.09	6.06	6.06	6.07	6.08	6.09	6.09	5.92	4.99	3.96	2.87	1.89	0.96	0.12

Note: values in the table are relative frequency x 100

The minimum possible value of the revenue A_S from annual sales is given by Equation (2.3-3) to be

$$\begin{aligned} A_S &= Rc_S \\ &= (1{,}000 \text{ ton/year})(\$750/\text{ton}) \\ &= \$750{,}000/\text{year} \end{aligned}$$

The maximum possible value of A_S is given by Equation (2.3-3) to be

$$\begin{aligned} A_S &= Rc_S \\ &= (2{,}000 \text{ ton/year})(\$900/\text{ton}) \\ &= \$1{,}800{,}000/\text{year} \end{aligned}$$

Divide this range of values of A_S into 22 intervals each of \$50,000/year. Note the frequency with which a random value of A_S falls inside a particular interval. The first random value of $A_S = \$1{,}167{,}900$/year falls inside the interval \$1,125,000/year to \$1,175,000/year. The relative frequency with which A_S falls inside a particular interval can be obtained from dividing the frequency by the total number of values of A_S calculated. Figure (7.2-1e) shows a histogram or plot of the relative frequency versus the midpoint value of each interval. Figure (7.2-1e) is used to plot the cumulative probability curve shown in Figure (7.2-1f). Table (7.2-1) lists a series of calculations done using a KDF9 digital computer up to a maximum of 10,000.

With 100 possible values of R and 100 possible values of c_S the frequency distribution of A_S can be determined exactly by 10,000 systematic calculations. It should be noted that even 10,000 random calculations do not duplicate exactly the frequencies given by systematic calculation. However, the frequency distribution could be adequately assessed with about 5,000 random calculations.

7.3 Utility Functions

Consider a proposed project in which there is a probability p_1 that a net present value of $(\text{NPV})_1$ will result, a probability p_2 that a net present value of $(\text{NPV})_2$ will result, etc. A weighted average $(\text{NPV})_w$ known as the expected value can be calculated from the equation

$$(\text{NPV})_w = p_1(\text{NPV})_1 + p_2(\text{NPV})_2 + \dots \qquad (4.5\text{-}2)$$

where

$$p_1 + p_2 + \dots = 1.0 \qquad (4.5\text{-}3)$$

Analogous equations may be written in terms of other quantities which measure profitability such as net profit.

Consider a contractor who stands to make a net profit of \$100,000 on a contract. The cost of preparing the bid on the contract is \$10,000. There are four competing contractors each with a probability $p_1 = 0.25$ of obtaining the contract. Thus each contractor has a probability $p_2 = 0.75$ of not obtaining the contract. Therefore the expected value of the project is (0.25)(\$100,000) + (0.75)(−\$10,000) = \$17,500. In this case the potential gain is ten times greater than the potential loss.

If the potential loss can bankrupt the company, then decisions are not necessarily made on the basis of expected value although the potential gain may be very high. Also decisions are not necessarily made on the basis of expected value if the potential loss is a relatively small amount of money to the company. Between these two extremes expected value can be a very useful criterion particularly for a company with a large number of projects.

A company may be considering a project with a very high potential rate of return and a low risk; yet it may prove impossible for the company to raise the money to start the project. Conversely, the company may be prepared to undertake an extremely risky project if the investment is trivial. Thus the attitude of a company to risk depends on the circumstances.

Money does not have the same value to each company or to each individual. A dollar may keep a pauper from starvation while being a trivial amount to the man who gave it to him. Attempts have been made to quantify a company's attitude to money, risk, and uncertainty[16] by asking businessmen a number of questions along the following lines:

Your company has signed a business contract with potential after tax proceeds of \$$P$. The probability of achieving this net gain of \$$P$ is say $p_1 = 0.75$ and the probability of a net loss of \$$P$ is $p_2 = 0.25$.

(i) If you would rather keep the contract, how much cash would you accept for your interest in it?

(ii) If you would rather be released from the contract, how much cash would you pay to be released from it?

The same questions may then be asked for different values of the probabilities p_1 and p_2. The answers to these questions can give an indication of the importance to the company of \$$P$ at various levels of risk.

The data in Table (7.3-1a) quantify an individual company's attitude to risk for the particular case of $P =$ \$100,000. These data are used to plot the utility curve in Figure (7.3-1). Positive values are the amounts of money which the company would accept in order to forgo their participation in the gamble. Negative values are the amounts of money which the company would pay in order to avoid participation in the gamble. It is only when the utility value and the expected value are the same that net present value (NPV) and discounted cash flow rate of return (DCFRR) can be justified as the investment criteria. However, since the utility curve has such a subjective basis, most companies prefer the objectivity of (NPV) and (DCFRR) over the range of

TABLE (7.3-1a)

The importance to the company of $100,000 at various levels of risk

probability of winning $100,000	money that the company would accept to avoid the gamble
0.0	- $100,000
0.1	- $ 25,000
0.2	+ $ 10,000
0.3	+ $ 35,000
0.4	+ $ 55,000
0.5	+ $ 70,000
0.6	+ $ 82,500
0.7	+ $ 90,000
0.8	+ $ 95,000
0.9	+ $ 97,500
1.0	+ $100,000

the normal income and expenditure budget. Subjective methods tends to be reserved for exceptional high risk projects.

It should be noted that a utility curve such as Figure (7.3-1) is specific to a certain sum of money. The curve is likely to be different for say $P = \$10,000$. Figure (7.3-1) can only be used to consider projects which fall within the range $-\$100,000$ to $+\$100,000$. Other utility curves must be used to cover projects which lie outside this range.

Swalm[20] found that many business executives had difficulty in appreciating fine shades of odds and confined his considerations to even money bets. He asked various business executives to state what guaranteed sum of money they considered equivalent to a gamble related to the toss of a coin. If the coin fell on one side they would win a given sum of money and if the coin fell on the other side they would get nothing. Swalm started by considering a sum of money equivalent to twice the maximum expenditure that the executive could authorize in one year. This was used to obtain a utility which in turn was used as the new prize to obtain a further utility. In this way a utility curve can be sketched. Swalm chose an arbitrary utility scale based on a range -120 utiles to $+120$ utiles. It should be noted that it is as incorrect to compare utiles by ratio as it is to imply that an object at 80 °F is twice as hot as an object at 40 °F.

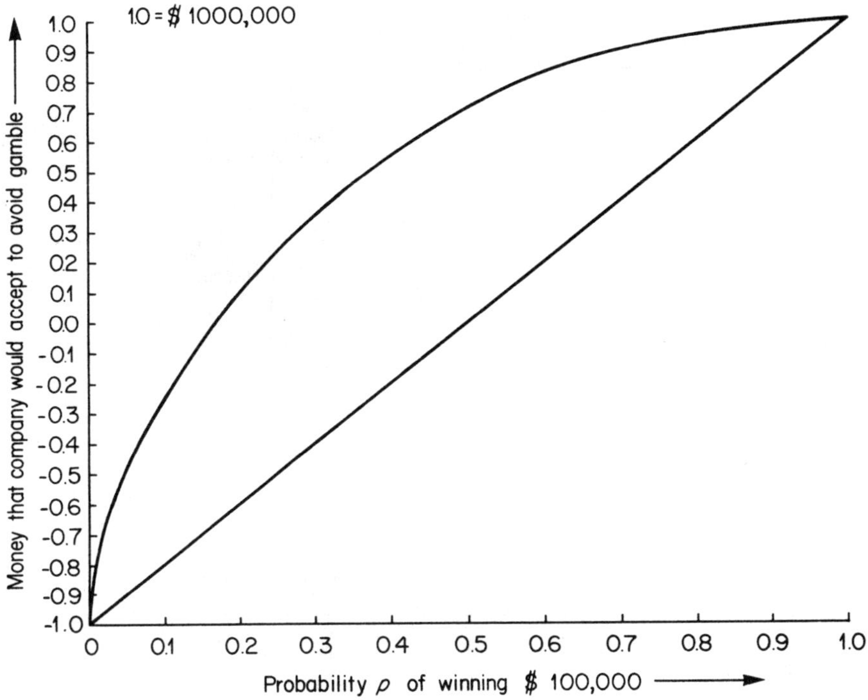

Figure (7.3-1) Utility function for $100,000

Swalm found that most executives are conservative and that the patterns of their curves are very similar when based on twice their authorized expenditure even though they may appear to differ quite widely when plotted in terms of absolute money values. The curves also show that executives tend to be more conservative when considering a loss than they do when considering a reduced gain.

Example (7.3-1)

A company is considering investment in one or more of three projects A, B, and C. Evaluate the investment priorities on the basis of the following data:

(i) the company's attitude to winning or losing $100,000 represented by the data on Table (7.3-1a) which are plotted in Figure (7.3-1)

(ii) the probabilities of attaining various net present values (NPV) listed in the third column of Table (7.3-1b).

Required equations:

$$(NPV)_w = p_1(NPV)_1 + p_2(NPV)_2 + \dots \qquad (4.5\text{-}2)$$

TABLE (7.3-1b)

Comparison of projects in terms of utility

project	(NPV) $	probability p	equivalent probability of winning $100,000	probable utility	expected value $	expected utility $
	95,000	0.1	0.80	0.080	9,500	8,000
A	45,000	0.8	0.34	0.272	36,000	27,200
	-75,000	0.1	0.03	0.003	- 7,500	300
		1.0		0.355	38,000	35,500
	50,000	0.2	0.37	0.074	10,000	7,400
B	20,000	0.6	0.23	0.138	12,000	13,800
	-60,000	0.2	0.04	0.008	-12,000	800
		1.0		0.220	10,000	22,000
	45,000	0.1	0.35	0.035	4,500	3,500
C	10,000	0.6	0.20	0.120	6,000	12,000
	-60,000	0.3	0.04	0.012	-18,000	1,200
		1.0		0.167	- 7,500	16,700

$$p_1 + p_2 + \ldots = 1.0 \tag{4.5-3}$$

Equation (4.5-2) gives the expected value of the net present value $(\text{NPV})_w$. For project A, $(\text{NPV})_w$ is given by Equation (4.5-2) to be

$$\begin{aligned}(\text{NPV})_w &= p_1(\text{NPV})_1 + p_2(\text{NPV})_2 + \ldots \\ &= (0.1)(\$95{,}000) + (0.8)(\$45{,}000) + (0.1)(-\$75{,}000) \\ &= \$9{,}500 + \$36{,}000 - \$7{,}500 \\ &= \$38{,}000\end{aligned}$$

The corresponding values for projects B and C are calculated in the same way and are listed in Table (7.3-1b).

In project A the probability $p = 0.1$ for (NPV) = \$95,000. Table (7.3-1a) and Figure (7.3-1) show that \$95,000 is the amount of money that this company would pay for a 0.8 probability of gaining \$100,000 together with a 0.2 probability of losing \$100,000.

In this case a probability $p = 0.1$ of attaining \$95,000 is equivalent to a probable utility of $(0.1)(0.8) = 0.08$ of gaining \$100,000.

Equation (4.5-2) can be used to calculate the expected utility if the probabilities p_1, p_2, etc., are replaced by the probable utilities and the net present values $(\text{NPV})_1$, $(\text{NPV})_2$, etc., are each replaced by \$100,000. For project A the expected utility

$$\begin{aligned} &= (0.1)(0.8)(\$100{,}000) + (0.8)(0.34)(\$100{,}000) \\ &\quad + (0.1)(0.03)(\$100{,}000) \\ &= \$8{,}000 + \$27{,}200 + \$300 \\ &= \$35{,}500 \end{aligned}$$

The corresponding values for projects B and C are calculated in the same way and are listed in Table (7.3-1b).

The straight line in Figure (7.3-1) represents the situation in which the expected value and the expected utility are equal over the range −\$100,000 to \$100,000. In this case decisions can be taken on the basis of the highest expected value as a routine matter. In other cases decisions should be made on the basis of the highest expected utility. The utility curve Figure (7.3-1) represents the attitude of the management to \$100,000. This curve should be updated as the company's business position changes.

In the present case, the utility curve is above the straight line. This represents a tendency on the part of the company's decision makers to gamble.

The investment priorities should be to implement project A and then, if finance is available, project B.

It might appear that project C should also be considered in view of the expected utility of \$16,700. However, it is better to do nothing than implement project C. The utility of doing nothing which is equivalent to paying \$0, is read from Figure (7.3-1) to be 0.17. This gives a corresponding probable utility of $(1.0)(0.17)(\$100{,}000) = \$17{,}000$. This is a better result than investing in project C.

In this example the order of priorities based on expected utilities is the same as that based on expected values. However, this will not necessarily be so in every case. In this example the order of priorities is clear cut on the basis of expected value but much less so on the basis of expected utility.

7.4 Curve Fitting and Trend Analysis

The conventional way of determining the relationship between two variables is to plot the available data on graph paper. This is done in a variety of ways until the shape of the data scatter suggests a form of equation. The best apparent curve may be drawn through the points. The constants of the equation which represents the curve may then be calculated. Alternatively statistical means may be used to calculate the constants of the equation which best fits the data. The curve can then be drawn from the resulting equation.

Although data points will rarely lie on the curve, confidence limits may be given which indicate the probability of actual values differing from those predicted by the curve by more than a given amount.

In addition to straight line relationships, power law, exponential, and S-shaped curves are all met with in economic studies.

Straight line relationships: These are represented by the equation

$$y = ax + b \tag{7.4-1}$$

It is the simplest and most generally useful of all curves. Quite small deviations from a straight line can be judged by eye. The best values of the constants a and b can readily be obtained by the method of least squares.

Consider a plot of y against x in which there are n pairs of values $(x_1,y_1),\ldots,(x_n,y_n)$. The vertical distance of any data point (x_i,y_i) from the straight line given by Equation (7.4-1) is $(y_i - ax_i - b)$. The best straight line through the points can be obtained by the method of least squares. This is based on choosing the constants a and b in Equation (7.4-1) so that the sum of the squares of these vertical distances $\sum (y_i - ax_i - b)^2$ is a minimum.

It can be shown[8] that for the best straight line, the constants in Equation (7.4-1) are given by the equations

$$a = \frac{n \sum x_i y_i - \sum x_i \sum y_i}{n \sum x_i^2 - (\sum x_i)^2} \tag{7.4-2}$$

and

$$b = \bar{y} - a\bar{x} \tag{7.4-3}$$

where the mean value of x is

$$\bar{x} = \frac{x_1 + x_2 + x_3 + \ldots x_n}{n} \tag{7.1-1}$$

and the mean value of y is

$$\bar{y} = \frac{y_1 + y_2 + y_3 + \ldots y_n}{n} \tag{7.4-4}$$

Since a straight line plot is more desirable than any other, data which cannot be represented by a straight line on ordinary Cartesian coordinate paper, should also be plotted on semi-log and log–log coordinate paper. If the data plotted on semi-log paper fall on a straight line, the line can be represented by one of the following two equations:

$$\log y = ax + b \tag{7.4-5}$$

$$y = a \log x + b \tag{7.4-6}$$

If the data plotted on log–log paper fall on a straight line, the line can be represented by the equation

$$\log y = a \log x + b \tag{7.4-7}$$

Power law curves: A curve with a single maximum or minimum can often be represented by the quadratic equation

$$y = ax^2 + bx + c \tag{7.4-8}$$

It is common for a curve to have a maximum followed by a minimum or vice versa. Such curves have a point of inflexion and can be represented by the cubic equation

$$y = ax^3 + bx^2 + cx + d \tag{7.4-9}$$

Equations containing higher powers are not normally met with in economic analysis.

Exponential curves: These curves represent natural growth and decay where the rate of change is proportional to the value of the independent variable. The parent curve is represented by the equation

$$y = a \exp(bx) \tag{7.4-10}$$

which is best handled in the form of Equation (7.4-5). The slope increases if b is positive and decreases if b is negative.

An extremely rapid rate of change can be represented by the equation

$$\log y = a \exp(bx) \tag{7.4-11}$$

S-*shaped curves:* These are common in economic studies. If a product is sold on the basis of personal recommendation, the rate of sale will depend on the number of people who have bought the product. Thus initially sales will increase exponentially. Eventually the market will be saturated and only replacement purchases will be made. This situation is represented by the logistic curve[11] which is defined by the equation

$$y = \frac{c}{1 + a \exp(-bx)} \tag{0.4-12}$$

This curve is asymptotic to $y = 0$ when $x \to -\infty$ and to $y = c$ when $x \to +\infty$. The position of the x axis may be adjusted by adding a suitable constant to the independent variable to ensure that the corrected variable, y, becomes asymptotic to zero. The point of inflexion of the logistic curve occurs at

$y = c/2$ and the curve is skew symmetric about this point. It is, therefore, not permissible to adjust the position of the y axis in a similar way.

It is often useful to fit such an equation to an existing curve. In general, after adjusting the range of y from 0 to c, the value of c can be read from the curve as the value of the upper asymptote. The value of b can be obtained with the aid of an auxiliary variable

$$T = x\ (\text{at } y = 0.88c) - x\ (\text{at } y = 0.12c) \tag{7.4-13}$$

and

$$b = \frac{3.985}{T} \cong \frac{4}{T} \tag{7.4-14}$$

If y has a readable positive value when $x = 0$ then

$$a = \frac{c}{y\ (\text{at } x = 0)} - 1 \tag{7.4-15}$$

If y is very close to zero when $x = 0$ then a is best obtained by substitution of the value of x at $y = c/2$ into Equation (7.4-12) when

$$a = \exp\left[bx\ (\text{at } y = 0.5c)\right] \tag{7.4-16}$$

The effect of an advertising campaign is usually to increase the rate of increase of sales at the beginning. It may also increase the level of the mature demand for the product, but satisfaction of the market demand will always lead to a finite upper limit of sales. This situation can often be represented by the Gompertz curve[11] which is defined by the equation

$$\ln y = \ln c - a \exp(-bx) \tag{7.4-17}$$

which has its point of inflexion at $y = c/\exp(1)$.

As with the logistic curve, y must range from 0 to c as x ranges from $-\infty$ to $+\infty$.

$$b = \frac{2.808}{T} \tag{7.4-18}$$

If y has a readable positive value when $x = 0$ then

$$a = \ln\left[\frac{c}{y\ (\text{at } x = 0)}\right] \tag{7.4-19}$$

If y is close to zero when $x = 0$ then a is best obtained by substitution of the value of x at $y = c/\exp(1) = c/2.7183$ into Equation (7.4-17) when

$$a = \exp\left[bx\ (\text{at } y = 0.3679c)\right] \tag{7.4-20}$$

These curves can represent cumulative frequency or probability density data. The frequency or probability density curves can be represented by the differentiated forms of the logistic and Gompertz equations written respectively as Equations (7.4-21) and (7.4-22).

$$f(x) = \frac{\mathrm{d}y}{\mathrm{d}x} = \frac{abc \exp(-bx)}{[1 + a \exp(-bx)]^2} \tag{7.4-21}$$

$$f(x) = \frac{\mathrm{d}y}{\mathrm{d}x} = yab \exp(-bx) \tag{7.4-22}$$

Since the mean and the mode of the logistic curve coincide, it can be used to represent the cumulative frequency curve of a symmetrical frequency curve such as a Normal curve.

The Gompertz curve can be used to represent a frequency curve with a moderate amount of positive skewness.

Business tends to be cyclic and sales and prices are subject to both short term and long term fluctuations. Regular patterns are frequently blurred by random variations. Hence, curves fitted to economic data will seldom pass through all the data points and there will be some uncertainty as to the exact location of the trend line. The standard deviation can be obtained from the scatter of data about the line. This in turn enables confidence limits to be established.

Seasonal trends can be examined by averaging the available data for corresponding days, weeks, or months. The data can often be made to lie on a simple curve, such as a straight line, by deliberately distorting the time axis. Long term fluctuations can often be smoothed out by using a moving average.

Example (7.4-1)

The annual sales history of product *A* is given in Table (7.4-1a). Make an estimate of the likely range of sales for 1971 with a certainty of 95 per cent.

Required equations:

$$y = ax + b \tag{7.4-1}$$

$$a = \frac{n \sum x_i y_i - \sum x_i \sum y_i}{n \sum x_i^2 - (\sum x_i)^2} \tag{7.4-2}$$

$$b = \bar{y} - a\bar{x} \tag{7.4-3}$$

$$\bar{x} = \frac{x_1 + x_2 + x_3 + \ldots x_n}{n} \tag{7.1-1}$$

$$\bar{y} = \frac{y_1 + y_2 + y_3 + \ldots y_n}{n} \tag{7.4-4}$$

TABLE (7.4-1a)

year	annual sales ton	five year moving average ton	predicted moving average ton
1951	5,800		
1952	6,800		
1953	7,800	6,900	6,865
1954	7,300	7,100	7,079
1955	6,800	7,100	7,294
1956	6,800	7,300	7,509
1957	6,800	7,500	7,724
1958	8,800	8,100	7,938
1959	8,300	8,400	8,153
1960	9,800	8,500	8,368
1961	8,300	8,800	8,582
1962	7,300	8,800	8,797
1963	10,300	9,100	9,012
1964	8,300	9,200	9,226
1965	11,300	9,400	9,441
1966	8,800	9,700	9,656
1967	8,300	9,800	9,871
1968	11,800	9,900	10,085
1969	8,800		
1970	11,800		

Plot the raw data as in Figure (7.4-1) which shows that the data are cyclic with a period of about five years.

Calculate the five-year average centered on 1953 which includes years 1951 through 1955 to be

$$\frac{(5{,}800 + 6{,}800 + 7{,}800 + 7{,}300 + 6{,}800)\ \text{ton}}{5} = 6{,}900\ \text{ton}$$

Values for subsequent years are calculated in the same way, listed in Table (7.4-1a), and plotted in Figure (7.4-1). The plot illustrates the dampening effect of the moving average on the variations.

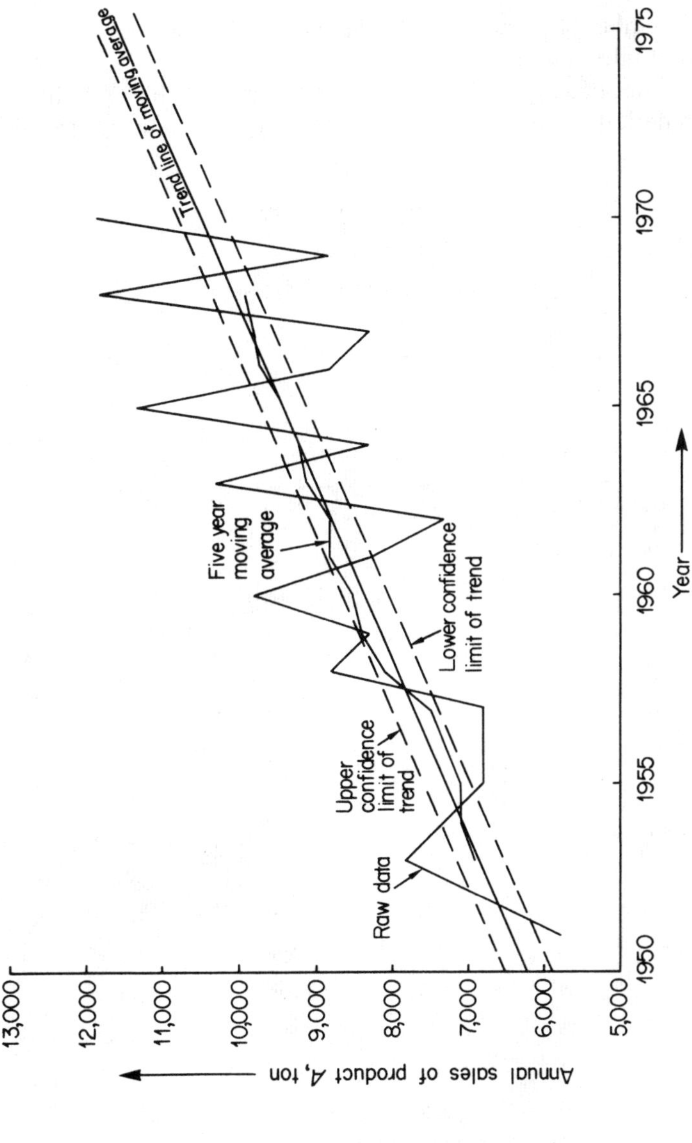

Figure (7.4-1) Annual sales of a product against time

Fit a straight line to the moving average data using the method of least squares. In Equation (7.4-1)

$$y = ax + b$$

let x be the number of years taking 1953 as year 3, 1954 as year 4 etc., and let y be the annual sales in tons.

List the values of x, $y/1{,}000$, x^2, and $xy/1{,}000$ as in Table (7.4-1b).

The summations of the individual values of x, y, x^2 and xy are calculated to be

$$\sum x_i = 168$$

$$\sum y_i = (135.6)(1{,}000)$$

$$\sum x_i^2 = 2{,}104$$

$$\text{and} \quad \sum x_i y_i = (1{,}496.8)(1{,}000)$$

respectively.

TABLE (7.4-1b)

year	x_i	$y_i/1{,}000$	x_i^2	$x_i y_i/1{,}000$
1953	3	6.9	9	20.7
1954	4	7.1	16	28.4
1955	5	7.1	25	35.5
1956	6	7.3	36	43.8
1957	7	7.5	49	52.5
1958	8	8.1	64	64.8
1959	9	8.4	81	75.6
1960	10	8.5	100	85.0
1961	11	8.8	121	96.8
1962	12	8.8	144	105.6
1963	13	9.1	169	118.3
1964	14	9.2	196	128.8
1965	15	9.4	225	141.0
1966	16	9.7	256	155.2
1967	17	9.8	289	166.6
1968	18	9.9	324	178.2
sum	168	135.6	2104	1496.8
mean	10.5	8.475		

The mean value of x is given by Equation (7.1-1) to be

$$\bar{x} = \frac{x_1 + x_2 + x_3 + \dots x_n}{n}$$
$$= \frac{\sum x_i}{n} = \frac{168}{16}$$
$$= 10.5$$

The mean value of y is given by Equation (7.4-4) to be

$$\bar{y} = \frac{y_1 + y_2 + y_3 + \dots y_n}{n}$$
$$= \frac{\sum y_i}{n} = \frac{(135.6)(1{,}000)}{16}$$
$$= (8.475)(1{,}000)$$

The value of a in Equation (7.4-1) is given by Equation (7.4-2) to be

$$a = \frac{n \sum x_i y_i - \sum x_i \sum y_i}{n \sum x_i^2 - (\sum x_i)^2}$$
$$= \frac{(16)(1{,}496.8)(1{,}000) - (168)(135.6)(1{,}000)}{(16)(2{,}104) - (168)^2}$$
$$= 214.7$$

The value of b in Equation (7.4-1) is given by Equation (7.4-3) to be

$$b = \bar{y} - a\bar{x}$$
$$= (8.475)(1{,}000) - (214.7)(10.5)$$
$$= 6{,}220.6$$

Substitute these values of a and b in Equation (7.4-1) to give

$$y = ax + b$$
$$= 214.7x + 6{,}220.6$$

which is a straight line representing the trend of the five-year moving average. This equation is used to calculate the predicted values of the moving average of annual sales listed in the fourth column of Table (7.4-1a).

The standard deviation of the data σ from this straight line is calculated by the method described in Example (7.1-1) to be $\sigma = 149.8$ ton so that $2\sigma = 299.6$ ton. Since $\pm 2\sigma$ represents the 95 per cent confidence limits, these are shown as ± 300 ton on either side of the trend line in Figure (7.4-1)

The equation

$$y = 214.7x + 6{,}220.6$$

predicts a moving average of 10,300 ton for 1969. This is equivalent to a total of (5)(10,300 ton) = 51,500 ton for the five-year period 1967 to 1971. Thus the predicted annual sales of product A for 1971 is

$$(51{,}500 - 8{,}300 - 11{,}800 - 8{,}800 - 11{,}800) \text{ ton} = 10{,}800 \text{ ton}$$

Since the moving average is within ±300 ton in 95 per cent of cases the predicted range of sales for 1971 is 10,500 to 11,100 ton.

The moving average should be used with caution. Predictions should be limited to one or two years ahead.

7.5 Linear Programming[9,10,13]

If a variable c is a linear function of several other variables x_1, x_2, etc., it can be written in the form

$$c = k_1 x_1 + k_2 x_2 + \dots k_n x_n \tag{7.1-9}$$

where k_1, k_2, etc. are constants.

Frequently variables are subject to constraints such that

$$k_1 x_1 + k_2 x_2 + \dots k_n x_n \leqslant c$$

or

$$k_1 x_1 + k_2 x_2 + \dots k_n x_n \geqslant c$$

where c is called the objective function. Linear programming is a method of maximizing or minimizing such an objective function which is subject to constraints. In Example (7.5-1) the annual cash income A_{CI} is the objective function which is to be maximized. Alternatively cost could be taken as the objective function which would need to be minimized.

Example (7.5-1) is a very simple problem concerned with the production of two products in the optimum ratio. It would not be possible to use a graphical solution with more than three products since graphical methods are limited to three dimensions. Dantzig[12] developed the simplex method to handle multidimensional problems. The simplex method is well adapted to iterative solution using a digital computer.

In addition to production planning, linear programming has been used in blending problems, transportation problems, and budget planning.

Example (7.5-1)

A company manufactures two alternative products using batch processing. Products 1 and 2 produce cash incomes of \$0.15/lb and \$0.12/lb respectively. Either product can be made in either of two batch processing units A and B. Both A and B units have a capacity of 1,000 lb/batch of either product.

The overall batch cycle times for product 1 are 3 hours in unit A and 4 hours in unit B. The overall batch cycle times for product 2 are 5 hours in unit A and 2 hours in unit B. Units A and B are available for processing for not more than 6,000 hour/year and 4,800 hour/year respectively. An annual cash income less than \$150,000/year is unacceptable.

Determine the usage of the processing units to give the maximum cash income. Plot a graph to illustrate the relationship between the variables and the constraints.

Let n_{A1} and n_{A2} be the number of batches processed per year of products 1 and 2 respectively in unit A. Let n_{B1} and n_{B2} be the number of batches processed per year of products 1 and 2 respectively in unit B.

Since the overall batch cycle times for products 1 and 2 are 3 hours and 5 hours in unit A and unit A is available for not more than 6,000 hour/year then

$$3n_{A1} + 5n_{A2} \leqslant 6{,}000$$

Since the overall batch cycle times for products 1 and 2 are 4 hours and 2 hours in unit B and unit B is available for not more than 4,800 hour/year then

$$4n_{B1} + 2n_{B2} \leqslant 4{,}800$$

Plot the linear equation

$$3n_{A1} + 5n_{A2} = 6{,}000$$

as line jf in Figure (7.5-1)
and the linear equation

$$4n_{B1} + 2n_{B2} = 4{,}800$$

as line ci in Figure (7.5-1).

Since products 1 and 2 produce cash incomes of \$0.15/lb and \$0.12/lb respectively and all batches are 1,000 lb/batch the annual cash income A_{CI} for the overall processing system is

$$A_{CI} = 150n_1 + 120n_2$$

in \$/year where n_1 and n_2 are the number of batches of products 1 and 2 respectively produced per year irrespective of the processing unit used. $A_{CI}(\text{min}) = \$150{,}000$.

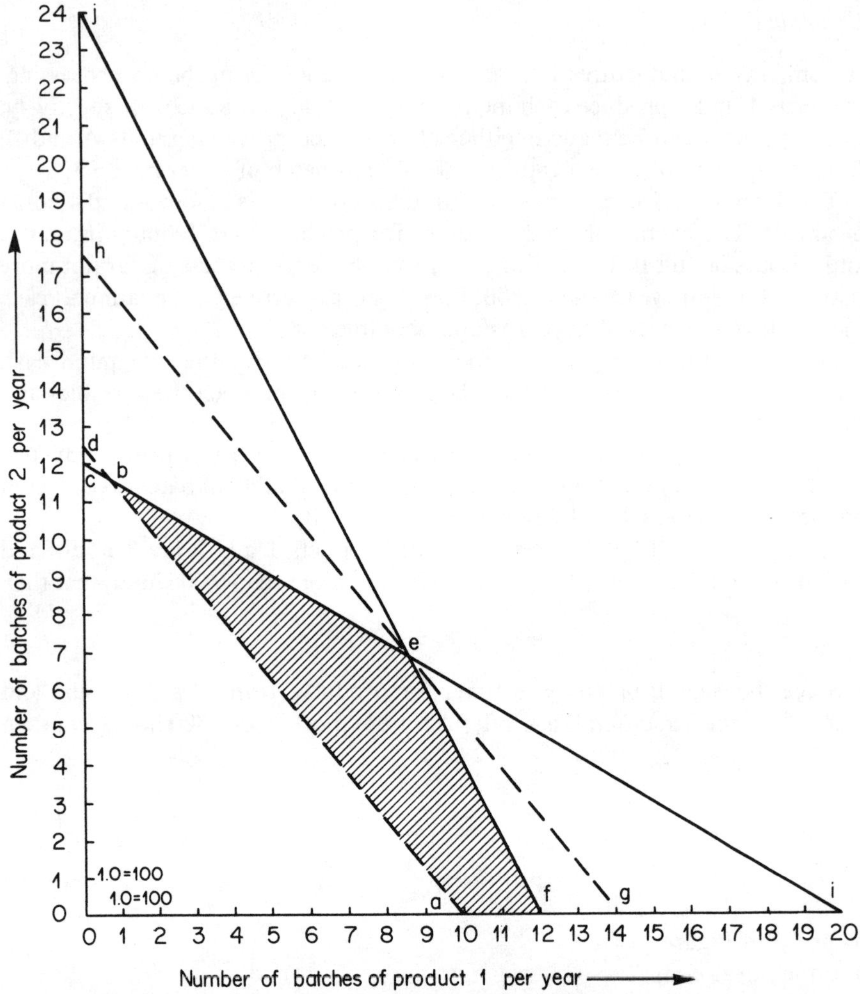

Figure (7.5-1) Graphical illustration of simple linear programming for batch processing

Plot the linear equation

$$150n_1 + 120n_2 = 150{,}000$$

as line ad in Figure (7.5-1).

The specified constraints limit the possible region of operation to the area shown as abef in Figure (7.5-1).

The two linear equations

$$3n_1 + 5n_2 = 6{,}000$$

and $4n_1 + 2n_2 = 4{,}800$

intersect at point e.
Solve the above simultaneous equations to give

$$n_1 = 857.1$$

and $n_2 = 685.7$ for point e.

Since only whole batches are produced write

$$n_1 = 857$$

and $n_2 = 685$.

The maximum utilization of the two processing units is accomplished at point e.
Thus the maximum cash income is

$$A_{CI} = (150)(857) + (120)(685)$$
$$= \$210{,}750/\text{year}$$

Plot the linear equation

$$150n_1 + 120n_2 = 210{,}750$$

as line gh in Figure (7.5-1).

It should be noted that lines ad and gh represent conditions under which the annual cash income is the same. Lines parallel to, and between, ad and gh, represent all possible, and acceptable, annual cash incomes lower than the maximum.

References for Chapter 7

1. Burlington, R. S., and May, D. C., 'Handbook of Probability and Statistics with Tables', 2nd ed., p. 105, New York, McGraw–Hill Book Co. Inc., 1970
2. Ibid., p. 110
3. Ibid., p. 347
4. Ibid., p. 367
5. Croxton, F. E., Cowden, D. J., and Bolch, B. W., 'Practical Business Statistics', 4th ed., p. 72, New Jersey, Prentice–Hall Inc., 1969
6. Ibid., p. 76
7. Ibid., p. 85
8. Davis, O. L. (Ed.), 'Statistical Methods in Research and Production', 3rd ed., p. 194, London, Oliver and Boyd, 1957
9. Gass, S. I., 'Linear Programming', New York, McGraw–Hill Book Co. Inc., 1958

10. Garvin, W. W., 'Introduction to Linear Programming', New York, McGraw–Hill Book Co. Inc., 1960
11. Gregg, J. V., Horsell, C. H., and Richardson, J. T., 'Mathematical Trend Curves', p. 24, London, Oliver and Boyd, 1964
12. Koopmans, T. C. (Ed.), 'Activity Analysis of Production and Allocation', Chapter XXI, New York, John Wiley and Sons, Inc., 1951
13. Loomba, N. P., 'Linear Programming', New York, McGraw–Hill Book Co. Inc., 1964
14. Reilley, P. M., and Johri, H. P., *Chem. Eng.*, **76**, No. 7 (1969)
15. Rudd, D. F., and Watson, C. C., 'Strategy of Process Engineering', p. 333, New York, John Wiley and Sons, Inc., 1968
16. Schlaifer, R., 'Probability and Statistics for Business Decisions', p. 34, New York, McGraw–Hill Book Co. Inc., 1959
17. Ibid., p. 176
18. Ibid., p. 209
19. Ibid., p. 275
20. Swalm, R. O., *Harvard Business Review*, **44**, 6 (1966)
21. Thorngren, J. T., *Chem. Eng.*, **74**, No. 17 (1967)

Problems for Chapter 7

(7.1-1) Consider an event which must either occur with a probability p_1 or fail to occur with a probability $p_2 = 1 - p_1$. The chance of x successes occurring in n trials is given by the term containing p_1^x in the binomial expansion of $(p_1 + p_2)^n$ provided that the value of p_1 does not vary from trial to trial. The combined probability of two independent events both occurring is the product of the probabilities of the individual events. If a six-sided dice is thrown, the probability of any particular number in the range 1 to 6 occurring is 1/6. Thus the probability of say 5 occurring followed by 6 is $(1/6)^2 = 1/36$. Use this information to deduce the relative frequency of various totals occurring in four throws of a six-sided dice. Plot the resulting data in the form of a histogram.

(7.1-2) Use Equations (7.1-2) and a modified form of (7.1-4) to calculate the mean and standard deviation for the distribution in Problem (7.1-1). Use these values in Equation (7.1-3) to calculate the relative frequency of occurrence of each total on the assumption that the distribution is normal. Compare the result with the distribution in Problem (7.1-1).

The modified form of Equation (7.1-4) is

$$s^* = \left[\frac{\sum (x_i - \bar{x})\, f(x_i)}{1 - (1/n)}\right]^{0.5}$$

where in this case $f(x_i)$ is the relative frequency and n is the total number of events in the distribution which is taken as continuous where $n \to \infty$.

(7.1-3) For a normal frequency distribution the mean may be taken at the centre of the range of certainty and the standard deviation as one-eighth of the range of certainty. On this basis use Equation (7.1-6) and Table (A2-1) to estimate the frequency distribution of totals of four throws of a six-sided dice. Compare the result with the distribution in Problem (7.1-1).

(7.2-1) A store, which opens five days per week, is to promote a new product. The manager believes that not more than five units will be sold in any one day but he cannot be more precise about the probable sales pattern. Stocks are delivered to the store once per week. What size should the first stock order be to give a 95 per cent certainty of meeting demand? For a normal frequency distribution the mean may be taken at the centre of the range of certainty and the standard deviation as one-eighth of the range of certainty.

(7.2-2) The IBM Manual 'Random Number Generation and Testing (IBM, 1959)' recommends the recursion formula

$$X_{j+1} = 10011 X_j \text{ (modulo 1)}$$

for the generation of pseudo-random numbers in the range zero to unity. The notation (modulo 1), requires that only the fractional part of the product is retained.

Write a computer subprogram RANDOM (N) to generate a series of pseudo-random numbers using this relationship. The first call of the subprogram, RANDOM (1), should read in an eight-digit integer to represent X_0. Subsequent calls of RANDOM (0) should generate successive members of this random number series.

Write a computer program to print out 50 rows each containing 10 four-digit integers.

(7.2-3) Write a computer program, using the subprogram RANDOM (N) of Problem (7.2-2), to produce frequency distribution data for Example (7.2-1). This is most directly done by increasing the frequency of occurrence of a mid-range value by unity each time a result falls in that range. The exact count will depend on the starting number chosen for RANDOM (1).

A relative frequency table such as Table (7.2-1) can be constructed by dividing each frequency by the total number in the Monte Carlo sample.

(7.3-1) The company in Example (7.3-1) is considering investment in one or more of three projects A, B, and C. Call this company X. Company X knows that competing companies Y and Z are also interested in projects A, B, and C. Past contracts indicate that an equal chance of gaining or losing \$100,000 has a utility of \$0 to company Y and a utility of −\$70,000 to company Z. Use this information and the method of Problem (7.4-2) to establish approximate utility curves for companies Y and Z.

Determine the expected utilities of contracts A, B, and C to companies

Y and Z by the method of Example (7.3-1). If company X has time to prepare a tender for only one project recommend the one most likely to be successful.

(7.4-1) A certain company's attitude to winning or losing \$100,000 is represented by the data in Table (7.3-1b). These data are plotted to give the utility curve in Figure (7.3-1).

Fit three quadratic equations of the form of Equation (7.4-8)

$$y = ax^2 + bx + c \tag{7.4-8}$$

to the data for the points $p = 0.0$, 0.2, 0.5, 0.8, and 1.0 listed in Table (7.3-1b). Plot the resulting composite curve and compare with Figure (7.3-1).

(7.4-2) The shape of the utility curve in Figure (7.3-1) is similar to the vapor–liquid equilibrium curve for an ideal binary mixture which is represented by the equation

$$y = \frac{ax}{1 + (a-1)x}$$

where x and y are variables in the range 0 to 1 and a is a constant.

On the basis of $P = +\$70{,}000$ for $p = 0.5$ in Figure (7.3-1b), construct an approximate utility curve using the above equation with y as a normalized value of P and $x = p$. Compare the curve with Figure (7.3-1).

(7.4-3) Fit a logistic curve, defined by Equation (7.4-12), to the curve of Figure (7.1-1b). Compare values calculated from the equation to this logistic curve with the data in Table (7.1-1a).

(7.4-4) Fit a Gompertz curve, defined by Equation (7.4-17), to the curve of Figure (7.1-1b). Compare values calculated from the equation to this Gompertz curve with the data in Table (7.1-1a).

(7.4-5) Use Equations (7.4-21) and (7.4-22) to establish the probability distribution curves underlying the logistic and Gompertz curves derived in Problems (7.4-3) and (7.4-4). Compare the distribution curves obtained.

Chapter 8

Management Considerations

Since top management operates within a broad context of financial and cost accounting, it is an advantage for process engineers to have some knowledge of these subjects. Process engineers involved in investment appraisal tend to be mainly influenced by the technical merits of a process. In contrast top management are more likely to be concerned with price and cost trends, value engineering, cost benefit analysis, marketing, risk, and insurance.

Risks for a company occur in the areas of finance, technology, and politics. The political risks range from Government legislation to labor problems which, although unavoidable, may be foreseeable. The seeds of business failure are sown in the early stages of planning and it is essential to recognize areas of potential failure as early as possible. It is the responsibility of process engineers to make top management aware of any areas of potential technological failure. In plant design, technological innovation should be kept to a minimum and should never be introduced merely for innovation's sake. The risk of technological failure can be reduced by incorporating well proven stages of processes in a plant design wherever possible. Sometimes a new plant will not work. Top management may have been aware that technical problems existed but may have been persuaded by the enthusiasm of their engineers that all such problems would be solved by the start up date.

Park[13] gave three criteria for business success: a superior product, a capable company, and a favorable business environment. Park said that if all three factors are merely comparable to competition, then the relative probability of venture success is only 25 per cent. If one factor is better than competition and the other two factors are comparable, then the relative probability of venture success is 40 per cent. This figure is increased to 60 per cent if two factors are better than competition and one factor is comparable. Park's method provides a rough but rapid and objective method for screening proposed new ventures.

8.1 Financial Accounting

Accounting is the language of business. Financial statements are both the basis and the result of management decisions. They can tell a manager a great deal about his company provided that he can interpret the information correctly. Since in the process industries a fair allocation of costs requires considerable technical knowledge of the operations, a close liaison between the senior process engineers and the accountants in a company is desirable. Thus the success of a company depends on a combination of financial, technical, and managerial skills.

In financial accounting, a double entry system is used to record completed transactions. The system can be represented by the equation

$$\text{debits} = \text{credits} \tag{8.1-1}$$

In each business transaction it is the convention that the account of the giver is credited and the account of the receiver is debited with the same amount of money. Transactions are entered daily into an account known as the journal. The data are subsequently summarized and transferred to an account known as the ledger. The procedure is called posting.

There are two main classes of accounts, real accounts and nominal accounts. Real accounts are divided into those representing the assets and those representing the liabilities of a company. Assets are the items owned and liabilities are the debts owed by a company. The debts may either be to the owners or to others. Ownership is the monetary value of the assets of a company. Ownership is also referred to as capital, equity or net worth.

All accounting is based on the equation

$$\text{assets} = \text{liabilities} + \text{ownership} + \text{profits} \tag{8.1-2}$$

Equation (8.1-2) is true at any given time. Although it may appear odd that ownership and profit are considered to be liabilities, it should be remembered that a business is regarded as a person in its own right. Thus even in a business owned by one individual, the business has a liability to repay to the individual his invested capital together with any profits.

Since profit is the revenue from sales minus the associated expenses, Equation (8.1-2) can be written in the form

$$\text{assets} + \text{expenses} = \text{liabilities} + \text{ownership} + \text{revenue from sales} \tag{8.1-3}$$

Nominal accounts are the revenue and expense accounts which form part of the ownership or capital accounts. At the end of each accounting period, nominal accounts are closed by transferring the balances to the capital accounts. The financial position of a company at a particular time is represented by the balance sheet. The latter is a graphic display of individual balances which are based on Equation (8.1-2). Nominal accounts are used to prepare the income statement for a given period which includes any necessary adjustments for depreciation and taxes etc.

For a period of one year, the total cash income A_{CI} arising from the sales of all the products of a company can be expressed by Equation (2.3-1).

$$A_{CI} = [A_S - (A_{VGE} + A_{VME})] - (A_{FGE} + A_{FME}) \tag{2.3-1}$$

where A_{VGE} and A_{VME} are the variable general expense and variable manufacturing expense respectively and A_{FGE} and A_{FME} are the fixed general expense and fixed manufacturing expense respectively.

A typical balance sheet is given in Table (8.1-1). It shows the financial

TABLE (8.1-1)

XYZ company balance sheet at December 31, 1973

assets		liabilities and stockholders' equity	
current assets		current liabilities	
cash	$ 38,893,000	notes payable	$ 34,507,000
notes and accounts receivable	110,740,000	accounts payable and accrued liabilities	106,433,000
inventories:		accrued taxes	7,264,000
finished products	17,396,000	total current liabilities	148,204,000
work in process	56,690,000		
raw materials and supplies (at cost)	35,790,000	long-term debt	67,677,000
total inventories	109,876,000	deferred income taxes	13,225,000
		other deferred credits	2,307,000
total current assets	259,509,000		
investments and long-term receivables (at cost)	94,009,000	stockholders' equity	
		common stock, $20	
		par value	
property, plant, and equipment (at cost)		shares authorized,7,750,000	
		shares issued, 4,794,450	$95,889,000
land	6,110,000		
buildings	63,848,000	capital in excess of par value of common stock	31,798,000
machinery and equipment	106,185,000		
	176,143,000		
less accumulated depreciation	75,163,000	retained earnings	101,492,000
		total stockholders' equity	229,179,000
net property, plant, and equipment	100,980,000		
prepaid and deferred charges	6,094,000		
total assets	$460,592,000	total liabilities and stockholders' equity	$460,592,000

condition of a company at a given date. It is usual to classify assets into current, fixed, and miscellaneous. Current assets are those readily converted into cash such as accounts receivable, inventories, cash and marketable securities, etc. They are also known as liquid assets. Fixed assets are those not readily converted into cash such as land, buildings, plant and equipment. The current book value of each fixed asset is obtained by deducting the accumulated depreciation from the cost. Miscellaneous assets consist of deferred charges, other investments and long term receivables which are not easily converted into cash yet are not considered to be fixed.

On the other side of the balance sheet the current liabilities are listed first. These include accounts payable, debts, and tax accruals which are due within twelve months of the balance sheet date. The net working capital is calculated by subtracting the total current liabilities from the total current assets. Other liabilities, such as long term debts, deferred income taxes, and deferred credits, are listed separately. The stockholders' equity, made up of issued shares, retained earnings, and any other surpluses, completes the liabilities side of the balance sheet. It should be noted that the depreciation reserve is not a separate fund. It merely records a decline in the value of the fixed assets.

A balance sheet shows the financial state of a company at a particular time. Subsequent transactions produce changes arising from the sale of goods or services and from the costs incurred by the manufacturing and selling operations. Accounts of all items of income and expense occurring in a given period are summarized at least once per year in the form of income statements. Table (8.1-2) shows a typical income statement for a period of one year.

The annual income before provision is made for income taxes can be calculated by applying Equation (2.1-1) to total revenue and total expenses.

$$A_{\mathrm{CI}} = A_{\mathrm{S}} - A_{\mathrm{TE}} \tag{2.1-1}$$

In Equation (2.1-1), A_{CI} is the annual cash income, A_{S} is the revenue from annual sales and A_{TE} is the annual total expense. Interest paid on borrowed capital is listed as an expense.

Equation (2.1-3) can be used to calculate the annual amount of tax A_{IT}.

$$A_{\mathrm{IT}} = (A_{\mathrm{CI}} - A_{\mathrm{D}} - A_{\mathrm{A}})\,t \tag{2.1-3}$$

In Equation (2.1-3) A_{D} is the annual depreciation charge, A_{A} is the annual amount of any other allowances, and t is the fractional tax rate. A_{D} and A_{A} are taken into account for each of the fixed assets.

The net annual cash income A_{NCI} is given by Equation (2.1-2).

$$A_{\mathrm{NCI}} = A_{\mathrm{CI}} - A_{\mathrm{IT}} \tag{2.1-2}$$

In Table (8.1-2) the earnings of related companies are added to give the net income (or net profit) for the whole company. The lower part of the table gives details of retained earnings and cash dividends distributed to stockholders.

TABLE (8.1-2)

XYZ company income statement for the year ending December 31, 1973

revenues	
net sales	$ 693,725,000
dividends from subsidiary and associated companies	4,500,000
miscellaneous - net	425,000
	698,650,000
expenses	
cost of goods sold	627,204,000
selling and administrative	50,995,000
interest	8,458,000
	686,657,000
income before provision for income taxes	11,993,000
provision for income taxes	5,313,000
income before equity in earnings of related companies	6,680,000
equity in earnings of related companies:	4,803,000
net income (net profit)	11,483,000
retained earnings at beginning of year	99,588,000
total surplus	111,071,000
cash dividends ($2.00 per share)	9,589,000
retained earnings at end of year	$101,482,000

The balance sheet and income statement can be used to calculate a number of ratios. These ratios indicate various aspects of the financial state of a company. Since long term debt holders have a prior claim to the assets of a company over stockholders, they should be aware of the book value of the security behind the long term debt. The appropriate ratio is the sum of the total assets (minus intangible assets) less the liabilities having a prior claim divided by the long term debt. For the state of the XYZ company represented in Table (8.1-1) this ratio is

$$\frac{\$460{,}592{,}000 - \$148{,}204{,}000}{\$67{,}677{,}000} = 4.62$$

The corresponding book value per share of common stock is

$$\frac{\$460{,}592{,}000 - \$148{,}204{,}000 - \$67{,}677{,}000 - \$13{,}225{,}000 - \$2{,}307{,}000}{4{,}794{,}450}$$

$$= \$47.8.$$

This value is useful for comparison with other companies. However, it has no significance in the event of liquidation.

Ratios which are useful in indicating the liquidity position of a company are the current ratio and the cash ratio. The current ratio is obtained by dividing the total current assets by the total current liabilities. The cash ratio is obtained by dividing the cash (plus easily marketable securities) by the total current liabilities. For the state of the XYZ company represented in Table (8.1-1) the current ratio is

$$\frac{\$259{,}509{,}000}{\$148{,}204{,}000} = 1.75$$

The corresponding cash ratio is

$$\frac{\$38{,}893{,}000}{\$148{,}204{,}000} = 0.262$$

A comparison of these ratios with those for previous years indicates the progress of a company. A lower value of either ratio signifies a deterioration in the ability of a company to pay its debts.

The operating ratio is obtained by dividing operating expenses by revenue. For the state of the XYZ company represented in Table (8.1-2) the operating ratio is

$$\frac{\$686{,}657{,}000}{\$698{,}650{,}000} = 0.982 \text{ (or 98.2 per cent)}$$

Improvements in operating efficiency are indicated by a decrease in the operating ratio. A ratio of 0.982 represents a rather low operating efficiency.

One of the best indicators of management efficiency is the net earnings per share of common stock. For the state of the XYZ company represented in Tables (8.1-1) and (8.1-2) the net earnings per share of common stock is

$$\frac{\$11{,}483{,}000}{4{,}794{,}450} = \$2.39$$

If the common stock of the XYZ company is selling at \$50 per share, the price to earnings ratio is

$$\frac{\$50}{\$2.39} = 20.9$$

The balance sheet and income statement are a record of the transactions which have been completed. They indicate to stockholders how those in charge of company funds have handled them throughout the year. The ability to interpret these records provides an insight into the way business is transacted and the methods by which the decisions are taken.

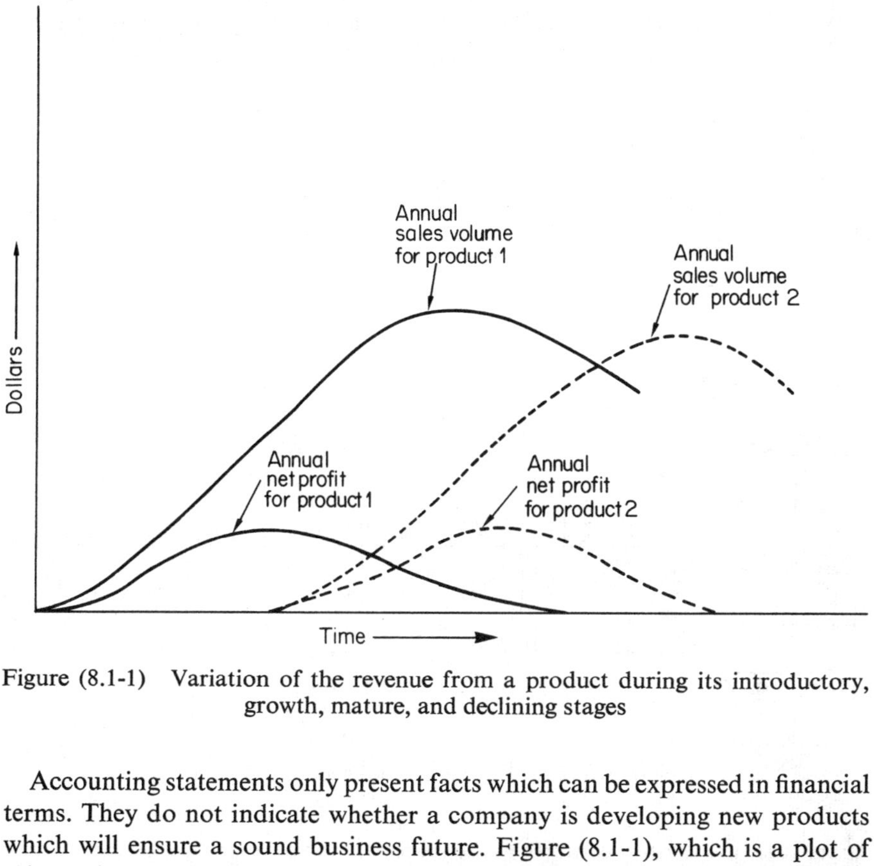

Figure (8.1-1) Variation of the revenue from a product during its introductory, growth, mature, and declining stages

Accounting statements only present facts which can be expressed in financial terms. They do not indicate whether a company is developing new products which will ensure a sound business future. Figure (8.1-1), which is a plot of sales volume and annual net profit against time for individual products, underlines the importance of looking beyond the accounting statements. A company may have impressive current financial statements and yet be heading for bankruptcy in a few years' time if provision is not being made for the introduction of sufficient new products or services.

8.2 Cost Accounting

Cost accounting forms an important part of managerial accounting. It is concerned with the determination and analysis of the cost of producing a product or rendering a service[3]. Its main use is in planning and control. The growth of modern managerial techniques has resulted in a demand for greater detail and accuracy in cost measurement and estimation.

The cost accountant needs to set up a recording system to control the manufacturing costs of a process. Although geared to the activities of the process, the system must be sufficiently flexible to cope with any changes. A cost accounting system is closely linked to the three stages of the production cycle shown in Figure 8.2-1. Measurements are recorded in suitable physical

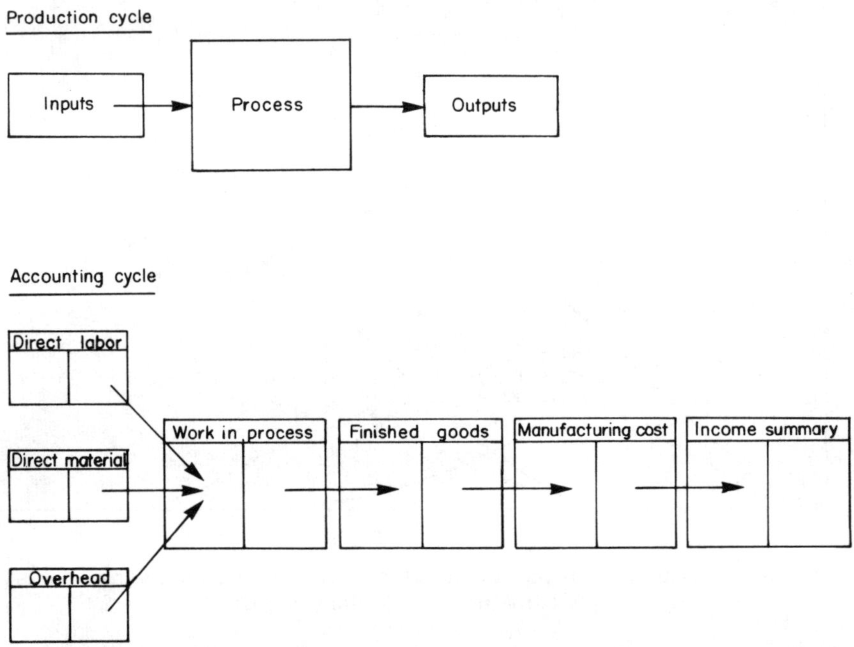

Figure (8.2-1) Production and accounting cycles

units such as number of units made, labor man hours or machine hours, or kilowatt hours of power used, etc. Inputs can be conveniently accumulated in the following accounts:

(1) direct material
(2) direct labor
(3) overhead

Direct material costs include those for materials and supplies used in the production process. The cost of a material is the purchase price including transportation costs, tariff duties, insurance, etc. The cost of materials is debited to the 'materials stores' accounts on receipt. Direct labor costs include the wages of workers involved in the production process. These costs are increased by adding overtime, social security, vacation pay, health, pension payments, etc. Overhead costs incorporate all other factors which affect the cost of the product. They are allocated according to some predetermined basis.

As production proceeds, the inventory accounts are credited with the costs of the input factors. Simultaneously the 'work in process' accounts are debited, usually by breaking them down into the three previously listed subaccounts. When a quantity of completed product is transferred to storage, the accumulated costs of production are debited to the 'finished products' account. Simultaneously the 'work in process' accounts are credited with the same amount. The balance remaining in the 'work in process' accounts will be the accumulated costs of unfinished product. The method of inventory valuation used for charging materials to the 'work in process' account has an important effect on the production costs.

The financial responsibility for manufacturing operations is usually divided between a number of departments. Each department has a supervisor and a small office staff. Costs are accumulated at cost centers placed at convenient points in the production process. These centers may not coincide with operating departments although it is more convenient if they do. Cost data should be related to a meaningful factor such as volume of production. All cost reports should show the unit cost as well as the total cost for a stated volume of production.

There are two basic methods for accumulating costs. These are known respectively as the job order cost system and the process cost system. The job order cost system is usually preferred for non-repetitive work, where each product or group of products tends to be quite distinctive. It is valuable both in the determination of costs and their control. Direct costs of labor and materials used for a particular job are obtained from time sheets and stock records. Indirect costs are allocated to jobs according to some agreed formula. As the various costs connected with the job are incurred, they are recorded in the 'work in process' account and also on the job cost sheet. Thus the 'work in process' account acts as a control over the job cost sheets. At all times, the total costs recorded on the latter should equal the balance in the 'work in process' account. The job order cost system is very accurate, but it does involve a considerable amount of effort and paper work.

The process cost system is normally used for production of large volumes of uniform products on a continuous basis. Costs are accumulated by cost centers and allocated to products according to some agreed basis. If the end products are all identical, the cost of each unit can be determined as an average value for the number of units produced over a period of time. The process cost system is less accurate than the job order cost method. However it is simpler and cheaper to operate. Stocks of both finished goods and raw materials must be physically checked at the beginning and end of the stated period. The 'work in process' must also be valued at the same time to obtain the necessary cost data.

In addition to the accumulation of historical costs, cost accountants are concerned with the estimation of costs and profits for new projects. These estimates form the basis for preparing budgets used in both long term and short term planning. It is common practice to prepare profit and loss statements for each new project. These statements can form the basis of research feasibility analyses. A typical profit and loss statement for a new product based on estimated mature year production data is shown in Table (2.5-1). The first part of the statement is based on a production level which in turn is based on the predicted market penetration and mature year sales revenue for the product. The direct manufacturing cost is estimated from the various cost components. Overheads are then added to give the total product cost. The estimate of mature year profits does not include pre-operating expenses incurred during the research and development stages of the project. These consist of research and development expenses, marketing expenses, start up and engineering expenses required to get the project to commercial operation. The inclusion of the total capital employed enables the return on investment after taxes to be calculated.

The profit and loss statement can also be used for the preparation of standard costs. The latter represent reasonable estimates of future costs per unit of product and can be used to advantage in managerial planning. Standard costs are based on estimated usages of materials and current prices prevailing for the period under consideration. Similarly the costs for direct labour are based on the estimated man hours required and the appropriate labor rates. Overhead costs are more difficult to standardize. They are normally allocated according to a formula. Standard cost differences are the deviations of actual costs from standard costs. Analysis of these deviations enables excessive differences to be pinpointed and reported to management. This information enables corrective action to be taken to improve any operating inefficiencies.

8.3 Price and Cost Trends

The primary objective of the accountant is to guide the financial policy of the company. A commercial enterprise will survive only as long as it provides acceptable rewards for its employees, pays the required taxes and levies, retains enough liquid assets to meet sudden demands on its resources, and distributes enough profits to satisfy the stockholders.

A forecast of the net income of a company for a given year is made by the accountants[1]. This forecast depends on fixing the level of dividend together with the amount of liquid assets to be retained. It also depends on forecasts of costs and expenditures such as labor costs, taxes etc., and on the estimated revenue from sales. The accountants advise management as to the proportion of this net income to be expected from each area of the business. This assessment will aim to spread the risk of failure.

The revenue from annual sales is the product of the number of units sold per year and the selling price per unit. Generally these two factors are not independent. When a new product is introduced it is necessary for a potential customer to know of its existence before he can buy. If each satisfied customer by word of mouth influences more than one purchaser, the sales curve will rise exponentially. There will usually be an upper limit to demand which is determined by the available number of purchasers. Demand will decrease exponentially as this limit is reached. This situation produces a logistic curve[6] which is represented by the equation

$$y = \frac{c}{1 + a\exp(-bx)} \tag{7.4-12}$$

where c is the asymptotic value of y at large values of x. A modified form of Equation (7.4-12) is

$$\ln y = \ln c - a\exp(-bx) \tag{7.4-13}$$

Equation (7.4-13) represents the Gompertz curve which allows for a skewness in the early years. This may be caused for example by an advertising campaign. Cost data can often be fitted by similar curves. Initially production and promotion costs are high. They fall rapidly as the product is accepted and then to a minimum level as production increases.

Predicted cost and price trends based on historical data can be very misleading if the mathematical model on which the extrapolation is performed is wrong. In the early or late years of a logistic or Gompertz curve, the data may be adequately fitted by a straight line. In the late years this causes little error. However, if this is done in the early years, predicted costs will be high and predicted sales will be low. As a consequence, the selling price will be fixed unnecessarily high. If the customer is prepared to pay this high price, then it is likely that competition will be attracted into the market at an early stage. This is likely to alter the assumed timing of the cash flows.

The classic approach to pricing is on a cost plus a fair profit basis. Although this method is simple it ignores demand. For a new product or for a product in a new market the basic pricing information must come from market research. One aim is to establish the asymptotic demand at maturity as a function of price. Another aim is to estimate the sales price which will maximize profits over a given phase of production for which the variable costs are constant. On the assumption that the market potential at any given price is independent of time, it can be deduced[19] that the optimum price c_S^* in \$/unit for the product is given by Equation (8.3-1)

$$c_S^* = \frac{c_{TVE}\,\alpha}{(\alpha - 1)} \tag{8.3-1}$$

where c_{TVE} is the total variable cost in \$/unit and α is the elasticity of demand which is given by Equation (8.3-2).

$$\alpha = \frac{-\mathrm{d}(\ln R)}{\mathrm{d}(\ln c_S)} \tag{8.3-2}$$

In Equation (8.3-2), R is the potential sales volume in units/year at a price of c_S in \$/unit. If $\alpha \leqslant 1$ no optimum price exists. If $\alpha > 1$, the optimum selling price falls as α is increased. This reflects the influence of increased competition on the market price.

In order to make use of Equation (8.3-1) it is necessary to know the relationship between the sales volume R and the sales price c_S. Suppose that a market survey has shown this to be given by the exponential equation

$$R = a \exp(-bc_S) \tag{8.3-3}$$

where a and b are constants. For this case

$$\alpha = \frac{-\mathrm{d}(\ln R)}{\mathrm{d}(\ln c_S)} = bc_S$$

Substitute this value of α into Equation (8.3-1), put $c_S = c_S^*$ and rearrange to give

$$c_S^* = c_{TVE} + \frac{1}{b} \tag{8.3-4}$$

For this case the value of α is greater than unity only if b is positive and greater than $1/c_S^*$. Equation (8.3-3) shows that this leads to a fall in R with an increase in c_S.

If the relationship between R and c_S is given by the general reciprocal equation

$$R = \frac{a_1}{c_S + a_2} + a_3 \tag{8.3-5}$$

where a_1, a_2, and a_3 are constants, the corresponding value of α is given by the equation

$$\alpha = \frac{-a_1 c_S}{(a_1 + a_2 a_3)(a_2 + c_S) + a_3 c_S^2} \tag{8.3-6}$$

For this case, unless a_1 is negative, there will be no optimum price. Again, for an optimum to exist, prices must fall as sales volume increases.

The cumulative net annual cash income over n years is given by the equation

$$\sum_1^n A_{NCI} = R(c_S^* - c_{TVE}) \int_1^n \kappa \, \mathrm{d}\theta - nA_{TFE} \tag{8.3-7}$$

where A_{NCI} is the net annual cash income in \$/year, A_{TFE} is the total annual fixed expense in \$/year, κ is the fraction of the sales potential R achieved at time θ, and θ is the time from the start of selling in years. The value of κ is obtained from a sales curve predicted for this product.

An alternative approach is to determine the long range economic price of a product[4]. This is the average price required to obtain a predetermined rate of return on all associated invested capital over the economic life of the process. This long range economic price is seldom the price which the customer actually pays for the product. The latter price is usually secret and differs from the manufacturer's published price because of discounts and other incentives.

Published prices are helpful in providing a rough guide to the possible prices of similar products. This is particularly so when the raw materials cost is available as a percentage of the product price as in Table (8.3-1)[7].

If the price of a new product is high competition is likely to enter the market, which will usually force prices down. Lowered prices will stimulate demand which may cause a slight rise in price. If the price falls much below the long range economic price, then prices are likely to fall drastically in an attempt to drive competition out of business and also to prevent other competitors entering the field. These low prices may also increase the potential market. This in turn could induce a price rise back to an economic level. Producers of established products often use this cut throat technique against a new product. Usually this is done by offering larger discounts rather than by making major changes in published prices. In extreme cases the price may fall to that determined by the breakeven point of the most efficient producer.

Just as price trends are generally downwards, costs are usually upwards. In an increasingly affluent society the cost of services tends to rise while the prices of finished products tends to fall. If this difference cannot be absorbed by increased efficiency then lower percentage returns on investment will result. In the past cost reductions have been made by using processes which have resulted in widespread pollution of the environment. Anti-pollution legislation is likely to lead to a sharp increase in the costs of such processes which will in turn be reflected in prices.

Activities ranging from plant operation to process design can be performed more efficiently as experience is gained. This can lead to some reduction in costs. The results can be approximated by so-called learning curves[8]. A learning curve is a plot of a cost ratio, or time ratio, etc., against, say, a production rate ratio. Learning curves are essentially exponential in type and can be represented by equations of the form

$$\frac{C_2}{C_1} = \left(\frac{x_2}{x_1}\right)^{\psi} \tag{8.3-8}$$

TABLE (8.3-1) [7]

Selling prices and raw material costs for common chemicals

product	raw materials	product price	raw materials cost	
		\$/lb	\$/lb product	% of product price
acetaldehyde	acetylene	0.09	0.0397	44
	ethylene, O_2, HCl, cat	0.09	0.0392	43
acetic acid	acetaldehyde, cat	0.09	0.0708	78
	butane, cat	0.09	0.0075	8
acetic anhydride	acetaldehyde, cat	0.14	0.1090	78
	acetic acid	0.14	0.1215	87
acetylene	natural gas, DMF	0.064	0.0218	34
	natural gas, DMF, O_2	0.064	0.0370	58
acronitrile	propylene, ammonia	0.145	0.0462	32
	acetylene, HCN	0.145	0.1074	74
adipic acid	cyclohexane	0.29	0.0257	9
	cyclohexane, HNO_3, cat	0.29	0.2054	71
benzoic acid	phthalic anhydride	0.1502	0.1050	70
butadiene	butylenes	0.1175	0.0726	62
	butane	0.1175	0.0200	17
chloral	ethanol, Cl_2, H_2SO_4	0.21	0.1672	80
crotonaldehyde	acetaldehyde	0.215	0.1460	68
ethylacetate	ethanol, acetic acid	0.13	0.1114	86
ethylene glycol	ethylene, Ag	0.135	0.0360	27
	ethylene, Cl_2, lime, caustic soda	0.135	0.1262	93
ethylene oxide	ethylene, Ag	0.155	0.0440	28
	ethylene, Cl_2, lime, caustic soda	0.155	0.1024	66
formaldehyde	methanol	0.035	0.0191	55
glycerol	propylene, Cl_2, lime, caustic soda	0.2375	0.0886	37
isopropanol	propylene, H_2SO_4	0.0733	0.0188	26
MIBK	acetone, H_2	0.13	0.0743	57
nitrobenzene	benzene, H_2SO_4, HNO_3	0.095	0.0513	54
phenol	benzene, HCl	0.1125	0.0434	39
phthalic anhydride	naphthalene	0.105	0.0469	45
	orthoxylene	0.105	0.0292	28
styrene	benzene, ethylene, cat	0.1246	0.0451	36
	benzene, ethylene	0.1246	0.0471	38
vinyl acetate	acetylene, acetic acid	0.115	0.0847	74
vinyl chloride	acetylene, HCl, $HgCl_2$	0.08	0.0638	80

The so-called 80 per cent curve is the one for which $C_2/C_1 = 0.8$ when $x_2/x_1 = 2$ corresponding to $\psi = -0.322$.

The learning curve depends both on the inherent susceptibility of an operation to improvement and the degree to which this is exploited. In the past it has been possible in many cases to raise the throughput of a plant well above its design capacity. In the future this will become increasingly difficult to do as a result of accurate computer aided design and optimization. Learning curves have been used for predicting both the cost and the installation time for replicate plant and equipment.

8.4 Value Engineering and Cost Benefit Analysis

The neglect of either value engineering or cost benefit analysis can put a company at a serious disadvantage compared with its competitors. Value engineering can lead to substantial savings in some existing processes while cost benefit analysis can provide a much more realistic picture on which to base profitability estimates.

In value engineering[12,16] an attempt is made to reduce costs by questioning the necessity for each action. The aim is to incorporate only such quality and reliability into the product as is absolutely necessary in order to meet specifications. The technique of value engineering is based on obtaining answers to questions such as the following:

(1) Is the production method under consideration the best possible?

(2) Have the needs of the customer changed since the product was last appraised?

(3) Are the cost data as reliable as is supposed?

(4) Can the specification be modified to permit less costly production?

(5) Can the materials currently specified be replaced by newer, more easily handled substitutes?

(6) Can unnecessary handling be eliminated?

Value engineering is a group exercise. It is useless to reduce the costs of raw materials and production to a minimum only to find that the product is unsaleable. It might be said that a completely successful value analysis would lead to a product which would totally disintegrate the day after the guarantee ran out. Such a degree of success in, say, a vehicle would be unlikely to encourage repeat orders. Clearly value engineering needs to be tempered with a degree of social responsibility.

In cost benefit analysis[5,9] an attempt is made to assign monetary values to actions such as the despoilation of the environment. The possible danger in neglecting cost benefit analysis is illustrated by the following hypothetical case. Several alternative processes for making product A were considered. Preliminary estimates showed that by far the most profitable process was one using a mercury based catalyst. A detailed design and cost estimate were made and eventually a site was acquired. A considerable amount of money had been spent before the cost of meeting a local by-law was assessed. This by-law prohibited the discharge of effluent containing more than 0.1 parts per million of mercury into the river which adjoined the site. The additional cost of the necessary purification rendered the process completely unprofitable, as could have been foreseen. In addition to the money lost in design, etc., the delay involved in changing to an alternative process had an adverse effect on the forecasts of sales volume and selling price.

The cost of meeting a legal requirement, or court action, can usually be forecast as accurately as most other costs. However, some costs are much more difficult to assess. These include costs of attracting workers from distant locations, avoiding law suits for nuisance, combating active propaganda against the product on non-technical grounds, etc. Nevertheless some of these factors can be costed. This is illustrated by the availability of insurance policies against the effects of some of them.

8.5 Marketing

In a society characterized by increasing competition and overproduction, it is no longer sufficient to produce a good product efficiently. A company must also be skilful in its marketing.

A fundamental tool of marketing is the marketing survey. Surveys are based on a questionnaire or similar kind of test. Questionnaires should always be checked for ambiguity before the cost of a survey is underwritten. The second step is to select a sample of the public to answer the questions. A desirable sample for a product of universal interest is a truly random sample. In practice random samples are often obtained from existing lists using a prearranged routine. For example every fifth name on a register of electors might be used. Although apparently unbiased, this selection automatically excludes children and visitors to the locality. The latter problem can be avoided by street interviewing. However, this tends to give prominence to the views of those willing or anxious to be interviewed. Quota random samples deliberately emphasize particular sections of the community. The aim is to match the samples to the predicted frequencies of different types of potential customer in the sales population. Double sampling is sometimes used to reduce the costs of surveys. In this method a sample selected as described is itself sampled randomly to provide the interview list. Many refinements of these basic techniques are possible.

A statistical analysis of the results of a survey can indicate the goodness of fit with an anticipated model[2]. If the model is wrong, the results of the survey may be used to produce a more realistic model by curve fitting and trend analysis. The results of market surveys often form the basis of advertising campaigns.

An essential part of marketing is the forecasting of both demand and prices at various stages in a feasibility study. The validity of a profitability analysis depends on the accuracy of the estimate of sales revenue. Factors such as transportation, warehousing, and stock control must also be considered[11] to ensure that the predicted sales demand can be satisfied when and where it occurs. It is essential that the views of the marketing director or manager are given due weight at all stages in the development of a project. Success in business is largely a question of accurate timing which in turn depends on team work.

8.6 Risk and Insurance

Capital is at risk until the breakeven point has been reached. It is common practice to consider the breakeven point (DBEP) discounted to time zero at the cost of capital. At any time after the (DBEP) the project will have provided a greater return on the capital than the cost of capital. It is customary for management to spread risk by diversifying the activities of their company among a portfolio of projects.

Business is an activity in which both skill and chance play a part. The theory of games teaches that in the long run the following events will happen:[10]

(1) The player with the largest capital will win all the available capital.
(2) Given equal capital, the most skilful player will win all the capital.
(3) Any player will lose all his capital if the odds are slightly against him.

Some of these factors can be seen to operate in the tendency of small businesses to be taken over by larger companies and also in the bankruptcy of companies which cannot raise sufficient funds to participate in business activity for a further period. However, what happens in the short run is far less predictable.

An event or outcome which will definitely occur has a probability $p = 1$. An event or outcome which will definitely not occur has a probability $p = 0$. If the probability of success is p, then the probability of failure is $(1 - p)$. The probability of at least one success p_1 in n similar tries is given by the equation

$$p_1 = 1 - (1 - p)^n \tag{8.6-1}$$

If a six-sided dice is thrown, the probability of a win is 1/6. For this case, Equation (8.6-1) can be written as

$$p_1 = 1 - \left(\frac{5}{6}\right)^n \tag{8.6-2}$$

and the probability of at least one win in four throws is $p_1 = 0.9952$. If each throw costs \$1 and the value of a win is \$4, there is at least a 99.52 per cent chance of breaking even in four throws.

Reul[14] has used Equation (8.6-1) to define a parameter (MSF) given by the equation

$$(\text{MSF}) = 1 - (1 - p)^{\beta} \tag{8.6-3}$$

where (MSF) is the probability that a portfolio of bets with a similar strategy will at least break even, and β is the amount of one win divided by the amount of each bet. Reul refers to (MSF) as the measured survival function. He has applied Equation (8.6-3) to the research and development activities of a company. From the derivation of Equation (8.6-3) it follows that $\beta \geqslant 1$ and hence $(\text{MSF}) \geqslant p$.

Equations (8.6-1) and (8.6-3) are based on the simplified assumption that a project either succeeds with probability p and achieves the expected reward or fails completely with probability $(1 - p)$. The (MSF) is therefore the probability of at least one success when β similar projects are undertaken. It represents a conservative measure of risk. Many projects may result in greater returns, or have an increased probability of attaining a given return, if more money is spent. Each alternative is treated as a separate risk in the portfolio.

Research and development activities do not, in themselves, produce a saleable product. Thus they cannot directly generate a return on capital outlay. A successful research and development project is one which results in an activity which earns revenue for the company. The life cycle of the revenue from an individual product is illustrated in Figure (8.1-1). This revenue has to pay not only for the successful project but for all the unsuccessful research and development activities. It is common practice to consider all research and development activities as a portfolio. Research and development disbursements are relatively flexible and can be switched from less favourable to more favourable projects at short notice. When considering individual projects, β should be taken as the lesser of

$$\beta = \frac{\text{expected proceeds if the project is successful}}{\text{disbursement on the project}}$$

or $$\beta = \frac{\text{total expenditure on all projects over the budget period}}{\text{expenditure on the project over the budget period}}$$

and p = probability of success for the project

As the projects in a portfolio will usually have different probabilities of success and different rewards for success, β and p in Equation (8.6-3) can be conservatively estimated as follows:

$$\beta = \frac{\text{total annual proceeds if all projects are successful}}{\text{total annual disbursements on all projects}}$$

$$p = \frac{\text{total expected value of all projects}}{\text{total proceeds if all projects are successful}}$$

In the case of net present value, the expected value can be calculated from the equation

$$(\text{NPV})_w = p_1(\text{NPV})_1 + p_2(\text{NPV})_2 + \ldots \qquad (4.5\text{-}2)$$

where there is a probability p_1 that a net present value of $(\text{NPV})_1$ will result, a probability p_2 that a net present value of $(\text{NPV})_2$ will result, etc.

The relationship between (MSF), p, and $1/\beta$ in Equation (8.6-3) is shown graphically in Figure (8.6-1). It is the responsibility of management to decide on an acceptable value for the measured survival function (MSF) for their particular company. The value chosen will depend on the individual company's attitude to risk which can be quantified in the form of a utility curve, such as the one shown in Figure (7.3-1) from which a value of equivalent (MSF) can be obtained[15]. It is also the responsibility of management to estimate the probabilities p for the success of individual projects after due consideration of all the data provided by the various departments. The rate of return on investment which is acceptable to management is a function of these probabilities. Each industry has a reasonably well defined return on investment which reflects the degree of risk inherent in that particular industry. If the management decisions are faulty, the company will either overspend or will miss opportunities.

For a disbursement of \$1,000 in year zero, the discounted breakeven point (DBEP) will be reached in three years for a compound interest rate of 30 per cent if the annual net profit $A_{\text{NP}} = \$550.63/\text{year}$. Thus a discounted cash flow rate of return (DCFRR) of 30 per cent/year corresponds to

$$\frac{1}{\beta} = \frac{\$1{,}000}{(3\ \text{year})(\$550.63/\text{year})} = 0.61$$

For $1/\beta = 0.61$ and a measured survival function $(\text{MSF}) = 0.999$, the probability of individual success is read from Figure (8.6-1) to be $p = 0.985$. Similarly it can be deduced that if $(\text{MSF}) = 0.999$ and $p = 0.95$ a (DCFRR) of 45 per cent/year is required if breakeven is to be achieved in four years. However if breakeven in twenty years is acceptable then a (DCFRR) of only 10 per cent/year is needed. It is interesting to note that if a measured survival function $(\text{MSF}) = 0.95$ is acceptable to management then a (DCFRR) of 10 per cent/year is equivalent to assuming that the process will break even in about two years.

In the venture premium method of assessment, risky investments are required to yield a rate of return which adds a premium to the cost of finance. Rudd and Watson[18] considered the equation

$$i_m = i + i_r \qquad (8.6\text{-}4)$$

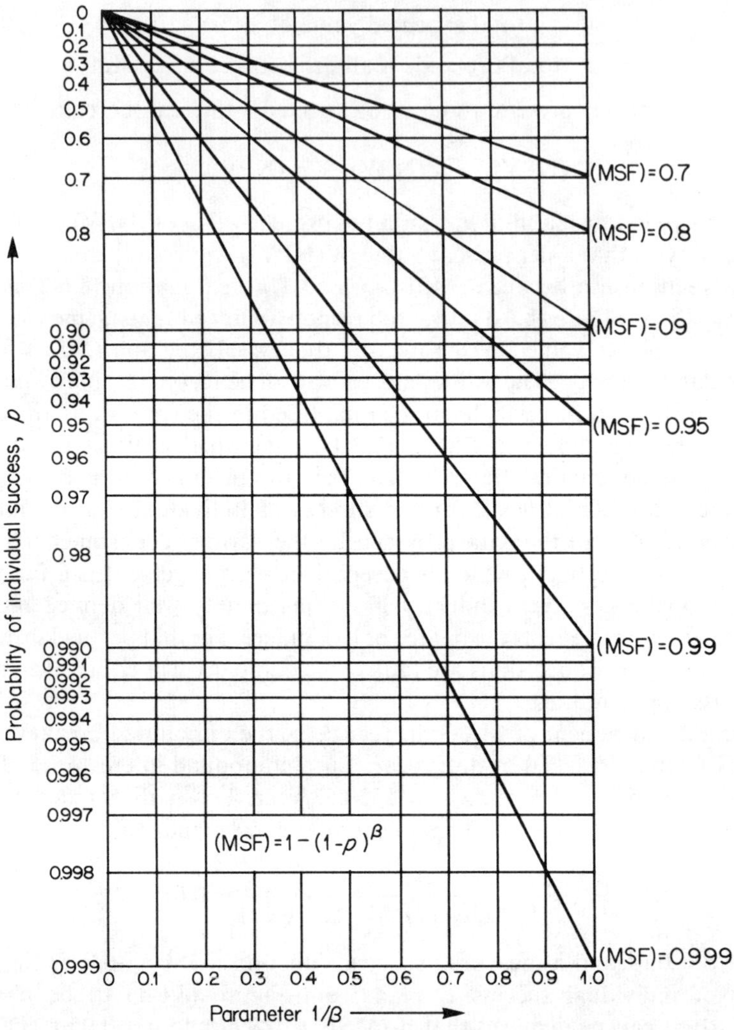

Figure (8.6-1) The measured survival function (MSF) as a function of its component parameters

where i is the cost of capital, i_m is the minimum acceptable interest rate of return on the investment, and i_r is known as the risk rate. Rudd and Watson[17] suggested that each project should pay an insurance premium i_r to guarantee the expected profits. The magnitude of i_r is proportional to the amount of capital to be risked. It is also a function of the degree of risk involved. Working capital and capital for auxiliary facilities are assumed to be risk free. Thus the risk rate i_r is only applied to the fraction of the capital investment likely to be lost if the project is unexpectedly terminated. The main objection to the venture premium method is that the assessment of the riskiness of a project may be too subjective. This could lead to the rejection of potentially attractive proposals and the acceptance of projects which merely appear to be risk free.

Insurance is protection against risk. Commercial insurance companies minimize their own risks by covering a large number of individuals against a given risk and also by offering cover on a wide variety of different types of risk. It is frequently quite difficult to assess the probability of success of a particular research and development project. It is much easier for an insurance company to assess its probabilities from its available tables of mortality, crime, fire, etc. Businesses tend to provide their own insurance cover when individual claims are likely to be a small fraction of the available capital. The cost of commercial insurance cover is about 30 per cent higher than would be necessary to cover the same risk in one's own company. However for low probability, high cost risks, most businesses prefer to insure with a commercial insurance company. Such risks include loss of plant or buildings due to fire, losses of revenue due to delays in start up or strikes, etc. It is also becoming increasingly necessary to insure against factors not normally considered until recently. These include possible law suits for polluting the environment. The cost of insurance increases the annual total expense A_{TE}. Thus overinsurance can lead to an unnecessary decrease in profitability. The management of a company must ultimately judge its own risks.

Without risk and the rewards for successfully accepting risks there would be no business activity. In a risk situation where skill plays a part, the skilled participant will prosper at the expense of his competitors provided that his resources enable him to continue in business for a sufficient length of time. This text has provided methods for assessing rewards and risks so that the reader may be encouraged to become a skilled participant.

Example (8.6-1)

Details of the estimates for the current research and development program of a company are given below. Estimate the probability that this portfolio will at least break even.

Required equation

$$(\text{MSF}) = 1 - (1 - p)^{\beta} \tag{8.6-3}$$

The total annual proposed disbursement for research and development is \$500,000. For project A the anticipated annual after tax income is \$600,000. As this exceeds the total annual disbursement, the correct value of β will be based on \$500,000, not \$600,000, and this is the value which should be used in computations. The effective total annual income if all projects reached their

project	proposed disbursement for the coming year	annual after tax income if successful	probability of success
	\$	\$	
A	125,000	600,000	0.95
B	100,000	400,000	0.90
C	100,000	125,000	0.80
D	80,000	100,000	0.75
E	50,000	60,000	0.70
F	20,000	30,000	0.65
G	20,000	70,000	0.50
H	5,000	15,000	0.20
	\$500,000	\$1,400,000	

anticipated income would be \$1,300,000 and

$$\beta = \frac{\text{total annual proceeds if all projects are successful}}{\text{total annual disbursement on all projects}}$$

$$= \frac{\$1{,}300{,}000}{\$500{,}000} = 2.600$$

Project A has an expected value of (0.95)(\$500,000/year) = \$475,000/year, project B has an expected value of (0.90)(\$400,000/year) = \$360,000/year, and so on. Sum these values to obtain the total expected value of the portfolio of \$1,109,500/year, hence

$$p = \frac{\text{total expected value of all projects}}{\text{total expected value if all projects are successful}}$$

$$= \frac{\$1{,}109{,}500/\text{year}}{\$1{,}300{,}000/\text{year}} = 0.8535$$

From Figure (8.6-1) for a probability of success $p = 0.8535$ and a value $1/\beta = 1/2.600 = 0.3846$ read the measured survival function (MSF) to be approximately 99.3 per cent. This is the probability that this portfolio will at least break even.

Alternatively, from Equation (8.6-3)

$$\begin{aligned}(\text{MSF}) &= 1 - (1 - p)^{\beta} \\ &= (1 - (1 - 0.8535)^{2.6} \\ &= 0.9932 = 99.32 \text{ per cent.}\end{aligned} \qquad (8.6\text{-}3)$$

Example (8.6-2)

Sketch a utility function curve equivalent to the following pattern of measured survival functions (MSF) which expresses the strategy of a particular manager to expending his authorized annual budget of \$1,000,000:

(i) for potential annual proceeds above \$600,000
(MSF) = 99.9 per cent
(ii) for potential annual proceeds between \$300,000 and \$600,000
(MSF) = 95 per cent
(iii) for potential annual proceeds between \$0 and \$300,000
(MSF) = 65 per cent
(iv) for potential losses
(MSF) = 75 per cent

Plot the resultant curve on a utility scale of ± 120 utiles against potential gain $\pm$\$1,000,000.

Required equation

$$(\text{MSF}) = 1 - (1 - p)^{\beta} \tag{8.6-3}$$

where $\beta = \dfrac{\text{total proceeds from the project}}{\text{total disbursement on the project}}$

The required axes range from −\$1,000,000/year to +\$1,000,000/year and from −120 utiles to +120 utiles. Utiles can be compared by ratio only on an absolute scale and hence, for purposes of calculation, the axes are moved to give a working range of \$0/year to \$2,000,000/year and 0 to 240 utiles. On these axes a potential gain of \$600,000/year corresponds to an absolute amount of (600,000 + 1,000,000) = \$1,600,000/year, and a potential loss of \$200,000/year to an absolute amount of (−200,000 + 1,000,000) = \$800,000/year. For annual proceeds above \$600,000, (MSF) = 99.9 per cent. If the certainty of an annual gain of \$600,000 had to be abandoned in an effort to obtain an annual gain of \$1,000,000 then, on an absolute scale,

$$\beta = \frac{\text{total proceeds from the project}}{\text{total disbursement on the project}}$$

$$= \frac{\$2{,}000{,}000/\text{year}}{\$1{,}600{,}000/\text{year}}$$

$$= 1.2500$$

From Equation (8.6-3)

$$(\text{MSF}) = 1 - (1 - p)^{\beta}$$

$$\text{or} \quad p = 1 - [1 - (\text{MSF})]^{1/\beta} \tag{8.6-3}$$

With $1/\beta = 0.8000$ and (MSF) = 99.9 per cent the required probability of success

$$p = 1 - (1 - 0.999)^{0.8000}$$
$$= 0.996$$

The utility of an amount of money is its utility when it is certain to be obtained multiplied by its probability of being attained. On a scale in which an absolute annual income of $2,000,000/year has a utility of 240 utiles the utility of $1,600,000/year to this manager is (0.996)(240 utiles) = 239 utiles.

For annual proceeds between $300,000 and $600,000, (MSF) = 95 per cent. If the certainty of an annual gain of $300,000 had to be abandoned to obtain an annual gain of $600,000 then, as above,

$$\beta = \frac{\$1{,}600{,}000/\text{year}}{\$1{,}300{,}000/\text{year}}$$

$$\text{or} \quad \frac{1}{\beta} = \frac{\$1{,}300{,}000/\text{year}}{\$1{,}600{,}000/\text{year}}$$
$$= 0.8125$$

With this value of $1/\beta$ and (MSF) = 95 per cent

$$p = 1 - (1 - 0.95)^{0.8125}$$
$$= 0.912$$

Since, to this manager, the utility of an absolute income of $1,600,000 is 239 utiles the value of $1,300,000 is (0.912)(239 utiles) = 218 utiles. On the original

TABLE (8.6-2)

potential gain $/year	absolute gain $/year	(MSF)	$\frac{1}{\beta}$	p	absolute utility utiles	utility utiles
1,000,000	2,000,000	0.999	1.0000	1.000	240	120
600,000	1,600,000	0.999	0.8000	0.996	239	119
300,000	1,300,000	0.950	0.8125	0.912	218	98
0	1,000,000	0.650	0.7692	0.554	120	0
-500,000	500,000	0.750	0.5000	0.500	60	-60
-1,000,000	0	0.750	0.000	0.000	0	-120

scales, potential annual proceeds of $300,000 have a utility of $(218 - 120) = 98$ utiles.

Values of utility at other potential annual gains are calculated in the same way and listed in Table (8.6-2). The results are presented graphically in Figure (8.6-2).

This strategy is extremely conservative when high gains are possible but becomes less so for smaller potential gains. Where potential losses are involved the strategy is a fair one for which net present value (NPV) would be an accurate guide to choose between alternatives.

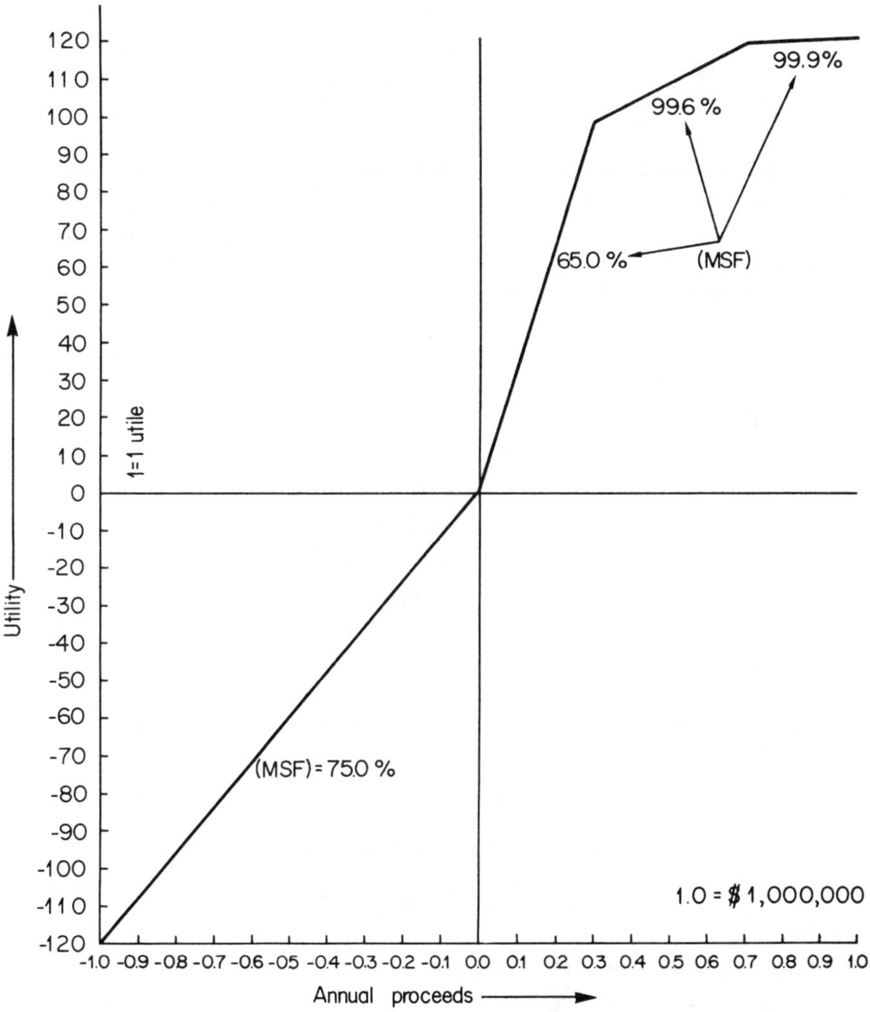

Figure (8.6-2) Utility function of Example (8.6-2)

Example (8.6-3)

For a minimum acceptable rate of return i_m of 15 per cent on an investment, construct a curve relating the anticipated project life in years to the minimum acceptable probability of success if the company attitude to the utility of money is represented by a measured survival function of 95 per cent.

Required equations

$$A = Pf_{AP} \tag{1.7-6}$$

where the annuity present worth factor

$$f_{AP} = \frac{i(1+i)^n}{(1+i)^n - 1}$$

$$(\text{MSF}) = 1 - (1-p)^{\beta}. \tag{8.6-3}$$

Consider a project in which \$1,000 is invested at a minimum acceptable interest rate of 15 per cent. Breakeven will be achieved in various periods of time depending on the cash flow pattern of the income. Assume, for purposes of standardization, that it is required to receive the same annual income x. This is the same situation as is expressed by Equation (1.7-6).

$$A = Pf_{AP} \tag{1.7-6}$$

The annuity present worth factor for $i = 0.15$ and $n = 3$ years is

$$\begin{aligned} f_{AP} &= \frac{i(1+i)^n}{(1+i)^n - 1} \\ &= \frac{0.15(1+0.15)^3}{(1+0.15)^3 - 1} \\ &= 0.437\,98 \end{aligned}$$

The required annual payment A is given by Equation (1.7-6) to be

$$\begin{aligned} A &= Pf_{AP} \\ &= (\$100{,}000)(0.437\,98) \\ &= \$437.98/\text{year} \end{aligned}$$

The total proceeds over three years are

$$(3)(\$437.98) = \$1{,}313.94$$

hence for this project

$$\beta = \frac{\text{total proceeds from the project}}{\text{total disbursements on the project}}$$

$$= \frac{\$1{,}313.94}{\$1{,}000.00} = 1.313\,94$$

From Equation (8.6-3)

$$(\text{MSF}) = 1 - (1-p)^{\beta}$$

$$\text{or} \quad p = 1 - [1 - (\text{MSF})]^{1/\beta} \tag{8.6-3}$$

TABLE (8.6-3)

year	f_{AP}	β	p
0	-	1.00000	0.9500
1	1.15000	1.15000	0.9261
2	0.61512	1.23024	0.9124
3	0.43798	1.31394	0.8977
4	0.35027	1.40108	0.8822
5	0.29832	1.49160	0.8658
6	0.26424	1.58544	0.8489
7	0.24036	1.68252	0.8314
8	0.22285	1.78280	0.8137
9	0.20957	1.88613	0.7957
10	0.19925	1.99250	0.7776
11	0.19107	2.10177	0.7596
12	0.18448	2.21376	0.7416
13	0.17911	2.32843	0.7237
14	0.17469	2.44566	0.7062
15	0.17102	2.56530	0.6889
16	0.16795	2.68720	0.6720
17	0.16537	2.81129	0.6555
18	0.16319	2.93742	0.6393
19	0.16134	3.06546	0.6237
20	0.14976	3.19520	0.6085

where for $n = 3$ years and (MSF) = 95 per cent the minimum required probability of success

$$p = 1 - (1 - 0.95)^{1/1.31394}$$
$$= 0.8977$$

Corresponding values of n and p are calculated in the same way and listed in Table (8.6-3). The relationship is presented graphically in Figure (8.6-3).

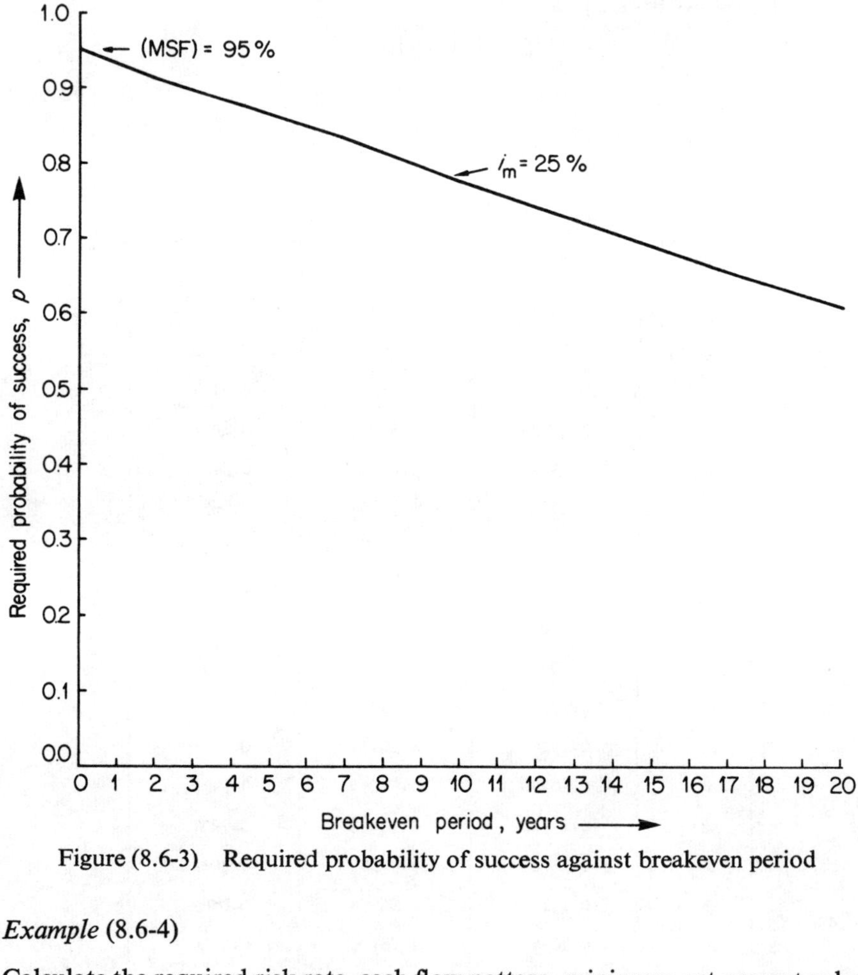

Figure (8.6-3) Required probability of success against breakeven period

Example (8.6-4)

Calculate the required risk rate, cash flow pattern, minimum net present value (NPV), and minimum discounted cash flow rate of return (DCFRR) for a project described by the following data:

(i) risk strategy equivalent to a measured survival function (MSF) of 99 per cent

(ii) payback of risk capital in three years
(iii) cost of capital $i = 10$ per cent/year
(iv) fractional tax rate $t = 0.50$
(v) no tax allowance other than depreciation, i.e. $A_A = 0$
(vi) straight line depreciation allowable over project life
(vii) estimated project life of ten years
(viii) risk capital $C_{FC} = \$200,000$
(ix) working capital $C_{WC} = \$100,000$
(x) probability of complete success of the project estimated as 95 per cent

The sales manager considers that, as a conservative estimate, it should be possible to establish the market in the first year, to double the net cash flow A_{CF} in the second year, and to double the net cash flow again to reach full output throughout the third year. To discourage competition, and so maintain full output, the company must be prepared to halve the before tax cash income A_{CI} after that time.

Required equations

$$A = Pf_{AP} \tag{1.7-6}$$

where the annual present worth factor

$$f_{AP} = \frac{i(1+i)^n}{(1+i)^n - 1}$$

$$A_{NCI} = A_{CI} - A_{IT} \tag{2.1-2}$$

$$A_{IT} = (A_{CI} - A_D - A_T)\,t \tag{2.1-3}$$

$$A_{CF} = A_{NCI} - A_{TC} \tag{2.1-4}$$

$$(\text{MSF}) = 1 - (1-p)^{\beta} \tag{8.6-3}$$

$$i_m = i + i_r \tag{8.6-4}$$

Risk rate required

From Equation (8.6-3)

$$(\text{MSF}) = 1 - (1-p)^{\beta} \tag{8.6-3}$$

For this project with $(\text{MSF}) = 0.99$ and $p = 0.95$

$$\beta = \frac{\text{total proceeds, \$}}{\text{total investment, \$}} = \frac{\log[1-(\text{MSF})]}{\log(1-p)} = \frac{\log 0.01}{\log 0.05}$$

$$= 1.597$$

To recover this amount of capital and interest in three years the average net annual cash flow A_{CF} required is

$$A_{CF} = \frac{1.597}{3} = 0.5124 \text{ (\$/year)/(\$ invested)}$$

From Equation (1.7-6)

$$A = Pf_{AP}$$

$$\text{or} \quad f_{AP} = \frac{A}{P} = 0.5124 \text{ (\$/year)/(\$ invested)} \qquad (1.7\text{-}6)$$

From the tables read the required value of the interest rate to be $i = i_m = 0.25$ to give $f_{AP} = 0.5124$ for $n = 3$ years.
From Equation (8.6-4)

$$i_m = i + i_r$$

Hence the risk rate i_r required is

$$\begin{aligned} i_r = i_m - i &= 25 \text{ per cent} - 10 \text{ per cent} \\ &= 15 \text{ per cent} \end{aligned}$$

All capital will be charged at the cost of capital $i = 10$ per cent. The working capital $C_{WC} = \$100,000$ is completely recoverable without risk; thus it requires interest only at 10 per cent. The unrecovered part of the risk capital C_{FC} attracts the additional interest rate of 15 per cent.

Cash flow pattern required

The conservative sales strategy is to obtain a net annual cash flow $(A_{CF})_1$ in year 1, to double this cash flow in year 2, and to double it again in year 3 with the plant operating throughout the year at full output. To meet the payback requirement that the risk capital should be recovered with interest by the end of the third year, the cash flow pattern must

(a) repay an interest of (0.1)(\$100,000) = \$10,000 due on the working capital in each year
(b) repay an interest of 25 per cent on the oustanding part of the risk capital
(c) reduce the outstanding part of the risk capital

The required payments are summarized in Table (8.6-4a). The risk capital carried forward to year 4 is required to be zero. Hence,

$$\begin{aligned} 428{,}750 - 8.0625(A_{CF})_1 &= 0 \\ (A_{CF})_1 &= \$53{,}178/\text{year} \\ &= \$53{,}200/\text{year} \end{aligned}$$

TABLE (8.6-4a)

year	1	2	3	4
net cash flow A_{CF}, \$	$(A_{CF})_1$	$2(A_{CF})_1$	$4(A_{CF})_1$	
working capital C_{WC}, \$	100,000	100,000	100,000	
interest on working capital at 10%,\$	10,000	10,000	10,000	
risk capital C_{FC}, \$	200,000	$260{,}000-(A_{CF})_1$	$335{,}000-3.25(A_{CF})_1$	$428{,}750-8.0625(A_{CF})_1$
interest on risk capital at 25%, \$	50,000	$65{,}000-0.25(A_{CF})_1$	$83{,}750-0.8215(A_{CF})_1$	

TABLE (8.6-4b)

Annual cash flows

year	cash income before tax	depreciation charge plus other allowances	taxable income	when t=0.5 amount of tax	net capital expenditure	after tax			
						net cash flow A_{CF} =	discount factor at i=10%	discounted net cash flow	net present value (NPV)
	A_{CI}	$A_D + A_A$	$A_{CI}-A_D-A_A$	$A_{IT} = (A_{CI}-A_D-A_A)t$	A_{TC}	$A_{CI}-A_{IT}-A_{TC}$	f_d	A_{DCF}	$= \Sigma A_{DCF}$
0	0	0	0	0	300,000	-300,000	1.00000	-300,000	-300,000
1	86,400	20,000	66,400	33,200	0	53,200	0.90909	48,364	-251,636
2	192,800	20,000	172,800	86,400	0	106,400	0.82645	87,934	-167,702
3	405,600	20,000	385,600	192,800	0	212,800	0.75131	159,879	- 3,823
4	202,800	20,000	182,800	91,400	0	111,400	0.68301	76,087	+ 72,264
5	202,800	20,000	182,800	91,400	0	111,400	0.62092	69,170	141,434
6	202,800	20,000	182,800	91,400	0	111,400	0.56447	62,882	204,316
7	202,800	20,000	182,800	91,400	0	111,400	0.51316	57,166	261,482
8	202,800	20,000	182,800	91,400	0	111,400	0.46651	51,969	313,451
9	202,800	20,000	182,800	91,400	0	111,400	0.42410	47,245	360,696
10	202,800	20,000	182,800	91,400	-100,000	211,400	0.38554	42,949	403,645

In year 3 the net annual cash flow is $4(A_{CF})_1 = \$212{,}800$/year. A depreciation allowance A_D of $\$200{,}000/10$ years $= \$20{,}000$/year may be set against a fractional tax rate $t = 0.5$ but other allowances A_A are zero. From Equation (2.1-3)

$$\begin{aligned} A_{IT} &= (A_{CI} - A_D - A_A)\,t \\ &= (A_{CI} - 20{,}000 - 0)\,t \\ &= 0.5A_{CI} - \$10{,}000/\text{year} \end{aligned} \tag{2.1-3}$$

From a combination of Equations (2.1-2) and (2.1-4)

$$A_{CI} = A_{CF} + A_{IT} + A_{TC}$$

The net annual cash flow A_{CF} in year 3 is \$212,800/year and the annual capital expenditure A_{TC} is zero. Hence for year 3

$$A_{CI} = 212{,}800 + 0.5A_{CI} - 10{,}000 + 0$$

$$A_{CI} = \frac{212{,}800 - 10{,}000}{0.5} = \$405{,}600/\text{year}$$

Annual cash incomes A_{CI} for earlier years are calculated in the same way. Annual cash incomes A_{CI} for year 4 and subsequently are specified as being at least half of that for year 3, or \$202,800/year. The resulting minimum expected cash flow pattern is presented in Table (8.6-4b).

Minimum net present value (NPV) *required*

The net present value (NPV) of the minimum required cash flow pattern, as given in Table (8.6-4b), is calculated in the same way as Example (3.3-1) to be \$403,645. The results of the calculations are listed in the last three columns of Table (8.6-4b). Any cash flow pattern which gives an (NPV) of at least \$403,645 is more conservative than the strategy provided that the risk capital can be paid back within three years. This will allow alternative pricing policies to be evaluated.

Minimum discounted cash flow rate of return (DCFRR) *required*

The discounted cash flow rate of return (DCFRR) for the minimum required cash flow pattern of Table (8.6-4b) is calculated by the method of Example (3.4-1) to be 34.7 per cent. Any cash flow pattern which allows for payback in three years and has a (DCFRR) of 34.7 per cent or more should be an acceptable alternative.

References for Chapter 8

1. Argenti, J., 'Corporate Planning', p. 70, London, George Allen and Unwin Ltd., 1968
2. Bass, F. M. (Ed.), 'Mathematical Models and Methods in Marketing', Homewood, Ill., Richard D. Irwin, 1961
3. Biermann, H. Jr., and Derbin, A. R., 'Managerial Accounting', p. 1, New York, The Macmillan Co., 1972
4. Cheslow, R. T., and Bates, A. G., *Chem. Eng.*, **72**, No. 24 (1965)
5. Frost, M. J., 'Value for Money: The Techniques of Cost Benefit Analysis', London, The Gower Press, 1971
6. Gregg, J. V., Horsell, C. H., and Richardson, J. T., 'Mathematical Trend Curves', p. 24, London, Oliver and Boyd, 1964
7. Grumer, E. L., *Chem. Eng.*, **74**, No. 9 (1967)
8. Hirschmann, W. B., *Chem. Eng.*, **71**, No. 7 (1964)
9. Kendall, M. G. (Ed.), 'Cost Benefit Analysis', London, The English Universities Press Ltd., 1971
10. Levinson, H. C., 'The Science of Chance', p. 83, London, Faber and Faber, 1952
11. Morrell, A. J. H. (Ed.), 'Problems of Stocks and Storage', London, Oliver and Boyd, 1967
12. Oughton, F., 'Value Analysis and Value Engineering', London, Sir Isaac Pitman and Sons Ltd., 1969
13. Park, W. R., 'Cost Engineering Analysis', p. 213, New York, John Wiley and Sons, 1973
14. Reul, R. I., *Trans. Inst. Chem. Eng.*, **48**, 238 (1970)
15. Reul, R. I., 'Selection and Monitoring of Research and Development Programmes', p. A-21, London, Industrial and Commercial Techniques Ltd., 1970
16. Ridge, W. J., 'Value Analysis for Better Management', Kingport, Ten., American Management Association, Inc., 1969
17. Rudd, D. F., and Watson, C. C., 'Strategy of Process Engineering', p. 91, New York, John Wiley and Sons, Inc., 1968
18. Ibid., p. 92
19. Seglin, L., *Chem. Eng.*, **70**, No. 19 (1963)

Problems for Chapter 8

(8.1-1) During early January 1972, the following transactions were recorded for the Zee company:

1972

Jan 2 the Zee company commenced business with a cash capital of $250,000

Jan 3 the company bought raw materials for cash for $125,000

Jan 4 further raw materials were bought on account from Alpha company for $62,500

Jan 6 the Zee company gave the Alpha company a note for $62,500

Jan 6 the Zee company paid expenses of $25,000 in cash

Jan 9 the Zee company sold half of the material purchased on January 3 for $87,500 cash

Jan 10 the Zee company sold the second half of the material purchased on January 3 for $87,500 to Beta company on account

Jan 11 a sum of $25,000 cash and a note for $62,500 were received from the Beta company.

List the journal entries and post the ledger accounts for the above transactions. Calculate the profit after paying expenses.

(8.1-2) Prepare a balance sheet for the Wye chemical corporation from the following information obtained as at December 31, 1972.

	$		$
bonds payable	300,000	wages payable	75,000
land	20,000	capital received from stockholders	275,000
inventories	195,000		
cash on hand	4,000	prepaid expenses	5,000
cash in bank	320,000	buildings	150,000
accounts payable	75,000	equipment	120,000
taxes payable	35,000	accounts receivable	65,000
retained earnings	164,000	marketable securities	45,000

Assume that depreciation has already been deducted from the original cost of property, plant, and equipment.

(8.1-3) Use the balance sheet obtained from Problem (8.1-2) and the information given below to discuss the financial position of the Wye chemical corporation as at December 31, 1972. Calculate any relevant financial ratios.

The issued common stock consists of 55,000 shares of par value $5 and market value $7 each. The total income amounts to $320,000 and the total expenses are $280,000 for the year. After payment of taxes, the net earnings are $24,000.

(8.2-1) The Beegee Company produces only one product and uses only one work in process account and one finished goods account. The company closes its books on December 31. Set up the necessary accounts showing the flow of costs and closing entries from the following information recorded during the year:

manufacturing costs incurred:

materials	$67,500
direct labor	$60,000
other factory costs	$27,000

The Beegee Company pays a rent of $36,000 per year for its factory building. The company's administrative section occupies one-fifth of the floor area, so that one-fifth of the rent is treated as an administrative expense; the remainder is treated as a manufacturing cost. Other administrative expenses amounted to $44,000 for the year. Selling expenses for the period were $37,300. The opening inventory for work in process was $13,500; at the end of the year it was $15,000. The opening inventory for finished goods was $27,000; at the end of the year it was $18,000. During the year the company received a revenue from sales of $300,000. All the manufacturing overhead was transferred to the work in process account.

(8.6-1) Analyse the utility function represented by Figure (7.3-1) and determine values of the measured survival function (MSF) implied by this attitude to an annual expendable budget of $100,000 using the equation

$$(\text{MSF}) = 1 - (1 - p)^{\beta} \tag{8.6-3}$$

(8.6-2) Repeat the calculations of Example (8.6-3) for minimum acceptable interest rate of returns of 5, 10, 15, 20, and 25 per cent when the risk strategy corresponds to a measured survival function (MSF) of 99 per cent.

Appendix 1
Money Tables

TABLE (A1-1)

Factors for a compound interest rate of 1 per cent

n years	f_i	f_d	f_{AF}	f_{AP}	f_K
1	1.01000	0.99010	1.00000	1.01000	101.00000
2	1.02010	0.98030	0.49751	0.50751	50.75124
3	1.03030	0.97059	0.33002	0.34002	34.00221
4	1.04060	0.96098	0.24628	0.25628	25.62811
5	1.05101	0.95147	0.19604	0.20604	20.60398
6	1.06152	0.94205	0.16255	0.17255	17.25484
7	1.07214	0.93272	0.13863	0.14863	14.86283
8	1.08286	0.92348	0.12069	0.13069	13.06903
9	1.09369	0.91434	0.10674	0.11674	11.67404
10	1.10462	0.90529	0.09558	0.10558	10.55821
11	1.11567	0.89632	0.08645	0.09645	9.64541
12	1.12683	0.88745	0.07885	0.08885	8.88488
13	1.13809	0.87866	0.07241	0.08241	7.69012
14	1.14947	0.86996	0.06690	0.07690	7.69012
15	1.16097	0.86135	0.06212	0.07212	7.21238
16	1.17258	0.85282	0.05794	0.06794	6.79446
17	1.18430	0.84438	0.05426	0.06426	6.42581
18	1.19615	0.83602	0.05098	0.06098	6.09820
19	1.20811	0.82774	0.04805	0.05805	5.80518
20	1.22019	0.81954	0.04542	0.05542	5.54153

$$f_i = (1 + i)^n$$

$$f_d = \frac{1}{(1 + i)^n}$$

$$f_{AF} = \frac{i}{(1 + i)^n - 1}$$

$$f_{AP} = \frac{i(1 + i)^n}{(1 + i)^n - 1}$$

$$f_K = \frac{(1 + i)^n}{(1 + i)^n - 1}$$

TABLE (A1-2)

Factors for a compound interest rate

of 2 per cent

n years	f_i	f_d	f_{AF}	f_{AP}	f_K
1	1.02000	0.98039	1.00000	1.02000	51.00000
2	1.04040	0.96117	0.49505	0.51505	25.75248
3	1.06121	0.94232	0.32675	0.34675	17.33773
4	1.08243	0.92385	0.24262	0.26262	13.13119
5	1.10408	0.90573	0.19216	0.21216	10.60792
6	1.12616	0.88797	0.15853	0.17853	8.92629
7	1.14869	0.87056	0.13451	0.15451	7.72560
8	1.17166	0.85349	0.11651	0.13651	6.82549
9	1.19509	0.83676	0.10252	0.12252	6.12577
10	1.21899	0.82035	0.09133	0.11133	5.56633
11	1.24337	0.80426	0.08218	0.10218	5.10890
12	1.26824	0.78849	0.07456	0.09456	4.72798
13	1.29361	0.77303	0.06812	0.08812	4.40592
14	1.31948	0.75788	0.06260	0.08260	4.13010
15	1.34587	0.74301	0.05783	0.07783	3.89127
16	1.37279	0.72845	0.05365	0.07365	3.68251
17	1.40024	0.71416	0.04997	0.06997	3.49849
18	1.42825	0.70016	0.04670	0.06670	3.33511
19	1.45681	0.68643	0.04378	0.06378	3.18909
20	1.48595	0.67297	0.04116	0.06116	3.05784

$$f_i = (1 + i)^n$$

$$f_d = \frac{1}{(1 + i)^n}$$

$$f_{AF} = \frac{i}{(1 + i)^n - 1}$$

$$f_{AP} = \frac{i(1 + i)^n}{(1 + i)^n - 1}$$

$$f_K = \frac{(1 + i)^n}{(1 + i)^n - 1}$$

TABLE (A1-3)

Factors for a compound interest rate of 3 per cent

n years	f_i	f_d	f_{AF}	f_{AP}	f_K
1	1.03000	0.97087	1.00000	1.03000	34.33333
2	1.06090	0.94260	0.49261	0.52261	17.42036
3	1.09273	0.91514	0.32353	0.35353	11.78435
4	1.12551	0.88849	0.23903	0.26903	8.96757
5	1.15927	0.86261	0.18835	0.21835	7.27849
6	1.19405	0.83748	0.15460	0.18460	6.15325
7	1.22987	0.81309	0.13051	0.16051	5.35021
8	1.26677	0.78941	0.11246	0.14246	4.74855
9	1.30477	0.76642	0.09843	0.12843	4.28113
10	1.34392	0.74409	0.08723	0.11723	3.90768
11	1.38423	0.72242	0.07808	0.10808	3.60258
12	1.42576	0.70138	0.07046	0.10046	3.34874
13	1.46853	0.68095	0.06403	0.09403	3.13432
14	1.51259	0.66112	0.05853	0.08853	2.95088
15	1.55797	0.64186	0.05377	0.08377	2.79222
16	1.60471	0.62317	0.04961	0.07961	2.65369
17	1.65285	0.60502	0.04595	0.07595	2.53175
18	1.70243	0.58739	0.04271	0.07271	2.42362
19	1.75351	0.57029	0.03981	0.06981	2.32713
20	1.80611	0.55368	0.03722	0.06722	2.24052

$$f_i = (1 + i)^n$$

$$f_d = \frac{1}{(1 + i)^n}$$

$$f_{AF} = \frac{i}{(1 + i)^n - 1}$$

$$f_{AP} = \frac{i(1 + i)n}{(1 + i)^n - 1}$$

$$f_K = \frac{(1 + i)^n}{(1 + i)^n - 1}$$

TABLE (A1-4)

Factors for a compound interest rate of 4 per cent

n years	f_i	f_d	f_{AF}	f_{AP}	f_K
1	1.04000	0.96154	1.00000	1.04000	26.00000
2	1.08160	0.92456	0.49020	0.53020	13.25490
3	1.12486	0.88900	0.32035	0.36035	9.00871
4	1.16986	0.85480	0.23549	0.27549	6.88725
5	1.21665	0.82193	0.18463	0.22463	5.61568
6	1.26532	0.79031	0.15076	0.19076	4.76905
7	1.31593	0.75992	0.12661	0.16661	4.16524
8	1.36857	0.73069	0.10853	0.14853	3.71320
9	1.42331	0.70259	0.09449	0.13449	3.36232
10	1.48024	0.67556	0.08329	0.12329	3.08227
11	1.53945	0.64958	0.07415	0.11415	2.85373
12	1.60103	0.62460	0.06655	0.10655	2.66380
13	1.66507	0.60057	0.06014	0.10014	2.50359
14	1.73168	0.57748	0.05467	0.09467	2.36672
15	1.80094	0.55526	0.04994	0.08994	2.24853
16	1.87298	0.53391	0.04582	0.08582	2.14550
17	1.94790	0.51337	0.04220	0.08220	2.05496
18	2.02582	0.49363	0.03899	0.07899	1.97483
19	2.10685	0.47464	0.03614	0.07614	1.90347
20	2.19112	0.45639	0.03358	0.07358	1.83954

$$f_i = (1 + i)^n$$

$$f_d = \frac{1}{(1 + i)^n}$$

$$f_{AF} = \frac{i}{(1 + i)^n - 1}$$

$$f_{AP} = \frac{i(1 + i)^n}{(1 + i)^n - 1}$$

$$f_K = \frac{(1 + i)^n}{(1 + i)^n - 1}$$

TABLE (A1-5)

Factors for a compound interest rate of 5 per cent

n years	f_i	f_d	f_{AF}	f_{AP}	f_K
1	1.05000	0.95238	1.00000	1.05000	21.00000
2	1.10250	0.90703	0.48780	0.53780	10.75610
3	1.15762	0.86384	0.31721	0.36721	7.34417
4	1.21551	0.82270	0.23201	0.28201	5.64024
5	1.27628	0.78353	0.18097	0.23097	4.61950
6	1.34010	0.74622	0.14702	0.19702	3.94035
7	1.40710	0.71068	0.12282	0.17282	3.45640
8	1.47746	0.67684	0.10472	0.15472	3.09444
9	1.55133	0.64461	0.09069	0.14069	2.81380
10	1.62889	0.61391	0.07950	0.12950	2.59009
11	1.71034	0.58468	0.07039	0.12039	2.40778
12	1.79586	0.55684	0.06283	0.11283	2.25651
13	1.88565	0.53032	0.05646	0.10646	2.12912
14	1.97993	0.50507	0.05102	0.10102	2.02048
15	2.07893	0.48102	0.04634	0.09634	1.92685
16	2.18287	0.45811	0.04227	0.09227	1.84540
17	2.29202	0.43630	0.03870	0.08870	1.77398
18	2.40662	0.41552	0.03555	0.08555	1.71092
19	2.52695	0.39573	0.03275	0.08275	1.65490
20	2.65330	0.37689	0.03024	0.08024	1.60485

$$f_i = (1 + i)^n$$

$$f_d = \frac{1}{(1 + i)^n}$$

$$f_{AF} = \frac{i}{(1 + i)^n - 1}$$

$$f_{AP} = \frac{i(1 + i)^n}{(1 + i)^n - 1}$$

$$f_K = \frac{(1 + i)^n}{(1 + i)^n - 1}$$

TABLE (A1-6)

Factors for a compound interest rate of 6 per cent

n years	f_i	f_d	f_{AF}	f_{AP}	f_K
1	1.06000	0.94340	1.00000	1.06000	17.66667
2	1.12360	0.89000	0.48544	0.54544	9.09061
3	1.19102	0.83962	0.31411	0.37411	6.23516
4	1.26248	0.79209	0.22859	0.28859	4.80986
5	1.33823	0.74726	0.17740	0.23740	3.95661
6	1.41852	0.70496	0.14336	0.20336	3.38938
7	1.50363	0.66506	0.11914	0.17914	2.98558
8	1.59385	0.62741	0.10104	0.16104	2.68393
9	1.68948	0.59190	0.08702	0.14702	2.45037
10	1.79085	0.55839	0.07587	0.13587	2.26447
11	1.89830	0.52679	0.06679	0.12679	2.11322
12	2.01220	0.49697	0.05928	0.11928	1.98795
13	2.13293	0.46884	0.05296	0.11296	1.88267
14	2.26090	0.44230	0.04758	0.10758	1.79308
15	2.39656	0.41727	0.04296	0.10296	1.71605
16	2.54035	0.39365	0.03895	0.09895	1.64920
17	2.69277	0.37136	0.03544	0.09544	1.59075
18	2.85434	0.35034	0.03236	0.09236	1.53928
19	3.02560	0.33051	0.02962	0.08962	1.49368
20	3.20714	0.31180	0.02718	0.08718	1.45308

$$f_i = (1 + i)^n$$

$$f_d = \frac{1}{(1 + i)^n}$$

$$f_{AF} = \frac{i}{(1 + i)^n - 1}$$

$$f_{AP} = \frac{i(1 + i)^n}{(1 + i)^n - 1}$$

$$f_K = \frac{(1 + i)^n}{(1 + i)^n - 1}$$

TABLE (A1-7)

Factors for a compound interest rate

of 7 per cent

n years	f_i	f_d	f_{AF}	f_{AP}	f_K
1	1.07000	0.93458	1.00000	1.07000	15.28571
2	1.14490	0.87344	0.48309	0.55309	7.90131
3	1.22504	0.81630	0.31105	0.38105	5.44360
4	1.31080	0.76290	0.22523	0.29523	4.21754
5	1.40255	0.71299	0.17389	0.24389	3.48415
6	1.50073	0.66634	0.13980	0.20980	2.99708
7	1.60578	0.62275	0.11555	0.18555	2.65076
8	1.71819	0.58201	0.09747	0.16747	2.39240
9	1.83846	0.54393	0.08349	0.15349	2.19266
10	1.96715	0.50835	0.07238	0.14238	2.03396
11	2.10485	0.47509	0.06336	0.13336	1.90510
12	2.25219	0.44401	0.05590	0.12590	1.79860
13	2.40985	0.41496	0.04965	0.11965	1.70930
14	2.57853	0.38782	0.04434	0.11434	1.63350
15	2.75903	0.36245	0.03979	0.10979	1.56849
16	2.95216	0.33873	0.03586	0.10586	1.51225
17	3.15882	0.31657	0.03243	0.10243	1.46322
18	3.37993	0.29586	0.02941	0.09941	1.42018
19	3.61653	0.27651	0.02675	0.09675	1.38219
20	3.86968	0.25842	0.02439	0.09439	1.34847

$$f_i = (1 + i)n$$

$$f_d = \frac{1}{(1 + i)^n}$$

$$f_{AF} = \frac{i}{(1 + i)^n - 1}$$

$$f_{AP} = \frac{i(1 + i)n}{(1 + i)^n - 1}$$

$$f_K = \frac{(1 + i)n}{(1 + i)^n - 1}$$

TABLE (A1-8)

Factors for a compound interest rate of 8 per cent

n years	f_i	f_d	f_{AF}	f_{AP}	f_K
1	1.08000	0.92593	1.00000	1.08000	13.50000
2	1.16640	0.85734	0.48077	0.56077	7.00962
3	1.25971	0.79383	0.30803	0.38803	4.85042
4	1.36049	0.73503	0.22192	0.30192	3.77401
5	1.46933	0.68058	0.17046	0.25046	3.13071
6	1.58687	0.63017	0.13632	0.21632	2.70394
7	1.71382	0.58349	0.11207	0.19207	2.40091
8	1.85093	0.54027	0.09401	0.17401	2.17518
9	1.99900	0.50025	0.08008	0.16008	2.00100
10	2.15892	0.46319	0.06903	0.14903	1.86287
11	2.33164	0.42888	0.06008	0.14008	1.75095
12	2.51817	0.39711	0.05270	0.13270	1.65869
13	2.71962	0.36770	0.04652	0.12652	1.58152
14	2.93719	0.34046	0.04130	0.12130	1.51621
15	3.17217	0.31524	0.03683	0.11683	1.46037
16	3.42594	0.29189	0.03298	0.11298	1.41221
17	3.70002	0.27027	0.02963	0.10963	1.37037
18	3.99602	0.25025	0.02670	0.10670	1.33378
19	4.31570	0.23171	0.02413	0.10413	1.30160
20	4.66096	0.21455	0.02185	0.10185	1.27315

$$f_i = (1 + i)^n$$

$$f_d = \frac{1}{(1 + i)^n}$$

$$f_{AF} = \frac{i}{(1 + i)^n - 1}$$

$$f_{AP} = \frac{i(1 + i)^n}{(1 + i)^n - 1}$$

$$f_K = \frac{(1 + i)^n}{(1 + i)^n - 1}$$

TABLE (A1-9)

Factors for a compound interest rate

of 9 per cent

n years	f_i	f_d	f_{AF}	f_{AP}	f_K
1	1.09000	0.91743	1.00000	1.09000	12.11111
2	1.18810	0.84168	0.47847	0.56847	6.31632
3	1.29503	0.77218	0.30505	0.39505	4.38950
4	1.41158	0.70843	0.21867	0.30867	3.42965
5	1.53862	0.64993	0.16709	0.25709	2.85658
6	1.67710	0.59627	0.13292	0.22292	2.47689
7	1.82804	0.54703	0.10869	0.19869	2.20767
8	1.99256	0.50187	0.09067	0.18067	2.00749
9	2.17189	0.46043	0.07680	0.16680	1.85332
10	2.36736	0.42241	0.06582	0.15582	1.73133
11	2.58043	0.38753	0.05695	0.14695	1.63274
12	2.81266	0.35553	0.04965	0.13965	1.55167
13	3.06580	0.32618	0.04357	0.13357	1.48407
14	3.34173	0.29925	0.03843	0.12843	1.42704
15	3.64248	0.27454	0.03406	0.12406	1.37843
16	3.97031	0.25187	0.03030	0.12030	1.33667
17	4.32763	0.23107	0.02705	0.11705	1.30051
18	4.71712	0.21199	0.02421	0.11421	1.26903
19	5.14166	0.19449	0.02173	0.11173	1.24145
20	5.60441	0.17843	0.01955	0.10955	1.21718

$$f_i = (1 + i)^n$$

$$f_d = \frac{1}{(1 + i)^n}$$

$$f_{AF} = \frac{i}{(1 + i)^n - 1}$$

$$f_{AP} = \frac{i(1 + i)^n}{(1 + i)^n - 1}$$

$$f_K = \frac{(1 + i)^n}{(1 + i)^n - 1}$$

TABLE (A1-10)

Factors for a compound interest rate of 10 per cent

n years	f_i	f_d	f_{AF}	f_{AP}	f_K
1	1.10000	0.90909	1.00000	1.10000	11.00000
2	1.21000	0.82645	0.47619	0.57619	5.76190
3	1.33100	0.75131	0.30211	0.40211	4.02115
4	1.46410	0.68301	0.21547	0.31547	3.15471
5	1.61051	0.62092	0.16380	0.26380	2.63797
6	1.77156	0.56447	0.12961	0.22961	2.29607
7	1.94872	0.51316	0.10541	0.20541	2.05405
8	2.14359	0.46651	0.08744	0.18744	1.87444
9	2.35795	0.42410	0.07364	0.17364	1.73641
10	2.59374	0.38554	0.06275	0.16275	1.62745
11	2.85312	0.35049	0.05396	0.15396	1.53963
12	3.13843	0.31863	0.04676	0.14676	1.46763
13	3.45227	0.28966	0.04078	0.14078	1.40779
14	3.79750	0.26333	0.03575	0.13575	1.35746
15	4.17725	0.23939	0.03147	0.13147	1.31474
16	4.59497	0.21763	0.02782	0.12782	1.27817
17	5.05447	0.19784	0.02466	0.12466	1.24664
18	5.55992	0.17986	0.02193	0.12193	1.21930
19	6.11591	0.16351	0.01955	0.11955	1.19547
20	6.72750	0.14864	0.01746	0.11746	1.17460

$$f_i = (1 + i)^n$$

$$f_d = \frac{1}{(1 + i)^n}$$

$$f_{AF} = \frac{i}{(1 + i)^n - 1}$$

$$f_{AP} = \frac{i(1 + i)^n}{(1 + i)^n - 1}$$

$$f_K = \frac{(1 + i)^n}{(1 + i)^n - 1}$$

TABLE (A1-11)

Factors for a compound interest rate

of 11 per cent

n years	f_i	f_d	f_{AF}	f_{AP}	f_K
1	1.11000	0.90090	1.00000	1.11000	10.09091
2	1.23210	0.81162	0.47393	0.58393	5.30849
3	1.36763	0.73119	0.29921	0.40921	3.72012
4	1.51807	0.65873	0.21233	0.32233	2.93024
5	1.68506	0.59345	0.16057	0.27057	2.45973
6	1.87041	0.53464	0.12638	0.23638	2.14888
7	2.07616	0.48166	0.10222	0.21222	1.92923
8	2.30454	0.43393	0.08432	0.19432	1.76656
9	2.55804	0.39092	0.07060	0.18060	1.64183
10	2.83942	0.35218	0.05980	0.16980	1.54365
11	3.15176	0.31728	0.05112	0.16112	1.46474
12	3.49845	0.28584	0.04403	0.15403	1.40025
13	3.88328	0.25751	0.03815	0.14815	1.34683
14	4.31044	0.23199	0.03323	0.14323	1.30207
15	4.78459	0.20900	0.02907	0.13907	1.26423
16	5.31089	0.18829	0.02552	0.13552	1.23197
17	5.89509	0.16963	0.02247	0.13247	1.20429
18	6.54355	0.15282	0.01984	0.12984	1.18039
19	7.26334	0.13768	0.01756	0.12756	1.15966
20	8.06231	0.12403	0.01558	0.12558	1.14160

$$f_i = (1 + i)^n$$

$$f_d = \frac{1}{(1 + i)^n}$$

$$f_{AF} = \frac{i}{(1 + i)^n - 1}$$

$$f_{AP} = \frac{i(1 + i)^n}{(1 + i)^n - 1}$$

$$f_K = \frac{(1 + i)^n}{(1 + i)^n - 1}$$

TABLE (A1-12)

Factors for a compound interest rate of 12 per cent

n years	f_i	f_d	f_{AF}	f_{AP}	f_K
1	1.12000	0.89286	1.00000	1.12000	9.33333
2	1.25440	0.79719	0.47170	0.59170	4.93082
3	1.40493	0.71178	0.29635	0.41635	3.46957
4	1.57352	0.63552	0.20923	0.32923	2.74362
5	1.76234	0.56743	0.15741	0.27741	2.31175
6	1.97382	0.50663	0.12323	0.24323	2.02688
7	2.21068	0.45235	0.09912	0.21912	1.82598
8	2.47596	0.40388	0.08130	0.20130	1.67752
9	2.77308	0.36061	0.06768	0.18768	1.56399
10	3.10585	0.32197	0.05698	0.17698	1.47487
11	3.47855	0.28748	0.04842	0.16842	1.40346
12	3.89598	0.25668	0.04144	0.16144	1.34531
13	4.36349	0.22917	0.03568	0.15568	1.29731
14	4.88711	0.20462	0.03087	0.15087	1.25726
15	5.47357	0.18270	0.02682	0.14682	1.22354
16	6.13039	0.16312	0.02339	0.14339	1.19492
17	6.86604	0.14564	0.02046	0.14046	1.17047
18	7.68997	0.13004	0.01794	0.13794	1.14948
19	8.61276	0.11611	0.01576	0.13576	1.13136
20	9.64629	0.10367	0.01388	0.13388	1.11566

$$f_i = (1 + i)^n$$

$$f_d = \frac{1}{(1 + i)^n}$$

$$f_{AF} = \frac{i}{(1 + i)^n - 1}$$

$$f_{AP} = \frac{i(1 + i)^n}{(1 + i)^n - 1}$$

$$f_K = \frac{(1 + i)^n}{(1 + i)^n - 1}$$

TABLE (A1-13)

Factors for a compound interest rate

of 13 per cent

n years	f_i	f_d	f_{AF}	f_{AP}	f_K
1	1.13000	0.88496	1.00000	1.13000	8.69231
2	1.27690	0.78315	0.46948	0.59948	4.61141
3	1.44290	0.69305	0.29352	0.42352	3.25786
4	1.63047	0.61332	0.20619	0.33619	2.58611
5	1.84244	0.54276	0.15431	0.28431	2.18703
6	2.08195	0.48032	0.12015	0.25015	1.92426
7	2.35261	0.42506	0.09611	0.22611	1.73931
8	2.65844	0.37616	0.07839	0.20839	1.60297
9	3.00404	0.33288	0.06487	0.19487	1.49899
10	3.39457	0.29459	0.05429	0.18429	1.41761
11	3.83586	0.26070	0.04584	0.17584	1.35263
12	4.33452	0.23071	0.03899	0.16899	1.29989
13	4.89801	0.20416	0.03335	0.16335	1.25654
14	5.53475	0.18068	0.02867	0.15867	1.22052
15	6.25427	0.15989	0.02474	0.15474	1.19032
16	7.06733	0.14150	0.02143	0.15143	1.16482
17	7.98608	0.12522	0.01861	0.14861	1.14314
18	9.02427	0.11081	0.01620	0.14620	1.12462
19	10.19742	0.09806	0.01413	0.14413	1.10873
20	11.52309	0.08678	0.01235	0.14235	1.09503

$$f_i = (1 + i)^n$$

$$f_d = \frac{1}{(1 + i)^n}$$

$$f_{AF} = \frac{i}{(1 + i)^n - 1}$$

$$f_{AP} = \frac{i(1 + i)^n}{(1 + i)^n - 1}$$

$$f_K = \frac{(1 + i)^n}{(1 + i)^n - 1}$$

TABLE (A1-14)

Factors for a compound interest rate of 14 per cent

n years	f_i	f_d	f_{AF}	f_{AP}	f_K
1	1.14000	0.87719	1.00000	1.14000	8.14286
2	1.29960	0.76947	0.46729	0.60729	4.33778
3	1.48154	0.67497	0.29073	0.43073	3.07665
4	1.68896	0.59208	0.20320	0.34320	2.45146
5	1.92541	0.51937	0.15128	0.29128	2.08060
6	2.19497	0.45559	0.11716	0.25716	1.83684
7	2.50227	0.39964	0.09319	0.23319	1.66566
8	2.85259	0.35056	0.07557	0.21557	1.53979
9	3.25195	0.30751	0.06217	0.20217	1.44406
10	3.70722	0.26974	0.05171	0.19171	1.36938
11	4.22623	0.23662	0.04339	0.18339	1.30996
12	4.81790	0.20756	0.03667	0.17667	1.26192
13	5.49241	0.18207	0.03116	0.17116	1.22260
14	6.26135	0.15971	0.02661	0.16661	1.19007
15	7.13794	0.14010	0.02281	0.16281	1.16292
16	8.13725	0.12289	0.01962	0.15962	1.14011
17	9.27646	0.10780	0.01692	0.15692	1.12082
18	10.57517	0.09456	0.01462	0.15462	1.10444
19	12.05569	0.08295	0.01266	0.15266	1.09045
20	13.74349	0.07276	0.01099	0.15099	1.07847

$$f_i = (1 + i)^n$$

$$f_d = \frac{1}{(1 + i)^n}$$

$$f_{AF} = \frac{i}{(1 + i)^n - 1}$$

$$f_{AP} = \frac{i(1 + i)^n}{(1 + i)^n - 1}$$

$$f_K = \frac{(1 + i)^n}{(1 + i)^n - 1}$$

TABLE (A1-15)

Factors for a compound interest rate

of 15 per cent

n years	f_i	f_d	f_{AF}	f_{AP}	f_K
1	1.15000	0.86957	1.00000	1.15000	7.66667
2	1.32250	0.75614	0.46512	0.61512	4.10078
3	1.52088	0.65752	0.28798	0.43798	2.91985
4	1.74901	0.57175	0.20027	0.35027	2.33510
5	2.01136	0.49718	0.14832	0.29832	1.98877
6	2.31306	0.43233	0.11424	0.26424	1.76158
7	2.66002	0.37594	0.09036	0.24036	1.60240
8	3.05902	0.32690	0.07285	0.22285	1.48567
9	3.51788	0.28426	0.05957	0.20957	1.39716
10	4.04556	0.24718	0.04925	0.19925	1.32835
11	4.65239	0.21494	0.04107	0.19107	1.27379
12	5.35025	0.18691	0.03448	0.18448	1.22987
13	6.15279	0.16253	0.02911	0.17911	1.19407
14	7.07571	0.14133	0.02469	0.17469	1.16459
15	8.13706	0.12289	0.02102	0.17102	1.14011
16	9.35762	0.10686	0.01795	0.16795	1.11965
17	10.76126	0.09293	0.01537	0.16537	1.10245
18	12.37545	0.08081	0.01319	0.16319	1.08791
19	14.23177	0.07027	0.01134	0.16134	1.07558
20	16.36654	0.06110	0.00976	0.15976	1.06508

$$f_i = (1 + i)^n$$

$$f_d = \frac{1}{(1 + i)^n}$$

$$f_{AF} = \frac{i}{(1 + i)^n - 1}$$

$$f_{AP} = \frac{i(1 + i)^n}{(1 + i)^n - 1}$$

$$f_K = \frac{(1 + i)^n}{(1 + i)^n - 1}$$

TABLE (A1-16)

Factors for a compound interest rate of 16 per cent

n years	f_i	f_d	f_{AF}	f_{AP}	f_K
1	1.16000	0.86207	1.00000	1.16000	7.25000
2	1.34560	0.74316	0.46296	0.62296	3.89352
3	1.56090	0.64066	0.28526	0.44526	2.78286
4	1.81064	0.55229	0.19738	0.35738	2.23359
5	2.10034	0.47611	0.14541	0.30541	1.90881
6	2.43640	0.41044	0.11139	0.27139	1.69619
7	2.82622	0.35383	0.08761	0.24761	1.54758
8	3.27841	0.30503	0.07022	0.23022	1.43890
9	3.80296	0.26295	0.05708	0.21708	1.35677
10	4.41144	0.22668	0.04690	0.20690	1.29313
11	5.11726	0.19542	0.03886	0.19886	1.24288
12	5.93603	0.16846	0.03241	0.19241	1.20259
13	6.88579	0.14523	0.02718	0.18718	1.16990
14	7.98752	0.12520	0.02290	0.18290	1.14311
15	9.26552	0.10793	0.01936	0.17936	1.12098
16	10.74800	0.09304	0.01641	0.17641	1.10259
17	12.46768	0.08021	0.01395	0.17395	1.08720
18	14.46251	0.06914	0.01188	0.17188	1.07428
19	16.77652	0.05961	0.01014	0.17014	1.06339
20	19.46076	0.05139	0.00867	0.16867	1.05417

$$f_i = (1 + i)^n$$

$$f_d = \frac{1}{(1 + i)^n}$$

$$f_{AF} = \frac{i}{(1 + i)^n - 1}$$

$$f_{AP} = \frac{i(1 + i)^n}{(1 + i)^n - 1}$$

$$f_K = \frac{(1 + i)^n}{(1 + i)^n - 1}$$

TABLE (A1-17)

Factors for a compound interest rate

of 17 per cent

n years	f_i	f_d	f_{AF}	f_{AP}	f_K
1	1.17000	0.85470	1.00000	1.17000	6.88235
2	1.36890	0.73051	0.46083	0.63083	3.71076
3	1.60161	0.62437	0.28257	0.45257	2.66220
4	1.87389	0.53365	0.19453	0.36453	2.14431
5	2.19245	0.45611	0.14256	0.31256	1.83861
6	2.56516	0.38984	0.10861	0.27861	1.63891
7	3.00124	0.33320	0.08495	0.25495	1.49969
8	3.51145	0.28478	0.06769	0.23769	1.39818
9	4.10840	0.24340	0.05469	0.22469	1.32171
10	4.80683	0.20804	0.04466	0.21466	1.26269
11	5.62399	0.17781	0.03676	0.20676	1.21626
12	6.58007	0.15197	0.03047	0.20047	1.17921
13	7.69868	0.12989	0.02538	0.19538	1.14928
14	9.00745	0.11102	0.02123	0.19123	1.12488
15	10.53872	0.09489	0.01782	0.18782	1.10484
16	12.33030	0.08110	0.01500	0.18500	1.08826
17	14.42646	0.06932	0.01266	0.18266	1.07448
18	16.87895	0.05925	0.01071	0.18071	1.06298
19	19.74838	0.05064	0.00907	0.17907	1.05334
20	23.10560	0.04328	0.00769	0.17769	1.04524

$$f_i = (1 + i)^n$$

$$f_d = \frac{1}{(1 + i)^n}$$

$$f_{AF} = \frac{i}{(1 + i)^n - 1}$$

$$f_{AP} = \frac{i(1 + i)^n}{(1 + i)^n - 1}$$

$$f_K = \frac{(1 + i)^n}{(1 + i)^n - 1}$$

TABLE (A1-18)

Factors for a compound interest rate of 18 per cent

n years	f_i	f_d	f_{AF}	f_{AP}	f_K
1	1.18000	0.84746	1.00000	1.18000	6.55556
2	1.39240	0.71818	0.45872	0.63872	3.54842
3	1.64303	0.60863	0.27992	0.45992	2.55513
4	1.93878	0.51579	0.19174	0.37174	2.06521
5	2.28776	0.43711	0.13978	0.31978	1.77654
6	2.69955	0.37043	0.10591	0.28591	1.58839
7	3.18547	0.31393	0.08236	0.26236	1.45757
8	3.75886	0.26604	0.06524	0.24524	1.36247
9	4.43545	0.22546	0.05239	0.23239	1.29108
10	5.23384	0.19106	0.04251	0.22251	1.23619
11	6.17593	0.16192	0.03478	0.21478	1.19320
12	7.28759	0.13722	0.02863	0.20863	1.15904
13	8.59936	0.11629	0.02369	0.20369	1.13159
14	10.14724	0.09855	0.01968	0.19968	1.10932
15	11.97375	0.08352	0.01640	0.19640	1.09113
16	14.12902	0.07078	0.01371	0.19371	1.07617
17	16.67225	0.05998	0.01149	0.19149	1.06381
18	19.67325	0.05083	0.00964	0.18964	1.05355
19	23.21444	0.04308	0.00810	0.18810	1.04502
20	27.39303	0.03651	0.00682	0.18682	1.03789

$$f_i = (1 + i)^n$$

$$f_d = \frac{1}{(1 + i)^n}$$

$$f_{AF} = \frac{i}{(1 + i)^n - 1}$$

$$f_{AP} = \frac{i(1 + i)^n}{(1 + i)^n - 1}$$

$$f_K = \frac{(1 + i)^n}{(1 + i)^n - 1}$$

TABLE (A1-19)

Factors for a compound interest rate

of 19 per cent

n years	f_i	f_d	f_{AF}	f_{AP}	f_K
1	1.19000	0.84034	1.00000	1.19000	6.26316
2	1.41610	0.70616	0.45662	0.64662	3.40327
3	1.68516	0.59342	0.27731	0.46731	2.45952
4	2.00534	0.49867	0.18899	0.37899	1.99469
5	2.38635	0.41905	0.13705	0.32705	1.72132
6	2.83976	0.35214	0.10327	0.29327	1.54355
7	3.37932	0.29592	0.07985	0.26985	1.42029
8	4.02139	0.24867	0.06289	0.25289	1.33097
9	4.78545	0.20897	0.05019	0.24019	1.26417
10	5.69468	0.17560	0.04047	0.23047	1.21301
11	6.77667	0.14757	0.03289	0.22289	1.17311
12	8.06424	0.12400	0.02690	0.21690	1.14156
13	9.59645	0.10421	0.02210	0.21210	1.11633
14	11.41977	0.08757	0.01823	0.20823	1.09597
15	13.58953	0.07359	0.01509	0.20509	1.07943
16	16.17154	0.06184	0.01252	0.20252	1.06591
17	19.24413	0.05196	0.01041	0.20041	1.05481
18	22.90052	0.04367	0.00868	0.19868	1.04566
19	27.25162	0.03670	0.00724	0.19724	1.03809
20	32.42942	0.03084	0.00605	0.19605	1.03182

$$f_i = (1 + i)^n$$

$$f_d = \frac{1}{(1 + i)^n}$$

$$f_{AF} = \frac{i}{(1 + i)^n - 1}$$

$$f_{AP} = \frac{i(1 + i)^n}{(1 + i)^n - 1}$$

$$f_K = \frac{(1 + i)^n}{(1 + i)^n - 1}$$

TABLE (A1-20)

Factors for a compound interest rate of 20 per cent

n years	f_i	f_d	f_{AF}	f_{AP}	f_K
1	1.20000	0.83333	1.00000	1.20000	6.00000
2	1.44000	0.69444	0.45455	0.65455	3.27273
3	1.72800	0.57870	0.27473	0.47473	2.37363
4	2.07360	0.48225	0.18629	0.38629	1.93145
5	2.48832	0.40188	0.13438	0.33438	1.67190
6	2.98598	0.33490	0.10071	0.30071	1.50353
7	3.58318	0.27908	0.07742	0.27742	1.38712
8	4.29982	0.23257	0.06061	0.26061	1.30305
9	5.15978	0.19381	0.04808	0.24808	1.24040
10	6.19174	0.16151	0.03852	0.23852	1.19261
11	7.43008	0.13459	0.03110	0.23110	1.15552
12	8.91610	0.11216	0.02526	0.22526	1.12632
13	10.69932	0.09346	0.02062	0.22062	1.10310
14	12.83918	0.07789	0.01689	0.21689	1.08447
15	15.40702	0.06491	0.01388	0.21388	1.06941
16	18.48843	0.05409	0.01144	0.21144	1.05718
17	22.18611	0.04507	0.00944	0.20944	1.04720
18	26.62333	0.03756	0.00781	0.20781	1.03903
19	32.94800	0.03130	0.00646	0.20646	1.03231
20	38.33760	0.02608	0.00536	0.20536	1.02678

$$f_i = (1 + i)^n$$

$$f_d = \frac{1}{(1 + i)^n}$$

$$f_{AF} = \frac{i}{(1 + i)^n - 1}$$

$$f_{AP} = \frac{i(1 + i)^n}{(1 + i)^n - 1}$$

$$f_K = \frac{(1 + i)^n}{(1 + i)^n - 1}$$

TABLE (A1-21)

Factors for a compound interest rate of 21 per cent

n years	f_i	f_d	f_{AF}	f_{AP}	f_K
1	1.21000	0.82645	1.00000	1.21000	5.76190
2	1.46410	0.68301	0.45249	0.66249	3.15471
3	1.77156	0.56447	0.27218	0.48218	2.29607
4	2.14359	0.46651	0.18363	0.39363	1.87444
5	2.59374	0.38554	0.13177	0.34177	1.62745
6	3.13843	0.31863	0.09820	0.30820	1.46763
7	3.79750	0.26333	0.07507	0.28507	1.35746
8	4.59497	0.21763	0.05841	0.26841	1.27817
9	5.55992	0.17986	0.04605	0.25605	1.21930
10	6.72750	0.14864	0.03667	0.24667	1.17460
11	8.14027	0.12285	0.02941	0.23941	1.14005
12	9.84973	0.10153	0.02373	0.23373	1.11300
13	11.91818	0.08391	0.01923	0.22923	1.09159
14	14.42099	0.06934	0.01565	0.22565	1.07451
15	17.44940	0.05731	0.01277	0.22277	1.06079
16	21.11378	0.04736	0.01044	0.22044	1.04972
17	25.54767	0.03914	0.00855	0.21855	1.04074
18	30.91268	0.03235	0.00702	0.21702	1.03343
19	37.40434	0.02673	0.00577	0.21577	1.02747
20	45.25926	0.02209	0.00474	0.21474	1.02259

$$f_i = (1 + i)^n$$

$$f_d = \frac{1}{(1 + i)^n}$$

$$f_{AF} = \frac{i}{(1 + i)^n - 1}$$

$$f_{AP} = \frac{i(1 + i)^n}{(1 + i)^n - 1}$$

$$f_K = \frac{(1 + i)^n}{(1 + i)^n - 1}$$

TABLE (A1-22)

Factors for a compound interest rate of 22 per cent

n years	f_i	f_d	f_{AF}	f_{AP}	f_K
1	1.22000	0.81967	1.00000	1.22000	5.54545
2	1.48840	0.67186	0.45045	0.67045	3.04750
3	1.81585	0.55071	0.26966	0.48966	2.22572
4	2.21533	0.45140	0.18102	0.40102	1.82282
5	2.70271	0.37000	0.12921	0.34921	1.58730
6	3.29730	0.30328	0.09576	0.31576	1.43529
7	4.02271	0.24859	0.07278	0.29278	1.33083
8	4.90771	0.20376	0.05630	0.27630	1.25590
9	5.98740	0.16702	0.04411	0.26411	1.20051
10	7.30463	0.13690	0.03489	0.25489	1.15861
11	8.91165	0.11221	0.02781	0.24781	1.12640
12	10.87221	0.09198	0.02228	0.24228	1.10129
13	13.26410	0.07539	0.01794	0.23794	1.08154
14	16.18220	0.06180	0.01449	0.23449	1.06587
15	19.74229	0.05065	0.01174	0.23174	1.05336
16	24.08559	0.04152	0.00953	0.22953	1.04332
17	29.38442	0.03403	0.00775	0.22775	1.03523
18	35.84899	0.02789	0.00631	0.22631	1.02870
19	43.73577	0.02286	0.00515	0.22515	1.02340
20	53.35764	0.01874	0.00420	0.22420	1.01910

$$f_i = (1 + i)^n$$

$$f_d = \frac{1}{(1 + i)^n}$$

$$f_{AF} = \frac{i}{(1 + i)^n - 1}$$

$$f_{AP} = \frac{i(1 + i)^n}{(1 + i)^n - 1}$$

$$f_K = \frac{(1 + i)^n}{(1 + i)^n - 1}$$

TABLE (A1-23)

Factors for a compound interest rate

of 23 per cent

n years	f_i	f_d	f_{AF}	f_{AP}	f_K
1	1.23000	0.81301	1.00000	1.23000	5.34783
2	1.51290	0.66098	0.44843	0.67843	2.94970
3	1.86087	0.53738	0.26717	0.49717	2.16162
4	2.28887	0.43690	0.17845	0.40845	1.77588
5	2.81531	0.35520	0.12670	0.35670	1.55087
6	3.46283	0.28878	0.09339	0.32339	1.40604
7	4.25928	0.23478	0.07057	0.30057	1.30682
8	5.23891	0.19088	0.05426	0.28426	1.23591
9	6.44386	0.15519	0.04225	0.27225	1.18369
10	7.92595	0.12617	0.03321	0.26321	1.14438
11	9.74891	0.10258	0.02629	0.25629	1.11430
12	11.99116	0.08339	0.02093	0.25093	1.09098
13	14.74913	0.06780	0.01673	0.24673	1.07273
14	18.14143	0.05512	0.01342	0.24342	1.05834
15	22.31396	0.04481	0.01079	0.24079	1.04692
16	27.44617	0.03643	0.00870	0.23870	1.03781
17	33.75879	0.02962	0.00702	0.23702	1.03053
18	41.52331	0.02408	0.00568	0.23568	1.02468
19	51.07368	0.01958	0.00459	0.23459	1.01997
20	62.82062	0.01592	0.00372	0.23372	1.01618

$$f_i = (1 + i)^n$$

$$f_d = \frac{1}{(1 + i)^n}$$

$$f_{AF} = \frac{i}{(1 + i)^n - 1}$$

$$f_{AP} = \frac{i(1 + i)^n}{(1 + i)^n - 1}$$

$$f_K = \frac{(1 + i)^n}{(1 + i)^n - 1}$$

TABLE (A1-24)

Factors for a compound interest rate

of 24 per cent

n years	f_i	f_d	f_{AF}	f_{AP}	f_K
1	1.24000	0.80645	1.00000	1.24000	5.16667
2	1.53760	0.65036	0.44643	0.68643	2.86012
3	1.90662	0.52449	0.26472	0.50472	2.10299
4	2.36421	0.42297	0.17593	0.41593	1.73302
5	2.93163	0.34111	0.12425	0.36425	1.51770
6	3.63522	0.27509	0.09107	0.33107	1.37948
7	4.50767	0.22184	0.06842	0.30842	1.28509
8	5.58951	0.17891	0.05229	0.29229	1.21789
9	6.93099	0.14428	0.04047	0.28047	1.16861
10	8.59443	0.11635	0.03160	0.27160	1.13168
11	10.65709	0.09383	0.02485	0.26485	1.10355
12	13.21479	0.07567	0.01965	0.25965	1.08187
13	16.38634	0.06103	0.01560	0.25560	1.06499
14	20.31906	0.04921	0.01242	0.25242	1.05176
15	25.19563	0.03969	0.00992	0.24992	1.04133
16	31.24259	0.03201	0.00794	0.24794	1.03307
17	38.74081	0.02581	0.00636	0.24636	1.02650
18	48.03860	0.02082	0.00510	0.24510	1.02126
19	59.56786	0.01679	0.00410	0.24410	1.01707
20	73.86415	0.01354	0.00329	0.24329	1.01372

$$f_i = (1 + i)^n$$

$$f_d = \frac{1}{(1 + i)^n}$$

$$f_{AF} = \frac{i}{(1 + i)^n - 1}$$

$$f_{AP} = \frac{i(1 + i)^n}{(1 + i)^n - 1}$$

$$f_K = \frac{(1 + i)^n}{(1 + i)^n - 1}$$

TABLE (A1-25)

Factors for a compound interest rate

of 25 per cent

n years	f_i	f_d	f_{AF}	f_{AP}	f_K
1	1.25000	0.80000	1.00000	1.25000	5.00000
2	1.56250	0.64000	0.44444	0.69444	2.77778
3	1.95312	0.51200	0.26230	0.51230	2.04918
4	2.44141	0.40960	0.17344	0.42344	1.69377
5	3.05176	0.32768	0.12185	0.37185	1.48739
6	3.81470	0.26214	0.08882	0.33882	1.35528
7	4.76837	0.20972	0.06634	0.31634	1.26537
8	5.96046	0.16777	0.05040	0.30040	1.20159
9	7.45058	0.13422	0.03876	0.28876	1.15502
10	9.31323	0.10737	0.03007	0.28007	1.12029
11	11.64153	0.08590	0.02349	0.27349	1.09397
12	14.55192	0.06872	0.01845	0.26845	1.07379
13	18.18989	0.05498	0.01454	0.26454	1.05817
14	22.73737	0.04398	0.01150	0.26150	1.04600
15	28.42171	0.03518	0.00912	0.25912	1.03647
16	35.52714	0.02815	0.00724	0.25724	1.02896
17	44.40892	0.02252	0.00576	0.25576	1.02304
18	55.51115	0.01801	0.00459	0.25459	1.01834
19	69.38894	0.01441	0.00366	0.25366	1.01462
20	86.73617	0.01153	0.00292	0.25292	1.01166

$$f_i = (1 + i)^n$$

$$f_d = \frac{1}{(1 + i)^n}$$

$$f_{AF} = \frac{i}{(1 + i)^n - 1}$$

$$f_{AP} = \frac{i(1 + i)^n}{(1 + i)^n - 1}$$

$$f_K = \frac{(1 + i)^n}{(1 + i)^n - 1}$$

TABLE (A1-26)

Time to double a sum of money for various discrete annual compound interest rates

rate per cent	years	rate per cent	years	rate per cent	years	rate per cent	years
0.25	277.6053	7.75	9.2861	15.25	4.8836	22.75	3.3815
0.50	138.9757	8.00	9.0065	15.50	4.8102	23.00	3.3483
0.75	92.7658	8.25	8.7438	15.75	4.7391	23.25	3.3158
1.00	69.6607	8.50	8.4965	16.00	4.6702	23.50	3.2840
1.25	55.7976	8.75	8.2634	16.25	4.6034	23.75	3.2528
1.50	46.5555	9.00	8.0432	16.50	4.5386	24.00	3.2223
1.75	39.9540	9.25	7.8349	16.75	4.4758	24.25	3.1924
2.00	35.0028	9.50	7.6376	17.00	4.4148	24.50	3.1631
2.25	31.1518	9.75	7.4504	17.25	4.3556	24.75	3.1344
2.50	28.0710	10.00	7.2725	17.50	4.2981	25.00	3.1063
2.75	25.5504	10.25	7.1033	17.75	4.2422	25.25	3.0787
3.00	23.4498	10.50	6.9422	18.00	4.1878	25.50	3.0517
3.25	21.6723	10.75	6.7886	18.25	4.1350	25.75	3.0252
3.50	20.1488	11.00	6.6419	18.50	4.0835	26.00	2.9992
3.75	18.8284	11.25	6.5017	18.75	4.0334	26.25	2.9737
4.00	17.6730	11.50	6.3677	19.00	3.9847	26.50	2.9487
4.25	16.6535	11.75	6.2393	19.25	3.9372	26.75	2.9241
4.50	15.7473	12.00	6.1163	19.50	3.8909	27.00	2.9000
4.75	14.9365	12.25	5.9982	19.75	3.8458	27.25	2.8763
5.00	14.2067	12.50	5.8849	20.00	3.8018	27.50	2.8531
5.25	13.5464	12.75	5.7761	20.25	3.7589	27.75	2.8303
5.50	12.9462	13.00	5.6714	20.50	3.7170	28.00	2.8079
5.75	12.3981	13.25	5.5707	20.75	3.6762	28.25	2.7858
6.00	11.8957	13.50	5.4737	21.00	3.6363	28.50	2.7642
6.25	11.4334	13.75	5.3802	21.25	3.5973	28.75	2.7429
6.50	11.0067	14.00	5.2901	21.50	3.5593	29.00	2.7220
6.75	10.6116	14.25	5.2031	21.75	3.5221	29.25	2.7015
7.00	10.2448	14.50	5.1191	22.00	3.4858	29.50	2.6813
7.25	9.9032	14.75	5.0379	22.25	3.4502	29.75	2.6615
7.50	9.5844	15.00	4.9595	22.50	3.4155	30.00	2.6419

TABLE (A1-27)

Effective annual interest rates equivalent to

nominal annual interest rates of ¼ per cent to 7½ per cent

rate per cent	compounded annually	compounded monthly	compounded daily	compounded continuously
0.25	0.25000	0.25029	0.25031	0.25031
0.50	0.50000	0.50115	0.50125	0.50125
0.75	0.75000	0.75258	0.75281	0.75282
1.00	1.00000	1.00460	1.00500	1.00502
1.25	1.25000	1.25719	1.25782	1.25785
1.50	1.50000	1.51036	1.51128	1.51131
1.75	1.75000	1.76410	1.76536	1.76540
2.00	2.00000	2.01844	2.02008	2.02013
2.25	2.25000	2.27335	2.27543	2.27550
2.50	2.50000	2.52885	2.53142	2.53151
2.75	2.75000	2.78493	2.78806	2.78816
3.00	3.00000	3.04160	3.04533	3.04545
3.25	3.25000	3.29885	3.30324	3.30339
3.50	3.50000	3.55670	3.56180	3.56197
3.75	3.75000	3.81513	3.82100	3.82120
4.00	4.00000	4.07415	4.08085	4.08108
4.25	4.25000	4.33377	4.34135	4.34161
4.50	4.50000	4.59398	4.60250	4.60279
4.75	4.75000	4.85479	4.86430	4.86462
5.00	5.00000	5.11619	5.12675	5.12711
5.25	5.25000	5.37819	5.38986	5.39026
5.50	5.50000	5.64079	5.65362	5.65406
5.75	5.75000	5.90398	5.91805	5.91853
6.00	6.00000	6.16778	6.18313	6.18365
6.25	6.25000	6.43218	6.44888	6.44945
6.50	6.50000	6.69719	6.71528	6.71590
6.75	6.75000	6.96279	6.98236	6.98303
7.00	7.00000	7.22901	7.25010	7.25082
7.25	7.25000	7.49583	7.51851	7.51928
7.50	7.50000	7.76326	7.78758	7.78842

TABLE (A1-28)

Effective annual interest rates equivalent to

nominal annual interest rates of $7\frac{3}{4}$ per cent to 15 per cent

rate per cent	compounded annually	compounded monthly	compounded daily	compounded continuously
7.75	7.75000	8.03130	8.05733	8.05822
8.00	8.00000	8.29995	8.32776	8.32871
8.25	8.25000	8.56921	8.59885	8.59987
8.50	8.50000	8.83909	8.87063	8.87171
8.75	8.75000	9.10958	9.14308	9.14423
9.00	9.00000	9.38069	9.41621	9.41743
9.25	9.25000	9.65241	9.69003	9.69131
9.50	9.50000	9.92476	9.96453	9.96589
9.75	9.75000	10.19772	10.23971	10.24114
10.00	10.00000	10.47131	10.51558	10.51709
10.25	10.25000	10.74551	10.79214	10.79373
10.50	10.50000	11.02035	11.06938	11.07106
10.75	10.75000	11.29580	11.34732	11.34909
11.00	11.00000	11.57188	11.62596	11.62781
11.25	11.25000	11.84859	11.90529	11.90723
11.50	11.50000	12.12593	12.18531	12.18734
11.75	11.75000	12.40390	12.46604	12.46816
12.00	12.00000	12.68250	12.74746	12.74969
12.25	12.25000	12.96174	13.02959	13.03191
12.50	12.50000	13.24160	13.31242	13.31485
12.75	12.75000	13.52211	13.59596	13.59849
13.00	13.00000	13.80325	13.88020	13.88284
13.25	13.25000	14.08503	14.16516	14.16790
13.50	13.50000	14.36744	14.45082	14.45368
13.75	13.75000	14.65050	14.73720	14.74017
14.00	14.00000	14.93420	15.02429	15.02738
14.25	14.25000	15.21855	15.31210	15.31531
14.50	14.50000	15.50354	15.60063	15.60396
14.75	14.75000	15.78917	15.88988	15.89333
15.00	15.00000	16.07545	16.17984	16.18342

TABLE (A1-29)

Effective annual interest rates equivalent to

nominal annual interest rates of 15¼ per cent to 22½ per cent

rate per cent	compounded annually	compounded monthly	compounded daily	compounded continuously
15.25	15.25000	16.36238	16.47054	16.47425
15.50	15.50000	16.64996	16.76195	16.76580
15.75	15.75000	16.93820	17.05410	17.05808
16.00	16.00000	17.22708	17.34697	17.35109
16.25	16.25000	17.51662	17.64058	17.64483
16.50	16.50000	17.80681	17.93491	17.93931
16.75	16.75000	18.09766	18.22999	18.23453
17.00	17.00000	18.38917	18.52579	18.53049
17.25	17.25000	18.68134	18.82234	18.82718
17.50	17.50000	18.97417	19.11963	19.12462
17.75	17.75000	19.26766	19.41765	19.42281
18.00	18.00000	19.56182	19.71642	19.72174
18.25	18.25000	19.85664	20.01594	20.02142
18.50	18.50000	20.15212	20.31620	20.32184
18.75	18.75000	20.44828	20.61722	20.62302
19.00	19.00000	20.74510	20.91898	20.92496
19.25	19.25000	21.04259	21.22150	21.22765
19.50	19.50000	21.34076	21.52477	21.53110
19.75	19.75000	21.63960	21.82880	21.83531
20.00	20.00000	21.93911	22.13359	22.14028
20.25	20.25000	22.23930	22.43913	22.44601
20.50	20.50000	22.54016	22.74544	22.75251
20.75	20.75000	22.84171	23.05252	23.05977
21.00	21.00000	23.14393	23.36036	23.36781
21.25	21.25000	23.44684	23.66896	23.67661
21.50	21.50000	23.75043	23.97834	23.98619
21.75	21.75000	24.05470	24.28849	24.29654
22.00	22.00000	24.35966	24.59941	24.60767
22.25	22.25000	24.66530	24.91111	24.91958
22.50	22.50000	24.97164	25.22359	25.23227

TABLE (A1-30)

Effective annual interest rates equivalent to

nominal annual interest rates of 22¾ per cent to 30 per cent

rate per cent	compounded annually	compounded monthly	compounded daily	compounded continuously
22.75	22.75000	25.27866	25.53685	25.54574
23.00	23.00000	25.58638	25.85088	25.86000
23.25	23.25000	25.89479	26.16571	26.17504
23.50	23.50000	26.20389	26.48131	26.49088
23.75	23.75000	26.51368	26.79771	26.80750
24.00	24.00000	26.82418	27.11489	27.12492
24.25	24.25000	27.13537	27.43286	27.44312
24.50	24.50000	27.44727	27.75163	27.76213
24.75	24.75000	27.75986	28.07119	28.08194
25.00	25.00000	28.07316	28.39155	28.40254
25.25	25.25000	28.38716	28.71271	28.72395
25.50	25.50000	28.70186	29.03467	29.04616
25.75	25.75000	29.01728	29.35744	29.36918
26.00	26.00000	29.33340	29.68101	29.69301
26.25	26.25000	29.65023	30.00538	30.01765
26.50	26.50000	29.96777	30.33057	30.34310
26.75	26.75000	30.28603	30.65656	30.66936
27.00	27.00000	30.60500	30.98337	30.99645
27.25	27.25000	30.92468	31.31099	31.32435
27.50	27.50000	31.24509	31.63944	31.65307
27.75	27.75000	31.56621	31.96870	31.98261
28.00	28.00000	31.88805	32.29878	32.31298
28.25	28.25000	32.21061	32.62968	32.64418
28.50	28.50000	32.53390	32.96142	32.97620
28.75	28.75000	32.85791	33.29397	33.30906
29.00	29.00000	33.18265	33.62736	33.64275
29.25	29.25000	33.50811	33.96158	33.97727
29.50	29.50000	33.83430	34.29663	34.31264
29.75	29.75000	34.16123	34.63252	34.64884
30.00	30.00000	34.48888	34.96925	34.98588

Appendix 2

Statistical Data

TABLE (A2-1)

Normal distribution curve

standard score z	ordinate of Normal curve f(z)	area under right hand side of curve $\int_0^z f(z)\,dz$
0.000	0.3989	0.00000
0.100	0.3970	0.03983
0.200	0.3910	0.07926
0.253	0.3864	0.10000
0.300	0.3814	0.11791
0.400	0.3683	0.15542
0.500	0.3521	0.19146
0.524	0.3478	0.20000
0.600	0.3332	0.22575
0.700	0.3123	0.25804
0.800	0.2897	0.28814
0.842	0.2798	0.30000
0.900	0.2661	0.31594
1.000	0.2420	0.34134
1.200	0.1942	0.38493
1.282	0.1953	0.40000
1.400	0.1497	0.41243
1.600	0.1109	0.44520
1.645	0.1032	0.45000
1.800	0.0790	0.46407
1.881	0.0680	0.47000
2.000	0.0540	0.47725
2.054	0.0484	0.48000
2.326	0.0266	0.49000
2.500	0.0175	0.49379
2.576	0.0145	0.49500
2.748	0.0092	0.49700
3.000	0.0044	0.49865
3.090	0.0034	0.49900
3.291	0.0018	0.49950
3.439	0.0011	0.49970
3.500	0.0009	0.49977
3.719	0.0004	0.49990
4.000	0.0001	0.49997
∞	0.0000	0.50000

Data abridged and recalculated from Fisher, Sir R.A. and Yates, F., "Statistical Tables for Biological, Agricultural and Medical Research", London, Oliver and Boyd, 5th Ed., p.42-43, 1957

TABLE (A2-2)

Uniformly distributed random numbers

3770	3221	4691	3352	6132	9203	0493	7174	8174	1665
7575	5076	5096	7807	5137	8258	0098	2829	0379	5920
4380	9931	8501	5262	7142	0313	2703	1484	5584	3175
4185	7786	4906	5717	2147	5368	8303	3139	3789	3430
6990	8641	4311	9172	0152	3423	6913	7794	4994	6685
2795	2496	6716	5627	1157	4478	8518	5449	9199	2940
1600	9351	2121	5082	5162	8533	3123	6104	6404	2195
3405	9206	0526	7537	2167	5588	0728	9759	6609	4450
8210	2061	1931	2992	2172	5643	1333	6414	9814	9705
6015	7916	6336	1447	5177	8698	4938	6069	6019	7960
6820	6771	3741	2902	1182	4753	1543	8724	5224	9215
0625	8626	4146	7357	0187	3808	1148	4379	7429	3470
7430	3481	7551	4812	2192	5863	3753	3034	2634	0725
7235	1336	3956	5267	7197	0918	9358	4689	0839	0980
0040	2191	3361	8722	5202	8973	7963	9344	2044	4235
5845	6046	5766	5177	6207	0028	9568	6999	6249	0490
4650	2901	1171	4632	0212	4083	4173	7654	3454	9745
6455	2756	9576	7087	7217	1138	1778	1309	3659	2000
1260	5611	0981	2542	7222	1193	2383	7964	6864	7255
9065	1466	5386	0997	0227	4248	5988	7619	3069	5510
9870	0321	2791	2452	6232	0303	2593	0274	2274	6765
3675	2176	3196	6907	5237	9358	2198	5929	4479	1020
0480	7031	6601	4362	7242	1413	4803	4584	9684	8275
0285	4886	3006	4817	2247	6468	0408	6239	7889	8530
3090	5741	2411	8272	0252	4523	9013	0894	9094	1785
8895	9596	4816	4727	1257	5578	0618	8549	3299	8040
7700	6451	0221	4182	5262	9633	5223	9204	0504	7295
9505	6306	8626	6637	2267	6688	2828	2859	0709	9550
4310	9161	0031	2092	2272	6743	3433	9514	3914	4805
2115	5016	4436	0547	5277	9798	7038	9169	0119	3060
2920	3871	1841	2002	1282	5853	3643	1824	9324	4315
6725	5726	2246	6457	0287	4908	3248	7479	1529	8570
3530	0581	5651	3912	2292	6963	5853	6134	6734	5825
3335	8436	2056	4367	7297	2018	1458	7789	4939	6080
6140	9291	1461	7822	5302	0073	0063	2444	6144	9335
1945	3146	3866	4277	6307	1128	1668	0099	0349	5590
0750	0001	9271	3732	0312	5183	6273	0754	7554	4845
2555	9856	7676	6187	7317	2238	3878	4409	7759	7100
7360	2711	9081	1642	7322	2293	4483	1064	0964	2355
5165	8566	3486	0097	0327	5348	8088	0719	7169	0610
5970	7421	0891	1552	6332	1403	4693	3374	6374	1865
9775	9276	1296	6007	5337	0458	4298	9029	8579	6120
6580	4131	4701	3462	7342	2513	6903	7684	3784	3375
6385	1986	1106	3917	2347	7568	2508	9339	1989	3630
9190	2841	0511	7372	0352	5623	1113	3994	3194	6885
4995	6696	2916	3827	1357	6678	2718	1649	7399	3140
3800	3551	8321	3282	5362	0733	7323	2304	4604	2395
5605	3406	6726	5737	2367	7788	4928	5959	4809	4650
0410	6261	8131	1192	2372	7843	5533	2614	8014	9905
8215	2116	2536	9647	5377	0898	9138	2269	4219	8160

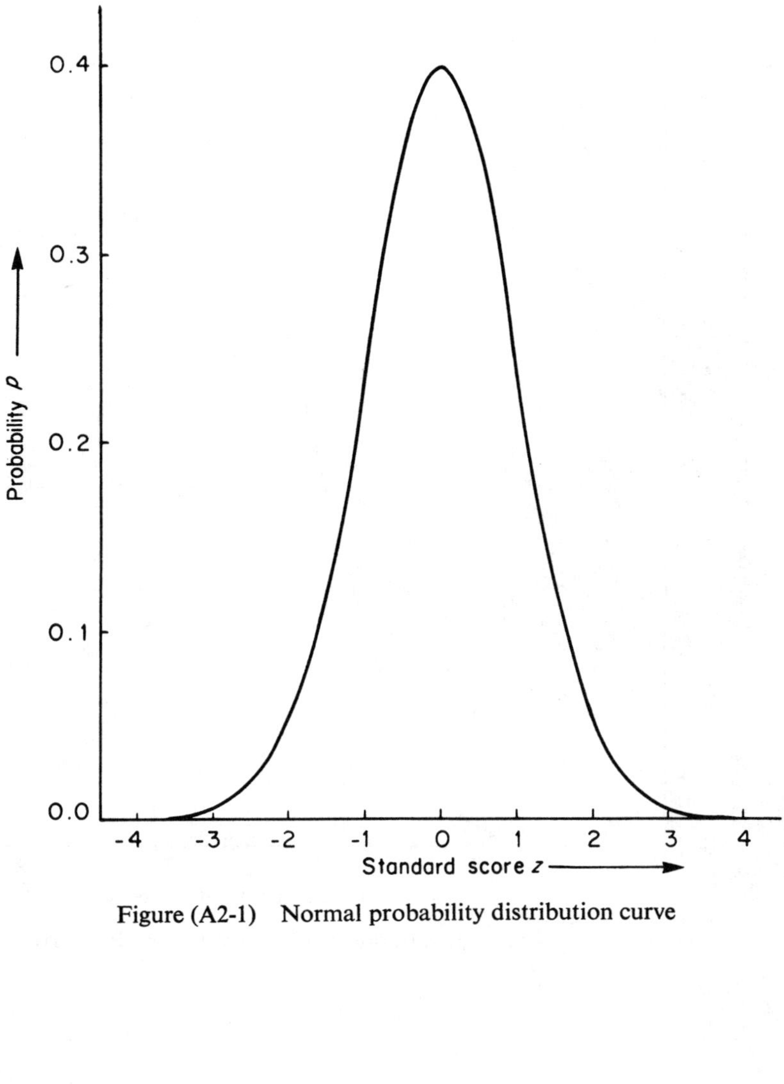

Figure (A2-1) Normal probability distribution curve

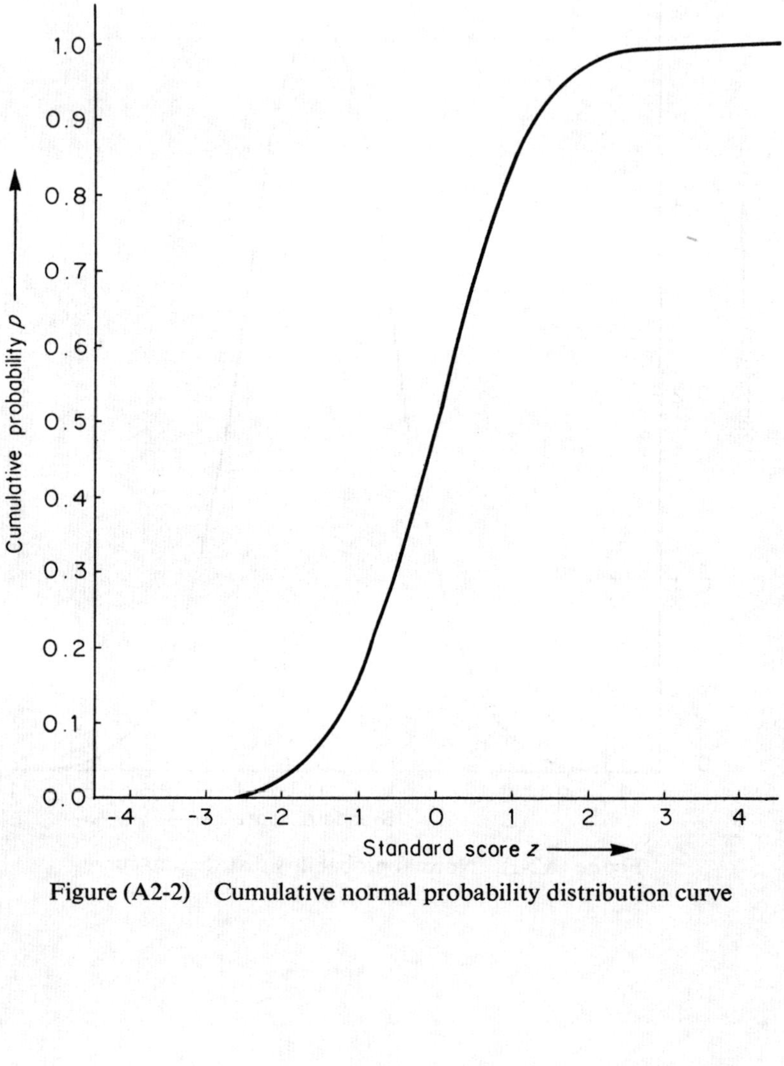

Figure (A2-2) Cumulative normal probability distribution curve

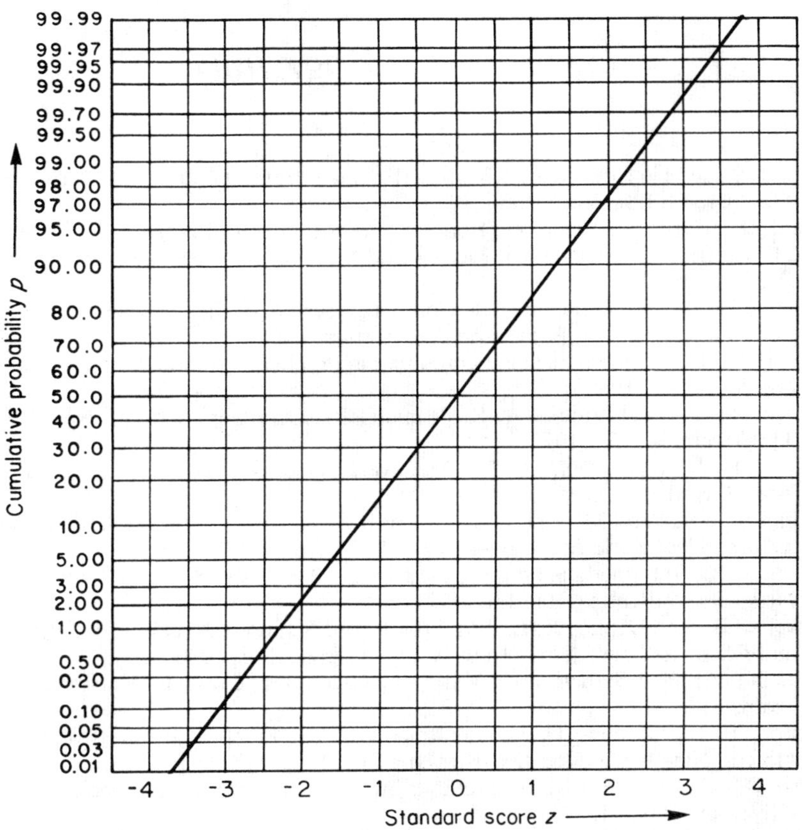

Figure (A2-3) Normal probability paper

Appendix 3

General Bibliography

Aries, R. S., and Newton, R. D., 'Chemical Engineering Cost Estimation', New York, McGraw–Hill Book Co. Inc., 1955

Argenti, J., 'Corporate Planning', London, George Allen and Unwin Ltd., 1968

Bass, F. M. (Ed.), 'Mathematical Models and Methods in Marketing', Homewood, Ill., Richard D. Irwin, 1961

Bauman, H. C., 'Fundamentals of Cost Engineering in the Chemical Industry', New York, Reinhold Publishing Corporation, 1964

Beale, E. M. L., 'Mathematical Programming in Practice', London, Sir Isaac Pitman and Sons Ltd., 1968

Bierman, H. Jr., and Drebin, A. R., 'Financial Accounting', 2nd ed., New York, The Macmillan Co., 1972

Bierman, H. Jr., and Drebin, A. R., 'Managerial Accounting', 2nd ed., New York, The Macmillan Co., 1972

Burlington, R. S., and May, D. C. Jr., 'Handbook of Probability and Statistics with Tables', New York, McGraw–Hill Book Co. Ltd., 1970

Canada, J. R., 'Intermediate Economic Analysis for Management and Engineering', New Jersey, Prentice–Hall Inc., 1971

Clarke, A. B., and Disney, R. L., 'Probability and Random Processes for Engineers and Scientists', New York, John Wiley and Sons, Inc., 1970

Croft, D., 'Applied Statistics for Management Studies', London, Macdonald and Evans Ltd., 1969

Croxton, F. E., Cowden, D. J., and Bolch, B. W., 'Practical Business Statistics', 4th ed., New Jersey, Prentice–Hall, Inc., 1969

Davis, O. L. (Ed.), 'Statistical Methods in Research and Production', 3rd ed., Oliver and Boyd, 1957

Dyckman, T. R., Smidt, S., and McAdams, A. K., 'Management Decision Making Under Uncertainty', New York, The Macmillan Co., 1969

Edgerton, R. A. D., 'Investment Decisions Under Uncertainty', Liverpool, England, Liverpool University Press, 1960

Frost, M. J., 'Value for Money, The Techniques of Cost Benefit Analysis', London, The Gower Press Ltd., 1971

Garvin, W. W., 'Introduction to Linear Programming', New York, McGraw–Hill Book Co. Inc., 1960

Gass, S. I., 'Linear Programming', New York, McGraw–Hill Book Co. Inc., 1958

Glicksman, A. M., 'An Introduction to Linear Programming and the Theory of Games', New York, John Wiley and Sons, Inc., 1963

Gregg, J. V., Horsell, C. H., and Richardson, J. T., 'Mathematical Trend Curves', London, Oliver and Boyd, 1964

Hackney, J. W., 'Control and Management of Capital Projects', New York, John Wiley and Sons, Inc., 1965

Hadley, G., 'Introduction to Business Statistics', San Francisco, Holden–Day, 1968

Happel, J., 'Chemical Process Economics', New York, John Wiley and Sons, Inc., 1958

Hemmerle, W. J., 'Statistical Computations on a Digital Computer', Waltham, Mass., Blaisdell Publishing Co., 1967

Imperial Chemical Industries Ltd., 'Assessing Projects', London, Methuen and Co. Ltd., 1968

The Institution of Chemical Engineers, 'Capital Cost Estimation', London, The Institution of Chemical Engineers, 1969

Jelen, F. C. (Ed.), 'Cost and Optimization Engineering', New York, McGraw–Hill Book Co. Inc., 1970

Kalton, S., 'Introduction to Statistical Ideas for Social Scientists', London, Chapman and Hall Ltd., 1966

Karger, D. W., and Murdick, R. C., 'New Product Venture Management', New York, Gordon and Breach Science Publishers, 1972

Keay, F., 'The Numerate Manager', London, George Allen and Unwin Ltd., 1969

Kendall, M. G. (Ed.), 'Cost Benefit Analysis', London, The English Universities Press Ltd., 1971

Koopmans, T. C. (Ed.), 'Activity Analysis of Production and Allocation', New York, John Wiley and Sons, Inc., 1951

Lambe, C. G., 'Statistical Methods and Formulae', London, The English Universities Press Ltd., 1967

Levinson, H. C., 'The Science of Chance', London, Faber and Faber Ltd., 1952

Lockyer, K. G., 'An Introduction to Critical Path Analysis', London, Sir Isaac Pitman and Sons Ltd., 1969

Lohnes, P. R., and Cooley, W. W., 'Introduction to Statistical Procedures with Computer Exercises', International ed., New York, John Wiley and Sons, Inc., 1968

Loomba, N. P., 'Linear Programming', New York, McGraw–Hill Book Co. Inc., 1964

Macniece, E. H., 'Production Forecasting, Planning and Control', New York, John Wiley and Sons, Inc., 1951

Marston, A., Winfrey, R., and Hempstead, J. C., 'Engineering Valuation and Depreciation', Ames, Iowa State University Press, 1936

Miller-Bakewell, J. B. C., 'Management Information for Producers', Brighton, England, The Machinery Publishing Co. Ltd., 1971

Moroney, M. J., 'Facts from Figures, 3rd ed., London, Penguin Books Ltd., 1956

Morrell, A. J. H. (Ed.), 'Problems of Stocks and Storage', London, Oliver and Boyd, 1967

Oughton, F., 'Value Analysis and Value Engineering', London, Sir Isaac Pitman and Sons Ltd., 1969

Park, W. R., 'Cost Engineering Analysis', p. 213, New York, John Wiley and Sons, 1973

Perry, J. H. (Ed.), 'Chemical Business Handbook', New York, McGraw–Hill Book Co. Inc., 1954

Perry, J. H., Chilton, C. H., and Kirkpatrick, S. D. (Ed.), 'Chemical Engineers Handbook', 4th ed., New York, McGraw–Hill Book Co. Inc., 1963

Pessemier, E. A., 'New Product Decisions', New York, McGraw–Hill Book Co. Inc., 1966

Peters, M. S., and Timmerhaus, K. D., 'Plant Design and Economics for Chemical Engineers', 2nd ed., New York, McGraw–Hill Book Co. Inc., 1968

Popper, H. (Ed.), 'Modern Cost Engineering Techniques', New York, McGraw–Hill Book Co. Inc., 1970

Quenouille, M. H., 'Rapid Statistical Calculations', 2nd ed., London, Charles Griffin and Co. Ltd., 1972

Richmond, S. B., 'Operations Research for Management Decisions', New York, The Ronald Press Co., 1968

Ridge, W. J., 'Value Analysis for Better Management', Kingport, Tennessee, American Management Association, Inc., 1969

Riggs, J. L., 'Economic Decision Models for Engineers and Managers', New York, McGraw–Hill Book Co. Inc., 1968

Rockley, L. E., 'Capital Investment Decisions', London, Business Books Ltd., 1968

Rudd, D. F., and Watson, C. C., 'Strategy of Process Engineering', New York, John Wiley and Sons, Inc., 1968

Salzman, L., 'Computerized Economic Analysis', New York, McGraw–Hill Book Co. Inc., 1968

Schlaifer, R., 'Computer Programs for Elementary Decision Analysis', Boston, Harvard University, 1971

Schlaifer, R., 'Probability and Statistics Business Decisions, An Introduction to Managerial Economics Under Uncertainty', New York, McGraw–Hill Book Co. Inc., 1959

Schweyer, H. E., 'Process Engineering Economics', New York, McGraw–Hill Book Co. Inc., 1955

Slater, L. J., 'Fortran Programs for Economists', Cambridge, England, Cambridge University Press, 1967

Spiegel, M. R., 'Theory and Problems of Statistics', SI Ed., New York, McGraw–Hill Book Co. Inc., 1972

Thuesen, H. G., Fabrycky, W. J., and Thuesen, G. L., 'Engineering Economy', 4th Ed., New Jersey, Prentice–Hall, Inc., 1971

Vilbrandt, F. C., and Dryden, C. E., 'Chemical Engineering Plant Design', New York, McGraw–Hill Book Co. Inc., 1959

Wright, M. G., 'Financial Management', London, McGraw–Hill Book Co. Inc., 1970

Wright, R. W., 'Investment Decision in Industry', London, Chapman and Hall, 1964

Index